Daf

Chris shook her head. Why couldn't Kevin understand? "You don't need a nursing degree to fluff pillows. Ask your daughter. She goes to Glen Eagles Hospital one afternoon a week. Alison doesn't want to be a nurse. She's working on a science project."

"Chrissy, I admit your idea has merit. But it will take a lot of time. Have you given any thought to that? It isn't something you can start and stop to suit your whim. It would have to be open every day. You don't have that kind of time. Or the attention span."

The more Kevin spoke, the angrier Chris became. It was as if he'd heard nothing she'd told him in the last few months. She'd expected him to be happy she'd found something that interested her. The children were at school all day and had after school activities. They barely got home in time for dinner. There was no need for Chris to sit in the house all day to wait for them. The servants took care of the house. They'd been doing it for so many years they didn't need her guidance. In fact, she was in their way when she was home.

Carrie Shearer
2002

Carrie Shearer
2250 N. Triphammer Rd.
Apt. K-1F
Ithaca, NY 14850-1506

Daffodils, Orchids and Roses

By

Carrie Shearer

ISBN: 0-9713971-1-2

This work is a novel and any similarity to actual persons or events is purely coincidental.

Cover Design by WORDPRO Press

Printed in the United States by WORDPRO Press

In memory of JoAnn Cooper who helped me bring this idea into reality. Without her support and friendship I might never have finished this project. I miss you.

Chapter 1
SARAH

Sydney, Australia
Tuesday, September 18, 1979

"Sarah, dear, please stand still. Martha can't fit the dress properly if you keep wriggling."

Sarah sighed inwardly, smiled outwardly, and stood frozen like a mannequin. For the last four days, it seemed all she'd done was try on clothes and pose like a statue while they were pinned and marked for alterations. She felt like a doll her mother and mother-in-law dressed. All the beautiful clothes didn't compensate for what she felt at the prospect of another move.

In less than a week Sarah, her husband Barney, and their son would be on their way to Singapore. Sarah didn't want to move again. This would be the fifth country she was expected to call home in as many years. It never failed; just as Sarah got used to a place, Barney was transferred.

Neither her mother mother-in-law Violet nor Sarah's mother Chloe would admit that Barney's drinking and gambling were the reason for the frequent transfers. They preferred to believe this was life in the international oil business. Sarah understood her new wardrobe, purchased by her in-laws, was the cost of her silence. By accepting the clothes, she was part of their deception.

They think if we keep moving, sooner or later Barney will stop drinking. Why can't they see the truth? Barney will never grow up. Even the baby can't keep him away from the liquor bottle, Sarah raged silently.

Both Barney and Sarah were only children, born late in their parents' marriages. Sarah's father died when she was five, leaving his wife and daughter with little other than memories. Barney's father founded Parker Oil, which was later bought by Trans Oil.

Sarah and Barney had been dating for a year when his father was offered a farewell tour of Trans Oil's global operations when he retired the following June. Violet was quite taken with Sarah and convinced herself that she was the proper wife for Barney. Sarah was young and innocent, interested in cultural events, and devoted to her mother, all qualities needed by an executive wife. Violet often stopped in the flower shop where Chloe worked to admire Sarah's deft ability to arrange flowers in new ways. No matter how demanding the customer, Sarah was always courteous. Violet wanted to see Barney settled before she and her husband left on their world tour, so she extolled Sarah's virtues to her son.

Sarah turned down Barney's proposal. She was just twenty and wanted to enjoy herself. When she told her mother, Chloe wouldn't hear of it. From the gossip at the flower shop, Chloe knew that if Sarah didn't act now, her chance might be lost forever.

"He's perfect, Sarah. An older man makes a better husband. He'll treat you like his princess. Believe me, you won't easily find someone better."

In the end Sarah agreed to marry Barney as much to placate her mother as anything. Chloe always orchestrated Sarah's life. Even on their meager budget, she exposed Sarah to fine things. If Sarah needed a new dress for a special occasion, Chloe would scrimp and save to make sure that her daughter had what she wanted. After all her mother's sacrifices, how could Sarah disappoint her?

When their engagement was announced, Barney's parents suggested Sarah quit her secretarial job in an art gallery and focus her efforts on the wedding preparations. They purchased a small terrace house for Chloe and gave Sarah an allowance larger than the salary she'd made working. The flurry of activity surrounding the wedding quickly took on a life of its own. The Parkers kept Barney and Sarah in a state of constant motion lest they have too much time to reflect upon the rushed marriage. At times Sarah fretted that she was marrying Barney so she'd never again have to eat beans on toast to make the grocery money stretch until her next paycheck.

If there were evenings when Sarah thought Barney drank too much, she put the thought out of her mind. After all he was as caught up in the frenetic celebration as she. And he had to work as well.

The day before the wedding, when she had second thoughts about what she was doing, Sarah thought longingly about the beautiful wedding gifts that had come from all over the world. The Georgian silver, Waterford crystal, and silk sheets were not articles found in her home. The closest Sarah had been to such finery before were the displays in the better shops. She was certain she'd be comfortable with the lifestyle they foretold.

Life with Barney didn't live up to the fairy tale Sarah imagined. Quickly she learned her husband was a glorified "gofer" at work, tolerated because of his father. More than that, Barney played at marriage, the same way he played at work.

Their first assignment was London. Sarah envisioned nights at the theater or opera, and dinner parties with a small circle of well-connected friends. It was not to be. Barney's idea of a night out was one where he gambled at the exclusive private clubs. Since the clubs were open to men only, Sarah spent most evenings alone.

Barney had little luck with cards. When his losing streak was prolonged, Sarah called his parents and asked for money to pay their creditors. The embarrassment she felt as she rang Barney Senior was intolerable. She'd have left Barney then, but she was pregnant. At the time, she was certain Barney would change once the baby was born.

Barney the Third, who they nicknamed Trey, was born in Hong Kong. At first Barney tried to make a success of his job, but his interest waned within a month. Once again he turned to gambling and drinking for entertainment. Unfortunately he couldn't beat the odds at the casinos. This time the people who came in search of money were frightening. Sarah was scared of a physical assault on her or the baby. She called her in-laws without hesitating.

Barney was transferred to New Zealand next, on the premise that being closer to home might be better for the family. Sarah loved New Zealand. In many ways Auckland was so similar to Sydney that she didn't feel as if she were living in a foreign country. The climate was temperate and there was a beautiful harbor where she could take Trey for walks in the afternoon. While Trey slept in his pram, Sarah sketched the sailboats and dreamed of a better life.

At first it looked as if her mental meandering were a harbinger of happier times. Barney made a friend at work, Geoff Melbourne, who had a settling influence on him. Geoff was a diligent worker, and Barney emulated his behavior. The two developed a friendly rivalry at work. Over time Geoff's enthusiasm spurred Barney to work harder.

Barney's efforts paid off. His next transfer was a promotion, but Zimbabwe turned into their worst posting. The expatriate community was mostly British and a closed circle to outsiders, which Sarah and Barney were. Barney drank more and more with each polite rebuff.

The only time he seemed happy was when he played with Trey. The minute Barney came home, Trey ran into his father's arms. Trey was happy to see Barney, a feeling Sarah didn't always share. Once they ate dinner and put Trey to bed, the couple had little to discuss. Often Barney finished a bottle of gin before stumbling into bed.

When Sarah and Barney returned to Australia, Violet recognized Sarah's apprehension about another move. In an attempt to take Sarah's mind off her trepidation, Violet and Chloe banded together to help Sarah select the perfect wardrobe for

Singapore. Care of Trey was turned over to a nanny while Barney went to the office.

Sarah wished she could talk to her mother about her fears, but knew that Chloe wouldn't hear a negative word about Barney. Four years earlier, while living in London, Sarah had turned to her mother for support. Rather than advice, her mother turned things around and made it sound as if any problems were Sarah's fault. Chloe insisted that if Sarah were a better wife, Barney would be a better husband.

Sarah tried so hard to be the model wife. No matter when Sarah had to get up, she ensured she was picture-perfect when her husband saw her. Barney never saw Sarah's hair in curlers or her face without at least powder and mascara. Each morning after Barney left for the office, Sarah exercised to guarantee that her weight never varied. At 5'2", her petite frame showed any excess weight quickly.

The seamstress gently pushed Sarah forward to see the pinned dress in the mirror. The subtle motion jolted Sarah from her memories and she opened her eyes with a start. Her eyes took in the buttercup yellow sundress with pink flowers on the bodice and skirt. The colors were perfect against her dark hair and porcelain complexion. She turned one way and the other to admire the dress, and then pouted. "It needs something," she said petulantly.

"A hat," Violet suggested. "Now, stay here, Sarah. Your mother and I will go find the perfect bonnet for this outfit."

Sarah tapped her foot impatiently. Much as she loved clothes, she detested the time being devoted to amassing her wardrobe. Each dress meant new underwear, shoes, purse, nail lacquer, and lipstick. Sarah couldn't be comfortable unless her clothes were completely color-coordinated, even the parts that no one but Barney would see.

While she was alone, she preened in the three-sided mirror. Her hair was flawless. It was cut just above her shoulders. The sides were swept off her face in combs that matched the outfit she'd worn to the store. Her makeup was carefully applied to accent some features and minimize others. Her nose turned up slightly at the tip, she had dimples, and dark brown eyes, which shone when she was happy. Since Sarah thought her eyes a bit too close together, she used five different shades of eye shadow to camouflage the deficiency.

Not too shabby, she thought. She turned to the side so she could see the dress from the back. Two thin strips of fabric crisscrossed from her shoulders to her waist. *I'll have to wear sun block.* Sarah took a notebook from her purse and made a note on the page marked yellow and pink sundress.

To make certain each dress was worn with the appropriate accessories, Sarah kept a notebook with a separate page for each outfit. Listed on the page were the jewelry, underwear, shoes, hose, purse, and makeup that should be worn with a dress. Later she would add the date and occasion it had been worn so she wouldn't be seen too frequently in the same clothes.

Violet and Chloe came rushing into the fitting room wearing self-satisfied grins. "We have it, dear," Violet said, "the perfect yellow straw hat. Now, put it on and let us see."

Sarah smiled at her reflection in the mirror. The hat did look nice. It was styled like a man's boater. “The sash will have to go," she said firmly.

"Not to worry. We can have the store remove it and put some of the fabric from the dress in its place. Do change quickly. We're to meet Barney Senior for lunch at his club. You know how he hates to be kept waiting."

The last thing Sarah wanted was to have lunch at Barney Senior's club. It was a sunny day, perfect for sitting at the pier and sketching people enjoying the spring day. However, she was resigned to the inevitable. If the in-laws wanted her to join them for lunch, they'd never consider she might prefer to do something else.

The oil club was one of the most fashionable private clubs in town, although Sarah couldn't understand why. The dark mahogany walls and heavy velvet drapes, that were always closed, blocked the scenery. Sarah preferred yacht clubs. They weren’t so depressingly dreary and provided sunny backdrops for her sketching.

Barney Senior was waiting at his table when the women arrived. He stood as he saw them approach and bowed gallantly. "I'll be the envy of every fellow here. The three most beautiful woman in the room all to myself."

Violet and Chloe laughed at the obvious line. Sarah smiled politely. No one would expect her to say anything. They never did. For the most part the three older adults spoke to one another as if Sarah weren't present. Sarah wondered why Barney hadn't picked up his father's social graces. Although Barney Senior was not her favorite man, he was a gentleman.

During the two-hour lunch Sarah puzzled over why Barney had been excluded. There must be a reason. It was only a matter of time before the purpose of this lunch would be placed on the table like their dessert soufflés had been.

As they sipped their espresso, Barney Senior smiled indulgently at Sarah. "Now, dear heart, we know how difficult it is for you two children to keep starting over. Singapore has some glorious old houses. I'm sure you'll find the perfect one for your little family. No doubt the house will require renovations and new furniture to make it into a showpiece. You'd make us very happy if you'd accept this check to help."

Sarah looked down and hung her head demurely. "Oh, you've been far too generous as it is. My new wardrobe is so grand. I couldn't accept anything more."

Barney Senior and Violet each took one of Sarah's hands and patted it. In a soothing voice, Violet said, "Now, dear, no reason to be shy. We know how much you enjoy decorating. It makes us happy we can give you a little something to ease the transition."

"Definitely," Barney Senior agreed. "You simply must have the finest house imaginable. After all, dear, you have Barney and Trey to consider. If you won't take the money for yourself, take it for them."

Sarah's dinner became a lead weight in her stomach. With each move, Barney's parents had become increasingly generous in their attempts to buy Sarah's love and affection. She was curious as to the amount of the check. It would give her an indication of how much trouble Barney was in.

She murmured, "I'll do my best to create a wonderful atmosphere for Barney and Trey. Thank you for your generosity." Without looking at it, Sarah opened her purse and put the check inside.

Violet spoke. "I'm positive the three of you will like Singapore. When Father and I did our world tour, we spent three weeks there. It's simply paradise."

Sarah smiled automatically, her mind a million miles away. "I've been reading the books you gave me. It does sound lovely."

"Now, Sarah, about the women. We were there long enough for me to get to know the wives. The woman you should cultivate is Chris Taylor. She and her husband Kevin seem to be the top of the heap. Kevin works for Trans Oil, so he and Barney will get to know each other at the office. Chris appears to be the social leader of the expat community. I'm sure she'll be happy to show you the ropes. She and her husband have been in Singapore for six or seven years now."

Imagine, the luxury of living in a country long enough to be anything but the new wife, Sarah thought wistfully. She asked the expected question. "What's she like?"

"Two children. Very active in all the groups that matter. Quite definitely the woman behind the man."

"Which one was Chris Taylor?" Barney Senior asked.

"You must remember her, Father. Mid-thirties. About five-feet-five-inches. Looks like she plays tennis every day. A pleasant face. Atrocious auburn hair."

"Oh, not the blonde? I'd have thought her to be an interesting sort."

Violet glared at her husband. "That woman is a little nobody. She actually works for a living. No, Father, I doubt our Sarah need worry her pretty little head about someone that trivial."

Although only half-listening to the conversation, Sarah picked up Violet's acid tone and was intrigued. "Is she a lady of the evening?" she asked. Had the question come from anyone but

Sarah, it would have sounded foolish. Sarah smiled at the knowledge that no one realized she was poking fun at Violet.

"No, dear. She's simply not our type. From what I heard at bridge, she's only tolerated because she's a friend of Chris Taylor. Most of the wives are just as happy she spends most of her time in the jungle. With luck, your paths will never cross."

Spends her time in the jungle. Sounds interesting. I wonder why. Not that Violet would know if I asked her, Sarah thought ruefully. At that moment she saw a look pass between Violet and Chloe. The two women stood in unison. Presuming it was the appropriate time to powder her nose, Sarah stood as well.

Barney Senior put out his hand and touched Sarah's arm. Even though his touch was gentle, Sarah sensed the command, and sat down.

"Stay with me a moment, dear. I'd like to have a little chat."

Sarah waited. She knew whatever Barney Senior had to say wouldn't be done in front of the ladies, even though they probably knew what was to come.

When the coast was clear, Barney smiled. "Sarah, dear, you've always impressed me as a bright young woman. I've spoken to the people at Trans Oil. This is the last time I'll be able to intercede on Barney's behalf. He sinks or swims in Singapore, and you and Trey with him. I'm expecting you to keep Barney's mind on the job."

"I do try, you know," Sarah answered defensively.

He patted her hand. "I know you do, dear. This time it's frightfully important. Barney could make his mark in Singapore. I want you to promise to ring me if things aren't going well. I'm sure if we put our heads together we can make it work. Do you understand?"

"I'll do my best."

"I want more than that, dear. I'm counting on your success. If something goes amiss, let me know immediately. Don't let things get too out of line before ringing me."

Sarah sighed. "I really hate to bother you with trivialities."

"I know that, dear. But I must insist. This is Barney's last chance. If he doesn't prove himself something other than a dilettante in Singapore, Trans Oil will make him redundant."

Sarah felt ill. It had never dawned on her that Trans Oil would fire her husband. Even if Barney weren't going to run one of the operations like his father had, Sarah presumed there would always be a job in the company for Barney.

Barney Senior moved a snifter of brandy to Sarah's lips. "Take a sip of this. It will make you feel better."

Visibly shaken, Sarah gulped the brandy and started to choke when the amber liquid burned her throat. After a few sips of ice water, she regained her composure. "I didn't realize how critical this posting was. I'll do everything in my power."

Barney Senior smiled at Sarah. "That's my girl. Please ring me if you sense any change in Barney. You know the warning signs."

Sarah wanted to throw the remaining brandy at Barney Senior. The pampering and coddling that he and Violet had given their son were the cause of Barney's problem. Since Barney had never been held responsible for his actions, he'd never learned to face problems head on. When things didn't go Barney's way, he buried himself inside a gin bottle.

Sarah would have traded every outfit she owned for a solution to Barney's problem.

Chapter 2
CHRIS

Singapore
Tuesday, September 18, 1979

The Taylor's white Colonial house had been built when the English ruled Singapore. Fifty years later it still retained the majesty of its bygone era. The palatial grounds were encircled by a ten-foot-high brick wall so covered in vines it was hard to see the wall. The house was set back and nestled amid dense foliage. If you didn't know the house was there, you wouldn't see it from the street.

There were twenty rooms on two floors. Most of the rooms were so large they needed three ceiling fans for cooling. The bedrooms and main living areas had been modernized to include wall-mounted air conditioners years before. Chris preferred the ceiling fans. The gentle motion of the blades was soothing compared to the air conditioners, which roared like lions.

As Chris walked down the staircase, her fingers traced the geometric light patterns on the teak banister. The shutters didn't completely bar the sun from the window; this morning Chris could make out only a faint hint of black on the wooden shutters. Bright colors never lasted in the tropics. Every six months the shutters were painted. It was time to schedule the job again. She took a second and jotted the name "Jeetu" in her appointment book in the comment section for Tuesday.

Her pruning shears and garden gloves were at the door to the garden. She slipped a hat on her head and walked outside to cut flowers for the breakfast table. One of the wonders of Singapore was the availability of fresh flowers every day.

The solarium had been a verandah when the Taylors rented the house seven years before. It was on the east side of the house and got the morning sun. Chris had convinced her husband Kevin and the landlord that enclosing the room with glass walls would make it appear a continuation of the garden. Over the years it had become the favorite spot for the family and close friends.

The house had a formal living room as well as a family room, yet this was Chris's favorite room. There was ample space for a rattan sofa and several chairs. The ceiling fans kept the room cool and she could control the amount of light by adjusting the rattan blinds. When she was alone, Chris let the sun shine into the room. But neither the children Alison and Marc, nor her husband were morning people. Bright sunlight in the morning irritated them.

Chris didn't understand why her family hadn't adapted to the early start of the day in Asia. Each morning they struggled, as if their wills would make the island community begin the day later.

Thirteen-year-old Alison was the first to stumble into the solarium, her wobbly gait indicating she was half-asleep. She wore the navy blue skirt and white blouse uniform of the American School. Her strawberry blond hair was askew. She thrust a navy headband and a hairbrush at her mother.

Chris smiled. It was so typical of her daughter to be half-ready. "You want your hair down today?" she asked.

"Mother, help. I can't do anything with it."

"It should be cut," Chris whispered as she took the brush to the tangle of curls that fell to Alison's shoulders.

"Not that again. I'm old enough to know how I want to wear my hair."

"Then you should be old enough to fix it."

Both females looked up at the sound of another voice. Chris stared at her twelve-year-old son Marc. He wasn't any more ready for school than his sister. His tie hung loose from the open neck of his shirt; and he'd missed a button when fastening his shirt.

"Did you sign my note, Mom?"

"It's next to your plate. You'd better look in the mirror before you leave."

"Looking in mirrors is for girls."

"And boys who can't button their shirts properly," Alison teased.

Marc stuck out his tongue at Alison. When he looked down at his shirt and saw the mess he'd made of the buttons, both children laughed.

Chris was pleased that the children were being pleasant to each other. They'd been at each other's throats since the start of school two weeks before.

"I'm starving," Marc whined. "Do we have to wait for Dad to eat?"

Chris put the finishing touches on Alison's hair and pushed her towards the table. "No. Start or you'll miss the bus. I'll see what's keeping your father."

Chris ran up the stairs two at a time. Kevin had been in the shower when she'd come downstairs. She couldn't imagine what was taking him so long. From the doorway of their bedroom, she watched Kevin fasten the latch to his carry-on suitcase. She'd forgotten he was going out of town. "What time's your plane?"

Kevin reached out and rubbed his hand against the furrows on Chris's brow. “There's time for breakfast. Are the children downstairs?"

"I told Marc he could start eating. After what he ate for dinner last night, how can he think about food again?"

"He's a growing boy." Kevin reached for Chris's hand and pulled her to him. "If you want, I'll have Suradmin drive the children so they won't have to take the bus."

“Thanks, sweetie." Chris squeezed her husband's hand as she led the way down the stairs.

Family breakfasts were a rarity. The school bus stopped for the children at 6:30 a.m. The children were often gone before Kevin woke. Kevin kissed Chris. "I know how much family time means to you."

When they reached the table, Marc regaled them with a story of his latest failed science experiment, which was so comical even Alison laughed.

Ah Soon, the children's amah, came into the room when the driver was ready. As they picked up their books, the children called goodbye to their parents. They were halfway out the door when Chris saw the envelope on the table. "Marc," she called. "You forgot your note."

"Thanks, Mom." He ran back into the room and grabbed the envelope from her hands without breaking his stride.

When the children were gone, Kevin gave Chris a questioning look. "What's he up to now?"

"A trip to Bangkok to see the alligator farms. It's over Thanksgiving."

Kevin shook his head, a puzzled frown on his face. "Can't Tory take him someplace safe? Alligators can be dangerous."

Chris laughed. "The school is doing this adventure. The trip was open to both the seventh and eighth grades. Marc's going; Alison isn't. I hope you don't mind. I thought with the party and all, we wouldn't go away."

Kevin reached over and stroked Chris's hand. "The children are your call, you know that. If you think the trip's a good idea, who am I to say differently?"

"Although why a child of yours wants to traipse through a swamp to see alligators is beyond you," Chris said with a smile, knowing Kevin wasn't fond of adventures.

Kevin nodded and squeezed Chris's hand, a loving gesture that caused her green eyes to sparkle. It was the little things that mattered to Chris. Family meals with flowers on the table were treasures worth far more than jewels.

"Did I mention we have a new guy at work?" Kevin asked.

"No. Why?"

"He's in his late thirties. And he's single. I thought you might want to introduce him to Tory."

"Kev, be serious. Tory has no interest in meeting anyone. Believe me, I've tried." She paused. Kevin and Tory often worked together on marketing campaigns. The introduction could be handled at Trans Oil. "When did you start playing matchmaker?"

"He reminds me of Tory."

Chris was immediately intrigued. Tory Winslow was her best friend and still single. For the past six years Chris had tried, unsuccessfully, to interest Tory in any number of men. "How's he like Tory?"

"He's been here a month and all he does is work. I've invited him home for dinner a couple of times. He always says he has too much work to do. From what I can see, work is the only thing that matters to him. Sounds just like Tory."

"That's not nice."

"Maybe not, but it's true. I met him years ago and Geoff's a nice guy. I thought if Tory were ready to come out of hiding and join the real world, they might hit it off. I'll leave it to you to work out the details."

"When will you be back?"

"Friday night. I'll probably stop at the office first to see what piled up while I was gone. Don't count on me for dinner. What are our plans that night?"

Chris opened her diary. "Janet and Phil Adams are having a party. It doesn't start until eight. Why don't I wait and go with you?"

Kevin nodded his agreement. "What will you be up to while I'm gone?"

"The garden, bridge," Chris shrugged. "What's there to say? My life's pretty much a routine."

Kevin got up and kissed his wife's auburn curls. "And you love it. Well, I've got to go. I'll send Suradmin back with the car."

Chris stood up and put her arms around Kevin's neck. "I'll miss you, sweetie."

"Me too. I'll call when I can. I love you, Chrissy."

After Kevin left, Chris poured herself another glass of mango juice. One of the advantages of being an expatriate wife in Asia was the household help. There was no need for Chris to clear the table. Wan Chan, the housekeeper, would do that when Chris left.

As she smoked a cigarette, Chris reflected on life in Singapore. It reminded her of a fairy tale world that existed in children's books. Imagine the wonder of living in constant summer. The temperature seldom varied and the sun shone every day. Even if it rained, the sun didn't stay hidden long. The city was spotless. In seven years, Chris had never seen as much as a gum wrapper on the street. There was no graffiti, even on the public housing. The government imposed heavy fines for behavior they didn't want. When an offense was committed, punishment was swiftly meted out.

After their cramped apartment in Bay Ridge, Brooklyn, the palatial house Trans Oil paid for was Utopia. With the allowances Kevin received they could afford servants to clean, do the laundry and ironing, and cook. Their house had both a regulation size swimming pool and tennis court. Daily tennis and swimming kept Chris's figure almost as thin as it had been in her youth, and the way Kevin preferred it.

Their lifestyle was idyllic. The only thing missing was the chance for Chris to work. Without a work permit, her nursing degree was useless. Although she'd only worked part-time after Alison was born, Chris missed the sense of accomplishment her career had given her. She volunteered two afternoons a week at Mount Elizabeth Hospital. It wasn't the same as nursing, but it was as close as circumstances allowed. It made Chris feel good to return something to the island that had been so magnanimous to her family.

Her cigarette finished, Chris went into the garden. Protecting her hands with heavy gloves, she spent the next two hours maintaining her creation. It had taken nearly two years to strip away the thick mangrove undergrowth that typified Singapore and transform her yard into a miniature botanical garden. Her garden was the talk of their community: a tranquil, serene oasis amid the city skyscrapers.

Before embarking on her grand design, Chris spent months studying horticulture. The ground was so fertile that, if the foliage weren't carefully tended, it would revert to jungle in a matter of weeks. It was a constant battle to maintain the atmosphere she wanted. For Chris, it was a labor of love.

With her hands in the warm, moist earth, Chris would think. Today she wondered about Kevin's suggestion Tory meet a bachelor from his office. At their first meeting, Chris had thought Tory utterly self-contained. In time Chris saw Tory's equanimity as a subterfuge, a device to keep people from getting too close. Since her work involved frequent travel, it was easy for Tory to maintain the distance she needed. In many ways she reminded Chris of a rose, beautiful yet fragile.

Chris smiled at the metaphor. The idea that Tory was other than a famous photographer who needed solitude to rejuvenate her creative spirit was absurd. Still she wondered why Tory was so guarded. In actuality she knew very little about the woman she thought of as her closest friend. Tory appeared in Chris's life when she felt like it. Years before Chris had learned that asking Tory a personal question would be met at best with stony silence. The few personal details she knew had been gleaned over a glass of wine late at night. Tory was uncomfortable when the topic of her past was raised. Chris decided that it wasn't a happy time in Tory's life. She wondered if Tory was happy now. On the surface she seemed content. Was that the same as happiness?

Chris was content and happy with her life. Her weeks seldom varied. The routine was comforting. Monday she had lunch and went shopping with women who either had children in school with Marc or Alison or whose husbands worked with Kevin. Shopping in Singapore was an experience, since there were no shopping malls. Once you knew what you wanted, you had to decide which section of town would most likely carry the item.

Stamford Raffles had laid out the city with a section for every nationality. His grand design still existed. There were shops in Little India, Chinatown and Arab Street as well as Orchard Road. Each area carried its own unique variety of goods. Prices were not fixed. Shopping was a battle of wits to get the best price.

Thursday afternoon Chris had lunch and played bridge. Friday afternoons were split between lunch, shopping and her chaperone activities for the children's field trips. The American

School planned one outing a month for each class, and Chris often went along with Marc or Alison's class. She enjoyed the involvement with her children.

"Hey, thought we were playing tennis. What are you still doing in the garden?"

Chris recognized Tory's voice and looked up. Tory stood with her hands on her hips, attempting to look stern. Chris held out her hands so Tory could help her up. "Guess the time got away from me. Kev left a bit late this morning."

Tory smiled slyly. "Sounds interesting."

Chris blushed at the innuendo. "He was going to the airport. Would you like to take me and the kids on an excursion tonight?"

Tory laughed so hard her long hair fell into her face. "Kev's gone, so it's safe to go to the hawker stands for dinner?"

Chris tried unsuccessfully to look indignant. They each knew Kevin would no more eat a meal from a street vendor than he'd eat a live mouse. "Kev was raised on meat and potatoes. It's what he likes." Hawker stands were Tory's territory. She delighted in exposing the Taylors to indigenous delicacies.

When Tory gave her a knowing grin, Chris presumed she was reacting to Kevin's lack of adventure.

"Something's come up. I may have to go to Sabah. Can I let you know about dinner later?"

Chris didn't return Tory's smile. Sabah was where Tory went to be alone. Every time Chris asked why she was going to the outlying area of Malaysia, Tory gave an outlandish reply. Knowing this, Chris still asked, "What do you find so fascinating in Sabah?"

"My pet orangutan Anna is in Sepilok. I like to visit her."

"A pet orangutan named Anna. That's rich."

"Anna Banana, thank you very much," Tory said in a teasing tone.

Chris carried a tray with a pitcher of juice and two glasses on it. She stretched out on the blue and green cushions of the sofa. Tory sat in her favorite rattan chair.

Chris wasn't certain what to make of Tory's comment. For years, she'd entertained the children with stories of an orangutan who took photographs. As a writer, Tory had a way of weaving tales, complete with such vivid details, that Chris would swear that they were true. Hours later, she'd realize it had been Tory's way to avoid answering a question.

Although Tory claimed to be thirty-five, a year younger than Chris, it was hard to know for sure. When she was with Chris's children, she seemed so young. Yet, when she talked about her work or journeys into the various Asian countries, it was obvious she was older than she appeared.

Despite the attention she received from men, Tory was oblivious to the opposite sex. It had been a long time since Chris had tried fixing Tory up. Chris thought it over, and decided to try one last time. "You'll never believe what Kev told me this morning," she said jokingly.

Tory helped herself to another glass of juice and grinned. "He loves you and wants to make an honest woman of you. After all these years, the man has finally proposed."

"Can't you ever be serious?" Chris paused. Tory was trying too hard to be funny. “There's a new guy at Trans Oil. He's single, about Kev's age. From the sound of things, he'd be perfect for you."

Tory raised her hand and held it out like a crossing guard halting traffic. "I thought we were done with this. I don't want to meet a man. Especially one Kevin thinks is perfect. I can see him now, a junior executive with a buttoned down mind that matches his three piece suit."

"You're wrong. Kev said he's known the guy for a while. He's smart, successful, and not bad looking." Chris changed the order of Kevin's description in an attempt to appeal to Tory's interests.

"If he's so wonderful, why isn't he taken? Anyway, I've told you a million times, I'll never get involved with an expat. I made that mistake once and it was more than enough."

Chris heard a hint of pain in Tory's voice. A discussion of men was the only time Tory ever lost her cool demeanor. "That affair was over before we got here. Isn't it time to give expats another chance?"

Tory rose, pacing in front of the coffee table. Chris watched and waited. When Tory was agitated, she walked to calm herself. There was no sense talking to her when she was in that state. Tory's reactions seemed more exaggerated than usual this morning. Chris wondered what was on her mind. Tory seldom discussed anything personal. It was obvious today wouldn't be different. A failed love affair didn't explain Tory's withdrawal from men.

Tory stopped and glared at Chris. "Why is it so hard for you to believe I'm happy with my life? Men always leave, and good-byes hurt. I never plan to say those words again."

Although she knew it was asking for another rebuff, Chris couldn't stop herself "You know, you've never said why you didn't marry. Or why you stayed here when he left."

"I have my career to consider. Can you see me lugging my photography equipment through the jungle with a baby on my hip?"

"Who said anything about children?" Chris looked at Tory and knew the topic was closed. Tory might joke about her lifestyle, but she had no intention of changing. Tory was still an enigma, even after all the time they'd been friends. *I shouldn't have said anything. I should simply have invited her to dinner and had him here. Heck, I can still do that,* Chris realized.

Tory gulped down her juice and slammed the glass on the table. "Time for tennis."

Usually Chris and Tory were equally matched. Today Tory's game was off. She missed several balls that were well within her reach, making it easy for Chris to win quickly.

After she showered and changed, Chris went into the kitchen for iced tea. She took two glasses into the solarium and waited for Tory. She was surprised when Tory came into the room wearing a silk dress instead of shorts. "Seeing a client?" she asked.

Tory shook her head. "I'm teaching a photography class at the American School on Tuesdays. Remember? Alison conned me into it. Look, um, I'm sorry I got hotheaded before. Tell Kev I'm sure his friend is great, but I'm not in the market."

"Stay for lunch. If you don't, you won't eat until you get to Sabah." Chris knew Tory was about to leave town. There was a look in her eyes, a far-away look Chris recognized as the precursor of Tory going into seclusion.

Tory shook her head no. "When's Kev due back?"

"Friday night. Why?"

"I'll be back before then. I have to get an article in the mail by Thursday. I'll call when it's done. We can take the kids to Little India." Tory paused with her hand on the doorknob. "I almost forgot. I picked this up for you at Jim Thompson in Bangkok." She tossed Chris a package wrapped in paper from the famous Thai silk factory.

Chris shuddered when she slit open the gold seal and saw several meters of dark green silk. The fabric was so dark it almost looked black. Chris preferred warm, pastel colors that matched her sunny disposition. Dark, somber colors didn't suit her. "Isn't it a bit austere?"

Tory put her things down and draped the fabric over Chris's chest and one shoulder. "I think it's dramatic. The color's wonderful with your hair. It'll bring out the green in your eyes. I thought you might want a new dress for Thanksgiving."

"Will you be here?"

"You know me, I'm a sucker for turkey and all the trimmings. Have I ever missed your Thanksgiving dinner?"

Although she shook her head, Chris wasn't convinced. Something was on Tory's mind. It was more than the mention of a new man in town. Tory's tone had been brittle, as if she were on the edge. Had Chris finally found a chink in Tory's self-possessed facade?

Chapter 3
TORY

Singapore, Malaysia and Indonesia
Tuesday-Thursday, September 18-20, 1979

"Miss Winslow?"

Tory groaned inwardly when she heard Laurel call her name. She didn't have time for questions today. Her body tense, she turned and smiled. "Yes?"

"My parents said I could get another lens for my birthday. What should I tell them I want?"

Tory paused. There were fifteen students in her photography class, each with different equipment. In two weeks, Tory had mastered their names and gotten a glimpse into their personalities. "What do you have now?"

"A normal lens and a telephoto," Laurel answered. Her tone indicated every thirteen-year-old had such treasures.

"How about a wide angle lens so you can take panoramic shots?"

"What would I need to take pictures of flowers like the ones you showed us today?"

"You could get tele-converters. They change your normal lenses into a close up lens. Or you could get a macro lens. I think the wide angle would be a better choice."

"Why? I want to take photos of the dew drops on the flowers."

Tory smiled. She could understand Laurel's interest in close up work. It was a fascinating form of photography, but hardly something she'd use often. Even had Laurel not been Alison Taylor's best friend, Tory wouldn't have wanted to squelch her enthusiasm.

She weighed her words carefully to be diplomatic. "I'm sure a wide angle lens will give you more opportunities than you think. Next Friday we're going to the Botanical Gardens. Why don't you show me where you think a macro lens would be good? I'll take those pictures and some with a wide-angle lens. When we look at the pictures the following week, you'll see what I mean."

Laurel grinned. "You'd do that for me?"

Tory nodded. "The best way to decide is to see the different effects of each. Make up your own mind. Don't be guided by what I say."

Before Laurel could say more, Tory glanced at her watch. "Oops, I've got to dash. See you next week, Laurel."

It took Tory several minutes to gather her paraphernalia from the staff lounge and call a taxi. Luckily, there was not much traffic and she made it to Paya Lebar Airport with enough time to pick up her ticket and board the plane to Sabah.

As the plane took off, Tory leaned back in her seat and sighed. At first, she'd been reluctant to teach at the American School. Now, she was pleased. The children were different from the ones at the small school she'd attended. Prior to teaching, the only children Tory spent time around were the Taylor's. She'd presumed their self-confidence came from living in a loving environment. She now saw that most children were assured and happy.

It was a marked contrast to her childhood. Tory frowned at the comparison. Her family never had enough money, and certainly not enough love. Her father was a lush who took his frustrations out on his wife and children.

Most families in rural North Dakota were poor. What cash they had went to necessities. Children who thought a new sweater or pair of boots great gifts would never have dreamed other children had the riches these expatriate children took for granted. Maybe it was different now. Tory hadn't been back to Prairie View for twenty years. She had no idea what had become of the town or most of its inhabitants.

Never happy thinking about the past, Tory diverted her attention to Halim's call. Halim was a director of Sepilok, the Animal Reserve where Tory had brought Anna years before. At the time, he warned Tory that domesticated orangutans often had difficulty adjusting to life in the wild. Although she'd been reluctant to move Anna, Tory had no choice. Anna had been her pet for nearly ten years when the government outlawed pet orangutans. When Tory no longer felt it was safe to leave Anna when she traveled, she took her pet to Sepilok.

No matter how busy her schedule, Tory went to Sabah every month. It was important Anna not feel she'd been abandoned. Tory understood that emotion only too well. Her family had deserted her while she was in high school. Whenever she thought of leaving her pet at Sepilok, Tory remembered her own tears when she left home. She imagined Anna felt the same rejection when she was crated and deposited at Sepilok.

At the start, Tory told herself her frequent trips were so she could be sure Anna was doing well. It took three years before she could admit she needed to see Anna. In a strange way the orangutan was her anchor. Anna was the ballast and she the sail. It was only with Anna that Tory felt safe enough to talk about her feelings. She shivered as she remembered the day she'd left Anna in Halim's care.

There were times like today when Tory wished she could open up and talk to Chris. It might ease her tension about Anna's impending death if Tory could share her pain. But how could she explain feeling so attached to a pet when she'd so cleverly built her persona as someone perfectly content by herself? It wouldn't make sense unless she explained much more.

By the time the plane landed at Sandakan, it was too late to go to Sepilok. Tory checked into a guesthouse and worked on her article until it was time for bed. In the morning, she ate a quick breakfast and dressed in jeans, thick socks, work boots, and a turtleneck sweater. The heavy clothing was hot in the dilapidated taxi without air conditioning.

Sepilok was a tropical rain forest, so her thick clothes were necessary, both as protection from leeches and mosquitoes and to combat the coolness that accompanied the heavy canopy of overgrowth.

Halim met Tory at the park gate. She smiled a greeting and asked about his family. No matter how much of a rush Tory was in to see Anna, she understood the Malaysian culture. It was imperative they chatter for at least forty-five minutes. Despite her dislike of social conventions, Tory enjoyed the opportunity to improve her Bahasa Malaysian.

Once Halim felt he and Tory had caught up with each other's lives, he led her to Anna. "She's a little better today."

Tory's face softened at the news. When she worried, her face assumed the look of a rigid mask of unyielding armor that shielded her from pain. "She's better? Wonderful."

"She's not cured," Halim hastened to add. "Malaria cannot be stopped. Today, though, she seems better. Maybe she knew you were coming."

Tory laughed. "Anna's clairvoyant. When we lived in Sembawang, she'd sense when I was coming home. According to my neighbors, she'd stay away the entire time I was gone and return an hour or two before I did."

"Orangutans are amazing animals. Oh, I nearly forgot, Barbara from the World Wildlife Federation rang. The time of your meeting in Jakarta is changed."

Tory nodded absently and shoved the piece of paper with the message into the pocket of her jeans. She could see Anna lying next to a tree stump. Tory ran to her pet and sat on the stump, cradling Anna's red-orange head on her lap. "Not feeling well?" she crooned. "You look tired."

Tory stood and helped Anna climb on to her back. She felt the fever that ravaged Anna's body and wanted to cry. As if she understood her fears, Anna patted Tory's hair.

Anna tugged at Tory's shoulder and pointed towards the side of the path. "Tired? Okay, we'll rest." Tory found a gentle area of sloping grass and placed Anna on a bed of soft underbrush. Tory reclined next to Anna and picked at the twigs matted in the orangutan's hair. She gazed at the sleeping orangutan, horrified by the changes in Anna. Her exuberant spirit had been replaced by lassitude. She'd lost weight. It was obvious the end was near.

"Don't you dare die on me. I'm not sure what I'd do if you weren't here." Tory thought Anna was asleep, and was startled when the orangutan wiped the tears that streamed from her eyes. Tory hadn't realized she was crying until she felt Anna's hand on her face.

Tory rested her head on Anna's chest and cried. When there were no tears left, she stood and picked up Anna. "Time for you to see Halim. Maybe he can give you something to help you feel better. I know you don't like medicine, Kiddo, but if it'd help, it might be worth a try."

Tory found Halim near the entrance to the park. "She's really bad. Can't you do something?"

"You should say good-bye. This may be the last time, you know."

Tory vigorously shook her head. There was no way she'd accept Halim's prognosis.

Tory stood with her left hip jutting out to create a place for Anna to sit. In a soft voice, she whispered to Anna, "Want me to take pictures of you? Someday I'll do a book on primates, and I'll need a photo of you."

The minute Anna heard the word "picture" she got down and did a slow, tired dance in front of the camera. Tory steadied the camera against her chest and shot a roll of Anna's antics. The charade made her feet better. Anna was prancing and smiling at the lens. For the moment, Tory could convince herself that both she and Anna were fine.

Out of the corner of her eye, she saw Halim frown. It didn't matter. She and Anna were going through a ritual that comforted them. When the roll of film was finished, Tory kissed Anna and waved to Halim. She left for Sandakan before Halim could tell her anything she didn't want to hear.

In Jakarta, Tory took a taxi to a small hotel. Her appointment with the man from the World Wildlife Federation was at five o'clock at the Mandarin. There was barely enough time for her to change clothes and get through the chaotic traffic.

Tory waited in one of the overstuffed club chairs in the lobby.

"Tory Winslow?" a voice asked tentatively.

The voice startled her from her reverie. Unsettled from her visit to Anna, Tory stared at her feet. Remembering that this was business, she stood, raised her head, and extended her right hand. "And you're...?"

"Greg Hampton. Barbara Harrisson said you'd be the woman to talk to. Sit down, please. Would you like a drink?"

"Scotch neat, water back."

"No ice?"

Tory shook her head. "Not in Jakarta. The water's bottled, so it's relatively harmless."

Once their drinks were served, Greg launched into a description of the information he wanted. The WWF was putting money into several Asian preserves where animals lived freely in the wild. They planned a mass mailing to collect donations and needed photos and copy about the various areas. Periodically, Tory interrupted Greg to ask a question or make a suggestion.

At the end of his sales pitch, Greg shifted uncomfortably in his seat. "The thing about it is we don't have much money. Barbara says you're the best and that's what we want."

Tory smiled inwardly. She was the best, and she knew it. Although money would have been nice, the assignment was interesting, and it would give her an excuse to see Anna again. "I'm sure we can come to terms. Money isn't my primary motivation. Barbara probably told you that, as well."

"Well, she did mention you often donate your services to what you see as worthy causes -- and you have a soft spot for animals."

Tory shrugged indifferently. There was no reason to explain she could stop working for several years, if she chose. "What's your time frame? I'll need to go to some of the places again. It'd be easier if I could combine the travel with a paying trip."

"We were thinking six months. Is that sufficient?" Greg looked troubled. Tory guessed he had no idea she could have the information to him in less than a week if she went through her vast library of photographs.

"Sure. One thing though, I reserve the right to review any changes to what I write. Only when I'm in agreement do we have a deal."

Greg nodded. "I can't see why anyone would object. Why don't you give me your card? I'll call if there's a problem. If not, you can send us the photos and write-ups as you finish them. We'll send you the galleys to review before publication."

Tory extended her arm again and smiled. "It's been a pleasure doing business with you."

"Are you free for dinner?"

Tory was surprised by the invitation. She'd made tentative plans to meet Kevin Taylor for dinner, but they could be changed. Then she saw the wedding band on Greg's left hand. If she were to eat with a married man, it would be Kevin. "Thanks, but I have plans."

"I understand. Well, it was nice to meet you."

Tory went to the reception desk and asked them to call Kevin's room. Luck was on her side; he was back from his meeting. They agreed to meet in the bar on the second floor.

Tory kissed Kevin on the cheek as she slipped into the booth next to him. "What's so important that I couldn't tell Chris I was meeting you?" she asked.

Kevin pulled at a twig in her hair and grinned. "See you've been playing Lady Tarzan again. What do you want to drink? I'm having a martini."

"Fine." Tory waited while he told the waiter. Spending the evening with Kevin would be pleasant. It was no surprise that Kevin and Chris were popular. They were fun to be around.

When their drinks were served, Kevin said, "Thanks for meeting me in Jakarta."

"What choice did I have?"

"You could've said no. But then you'd never know what I wanted. And your innate curiosity couldn't tolerate that."

Tory smiled at his apt description of her motivation.

"I want to buy Chris something really nice."

Tory looked up from her drink. Kevin and Chris rarely exchanged gifts. Their money was spent on family trips. "What's the occasion?" she asked.

"I was thinking I might get her a necklace for Thanksgiving."

Tory waited. Kevin would explain without her prompting.

"I've got a chance to move out of marketing. It'll mean more time away from Chris and the kids."

"And you think a necklace will compensate? Who are you kidding?"

Kevin hung his head. "We both know how much family time means to Chris. But this is my chance at the brass ring. I don't want to pass it up."

"Tell her the truth, Kev. Chris can't be bought."

"It's not bribery! If I take this job, it'll start around Thanksgiving. You know how busy the social scene gets then. All the wives struggle to outdo each other. Chris never says anything, but I see her eyeing the jewelry the other women wear."

"So?"

"I'd like her to have one piece she really likes. Chris makes my life so easy. I'd like to do something in return."

Tory thought about the time that Chris spent preparing for parties. She agonized over the guest list, careful to invite people who were important to Kevin's career, as well as people they enjoyed. Chris kept her ears open to any gossip that might give Kevin some important information.

"There's a jewelry store on L Street that has some things Chris likes. We can go there after dinner."

"Great! I knew I could count on you."

"Not so fast. What's this I hear about you wanting me to meet some new guy at Trans Oil? I thought we understood each other better than that."

"He asked about you."

Kevin's tone hadn't been joking, yet Tory expected to see a grin on his face when she looked at him. Instead he was poker faced, as if he'd said the sky was blue.

"Right," she snickered. "This guy gets off a plane and the first words out of his mouth are 'Can you introduce me to Tory Winslow?'"

"I know it sounds strange, but it's important to him. Anyway, I think you'd like him."

"Just what I need, another matchmaker. I finally get Chris to stop, and now you want to pick up where she left off. The dynamic duo! No wonder you're the perfect couple, you share one mind." Tory took her napkin from her lap and tossed it on the table in feigned disgust.

Kevin put his hand on her arm to keep her from leaving. "Chris and I care about you. We want you to be happy."

"I am," she said defiantly. "I won't become part of Noah's Ark."

"Why do you insist on calling Singapore that?"

"Because you expats think the world only exists if you're part of a couple. You can't understand there are people who enjoy solitude."

At the same time she ridiculed her friends, Tory was jealous of them. Chris and Kevin had a closeness she didn't share with anyone. Long-term liaisons weren't for her. It had taken years to build the perfect fortress to hide behind. She wouldn't give anyone the key to her past.

The one time she had let down her guard had been with Tim Hammond. They'd met one Saturday morning in Chinatown where they'd each gone to watch the funeral processions. It had been hot and muggy. When he invited her into a nearby bar for a shandy, she accepted. Tim had been so full of dreams of where his career would go. If she closed her eyes, Tory could almost hear his Australian twang, "Luv, this is my place. Been here a week and already I know this is the start of something big in my life."

Tim thought the world existed for him to conquer. He never doubted he'd one day run a brewery. At a time when Tory was barely making enough money to scrape by, his confidence was the bromide she needed.

Tim hadn't been interested in her past. He never asked why Tory lived in Asia. They enjoyed an easygoing romance for five years. Tory had been amazed at how upset she was when Tim returned to Australia.

She shook her head as if to stop the painful memories. She looked across the table and grinned at Kevin. "Ready to go shopping?" She smiled when Kevin nodded. "I'll go along with the necklace if you promise you'll explain about the new job to Chris."

"Sure."

Something in Kevin's tone made Tory wonder. "I'm serious, Kevin. Chris will understand."

"How long are you in Jakarta?"

"I leave in the morning. Why?"

"Dinner was fun. I thought we might do it again tomorrow night."

"You don't like eating alone, do you?"

Kevin shook his head.

Tory smiled at their differences. Eating alone was commonplace for her. A shared meal provided an interesting diversion. It was not something she'd want to do on a daily basis.

Chapter 4
CHRIS

Singapore
Saturday, October 6, 1979

Kevin kissed Chris as he joined her at the table in the solarium. "I thought you were playing tennis with Lady Tarzan this morning. Have I missed Tory?"

Chris looked at her tennis clothes and frowned. "Tory's off somewhere, I guess. Are you avoiding Tory? Is that why you didn't come downstairs? I know you were awake when I got out of bed."

Kevin grimaced, his boyish freckled face trying hard to look stern, an act that wasn't entirely successful. "It's the weekend," he said. "I wasn't up to Tory." He reached for the pitcher of papaya juice and poured himself a glass of the sweet nectar. "There are times when I find your friend a bit too much to take on an empty stomach. She can be so certain she knows what's right for everyone."

"Oh, Kev," Chris laughed, "you're being ridiculous. What's Tory done to you?"

"Nothing." Kevin reached for her hand and squeezed it gently. "You promised to take Sarah Parker looking at houses today. I don't think she needs to be exposed to Tory. Singapore's enough for now. Your friend takes time to appreciate. She's like mildew. At first, it's unpleasant. Then, after a while, you hardly notice it."

Chris swatted her husband. How could he compare Tory to mildew? Kevin enjoyed bantering with Tory. Both she and Kevin adored Tory, as did their children. Tory was the children's unofficial aunt, the adult they discussed things with which they sometimes were hesitant to broach with their parents. The fact that Tory was so much a part of their lives made Kevin's reaction odd. It wasn't like him.

"Have you and she quarreled about creative license again?" she asked.

"No." Kevin looked at the piece of fruit in front of his wife. "Is that all you're eating?"

"I'm dieting again. I thought Sarah might want to stop for lunch."

Kevin lifted his newspaper and Chris pulled the paper down. "Why are you so protective of the Parker woman? If she's going to live here, she'll meet Tory sooner or later."

"I simply think later would be better. Her husband Barney is about our age, and a good ten years older than his wife. Sarah gives the impression of being a babe in the woods. I get the feeling she didn't want to move."

"Neither do half the women who come here," Chris parried.

"Point taken. It's just ... you know how intimidating Tory can be if she's on about something."

Chris gave him a quizzical look. Kevin had never before been so protective about the wife of a business associate.

Kevin patted her hand. "My jungle drum says the Parkers had a rough time in Harare. I'd like you to make her feel welcome. You can show her the ropes like no one else can, Chrissy."

Chris beamed at the compliment. She reveled in her position within their community. "I better get dressed. Suradmin should be back with the car soon."

"Back?" Kevin asked.

"I sent him to get Marc. Janet and Phil Adams are going to Penang for the weekend, so I said Steven could stay with us. Make sure Marc and he don't drown each other in the pool."

"Sure. Where's Alison?"

Chris laughed. "Where else? With Laurel."

"They were both here for dinner last night. When did she leave?"

"Laurel spent the night. The two of them stayed up half the night talking. You probably won't see or hear from them for hours."

By the time Suradmin returned with Marc and Steven, Chris was ready. As the car made its way through the Saturday morning traffic, Kevin's comments were on her mind. Chris hadn't seen Tory since the morning they played tennis two weeks before. Alison's friend Laurel said Tory hadn't taught her photography class last week. Chris wondered if something had happened.

Diverting her concerns about Tory, Chris wondered about the woman that she was about to visit. Why had the Parkers come to Singapore now? There was an unwritten rule at Trans Oil that couples didn't move between October and December. They spent their holidays where they were and moved the next year.

The Goodwood Park was one of the most expensive and exclusive hotels on the island. It was not where expats typically stayed until they found a place to live. Chris had expected the Parkers to be at the Shangri-La.

The second Chris saw Sarah Parker sitting in the lobby she knew Sarah wasn't American. Even before Sarah opened her mouth, her clothes gave her away. Sarah wore a stylish but form-fitting dress, the skirt so full Chris was certain there was a crinoline petticoat underneath. Sarah's accent was pure Australian. She had their strange way of pronouncing an A like an I. "Why don't we have some coffee?" Chris suggested.

"If you'd like," Sarah answered timidly.

Immediately, Chris saw what so captivated Kevin. Sarah looked like the Dresden dolls Alison collected. She was exquisite. Her small frame was perfectly proportioned. Tory would want to photograph her immediately. *No wonder Kevin's gone gaga*, she thought.

Despite her picture-perfect appearance, there was hesitancy about Sarah, as if she were frightened of life in Singapore. Chris wanted to reach out, comfort Sarah, and tell her everything would be fine and she had nothing to worry about.

"If we talk a while, we can probably cross out half the places on this list," she offered. If Sarah were uneasy about

Singapore, finding the right house quickly might help her feel more comfortable.

"I'd feel simply terrible taking up too much of your time."

Chris frowned; Sarah had misunderstood. "I love showing off Singapore. I also know how important finding the right house is. I couldn't wait to move out of the hotel."

Sarah looked pensive, then said, "I think the hotel is wonderful."

"Don't you find the traffic unsettling?"

Sarah glanced up, a startled look on her face. "How did you know?"

"Everyone does at first. Have you left the hotel at all?"

Sarah shook her head. "My husband Barney went into the office yesterday. When your husband picked him up, he volunteered your services instead of a realtor."

Chris smiled. "I like showing people around. It's better to get the lay of the land from another wife. All realtors care about is getting Trans Oil to sign the most expensive lease and collecting their commission."

Sarah helped herself to another cup of coffee. The longer they spoke, the more she appeared to relax. "My mother-in-law met you when she and her husband visited here five years ago."

"The Parkers, of course." The pieces were falling into place. The Parkers were part of the fabric of Trans Oil. No wonder Kevin was concerned that Sarah's introduction to the island be perfect. *Why didn't he tell me,* she wondered. "I remember. I'm surprised Violet remembers me."

"Oh, she did. She said you knew everyone and everything about Singapore."

Chris blushed at the way Sarah gushed. "Kevin and I have been here longer than most people. That gives us the home court advantage."

"I can't imagine living anywhere long enough to stop being the new wife."

"You've never lived in Singapore. It's different."

"How?"

"It's very small. There are over a hundred companies, each with thirty or more expatriates. More people arrive every day. No one stays new for long."

"What are the women like?"

Chris paused. How could she explain without frightening Sarah? There were three main groups. The first stayed safely within the confines of each other's houses and complained bitterly about life in Asia. To them, nothing about the area was worthwhile. They relied upon each other to maintain their memories of what had been so perfect at home. The second group was comprised of women who no longer noticed where they lived. They coped with their frequent moves by staying ensconced in the confines of their houses, usually with a bottle, their remedy to counteract the alien environment. Whenever possible, Chris stayed with the third and smallest group, the women who indulged in all the wonders Singapore had to offer.

Realizing she'd been lost in thought, Chris apologized. "Your last question made me think. There's no set type. It depends on what you want."

"How do you make friends?"

"Women I meet at parties or who have children in school with my two. I've also met some playing tennis. Do you play?"

"In this heat? I could barely get my hair to behave this morning."

Chris stared at Sarah; her hair was faultless. "You did a wonderful job. Most of us give into the heat and keep our hair cropped."

Sarah touched the tips of her hair with trembling fingers. "Barney likes my hair long. I don't think he'd be too keen on my cutting it."

"Maybe you'll find a way to cope with the heat. My hair's not important to me. If you don't play tennis, what hobbies do you have?"

Sarah frowned. "I'm not interested in that much. I sketch a little. Every place we've lived I've tried to decorate our house with native artifacts. I'm no interior decorator though." She flushed, as if her accomplishments were meaningless. "Being Barney's wife takes up most of my time. He works so hard. I try to make where we live a place he likes coming home to."

Chris smiled; Sarah had unwittingly described Chris. She and Kevin were a team. He left his problems at the office; the only times he discussed work were when he wanted her opinion. In exchange, Chris ran their large house without troubling him about the myriad of details involved.

"I have a friend who's artsy, a photographer. She'd be the person to show you where to find fascinating things to draw. Do you want a house or an apartment?"

"A house, of course. Trey will need a place to play."

"Trey?'

"Our son. He just turned three. I had a devil of a time finding someone to stay with him today. The hotel came up with several candidates, but they were utterly unsuitable. Barney claims he'll tend him, but he's so easily diverted." Sarah stopped, as if she'd said too much. She sipped her coffee and tapped her foot uncomfortably. "What I mean is, Barney was at the office and I just know he has a briefcase full of papers. The poor dear won't mean to, he'll honestly think Trey is safely playing with a toy, but, before you know it, he'll be buried in work and forget he even has a son."

To put Sarah at ease, Chris giggled. "I know that routine. Kevin's the same. This morning I had to remind him where his children were. If it weren't for the servants, I'd never trust him alone with the children."

Struck by an inspiration, Chris turned to Sarah with a grin. "Will you be looking for an amah to help with Trey? If so, I know just the woman. Marc's twelve now and Alison's thirteen. They're too old for an amah, a fact they mention at every opportunity. Ah Soon's been part of our family for so long, I've been reluctant to let her go. She takes some getting used to, but she's simply wonderful with small children."

"What takes getting used to?"

"She's what's called a black and white amah. She wears starched white cotton blouse and black silk trousers. The colors symbolize her spinsterhood. Amahs like her were common twenty years ago. They're hard to come by these days. I'd feel better if I thought she were going to work for a good family."

"She sounds perfect. I know I'll need help with Trey."

"Once we find you a place to live, I'll mention it to Kevin. I'm sure he'll have no objection."

While Sarah motioned for the check, Chris's thoughts returned to Kevin's earlier comments. Sarah seemed worried about fitting in. The only time she relaxed was when Chris suggested introducing her to Tory. Chris made a mental note to ask her friends to be especially nice to Sarah. She knew that the women would do as asked.

Since junior high school, she and Kevin had always been the leaders of their group. They were outgoing and friendly and enjoyed having friends over for an evening, even if only for a potluck supper. In Singapore, Chris determined which couples were admitted to the most popular crowd. The other wives followed her example, almost blindly. If she snubbed a woman, they ignored her as well. Likewise, they'd feign interest in a seemingly boring woman if Chris felt the woman had something to offer.

Chris wondered what to make of Sarah. She remembered Barney and Violet Parker well. The husband was gracious, a true gentleman of the old school, whereas Violet was a pretentious snob. Chris wondered if Sarah would turn out to be the same.

From her earlier comment about her hair, Chris presumed Sarah had made a career of always doing the proper thing. At the same time, Sarah's face lit up when she spoke about the things she enjoyed. There was a person buried underneath the perfect clothes and hair. She hoped Sarah would soon be comfortable enough to let the world see the real woman.

Chapter 5
SARAH

Singapore
Saturday, October 6, 1979

Violet had been right when she promised Sarah would like the hotel. "Father's arranged for you to be put up in the Goodwood Park Hotel. It's the poshest on the island. If one of the wives suggests you move to the Shangri-La, don't be swayed. The Goodwood is far better."

As she sat in the lobby sharing coffee with Chris, Sarah stared at the woman sitting opposite her. Violet hadn't been far off the mark in her description. The dress she wore was dreadful. It was more a shift worn to the beach than a proper dress. The style would not flatter anyone. It certainly wasn't appropriate for looking at houses. If her hair were an inch longer, the cut would be dramatic. Instead of her crowning glory, Chris's hair was utilitarian, like her dress. When Sarah saw the sandals on Chris's feet, she winced. Her entire look was wrong. If this was the best of the best, Sarah couldn't imagine what the other women must look like. *How on earth could Mother Parker think this woman anything but a frump? I hope she doesn't have such atrocious taste in houses.*

Despite her first impression, Sarah smiled at Chris. Violet Parker was seldom wrong about social matters. If Chris was the leader of the pack, there must be more to her than was apparent.

At that moment, the waiter came with their check. Sarah reached for the maroon leather folder with lacquered pink nails that matched her dress perfectly. The color was a dusty pink that went with many of her floral print dresses. She signed her name to the check with a flourish. "Shall we be off then? I'm terribly anxious to get settled. It just won't do for poor Barney to live in the hotel for long. He'll get spoiled and be cross with me when I don't wait on him hand and foot the way room service does."

Chris grinned as if Sarah had just told her a joke. When she smiled, Chris looked pretty. The thought made Sarah question her initial misgivings. Chris had looked older while she was serious. Now that she was smiling, it was obvious she was in her thirties. It was older than Sarah, but most of the people she met were closer to Barney's age than hers.

When the car pulled up in front of an iron gate, Sarah's jaw dropped. The house was hidden from the street by bushes that covered the wall surrounding the property. Inside the house wasn't magnificent at all. Paint peeled from the walls and several light fixtures were broken. The two staircases to the second floor were in poor repair. It would take a small fortune to make the house habitable. "Ugh," she said when she spied a lizard on the marble floors. "What's that filthy thing doing here?"

Chris laughed. "It's a cicak. Don't worry; it's harmless. They're everywhere. They eat mosquitoes, so you learn to ignore them. The house is the pits, though. Unless you can see something I've missed, we might as well be on our way. There's a house on Cluny Road I think you'll like."

Sarah wondered if she'd ever be as nonchalant as Chris about a lizard. The thing had startled her. It had taken restraint for her not to scream.

The house on Cluny Road was lovely. It was an old Colonial, complete with white columns by the front door. The rooms were large, and the only one that would need a makeover was the kitchen. There was no way she'd be able to create her masterpieces in that kitchen. "The kitchen will have to go."

"The people who lived here before never set foot there. Myra thought kitchens were for servants. If you like the house, let's see the grounds. I think there's a pool."

The house did have a pool. Sarah was overjoyed. Perhaps Singapore wouldn't be so bad after all. Although smaller than the first house, it was still large. The grounds were manicured. The shrubbery was different from what she was accustomed to. There were several palm trees in the backyard. She wondered what a gardener would cost. She couldn't imagine Barney tending the lawn.

She turned to Chris and gave her a coaxing smile. "Would you mind terribly if we stopped for lunch? I'm famished. I think this house will be perfect, but I've so many questions. If you have the time, I'd appreciate it if you could give me some advice."

As Sarah expected, Chris agreed. While they drove, Sarah fretted about raising the topic of costs without sounding crass. Money was a subject she was uncomfortable discussing. She knew Trans Oil would pay for the house. If Chris had shown it to her, it must be on their approved list. What would it cost to maintain? There was no way she could clean the house; it was much too large. She desperately wanted to live there though.

When the car pulled up in front of a hotel, Sarah was surprised. She expected them to go to a restaurant.

Chris smiled at Sarah's perplexed face. "Most of the hotels have several good restaurants. I thought we'd go to the Bistro at the Marco Polo. It has an interesting menu, a mixture of French and Italian."

The hotel enchanted Sarah. A guard in a starched and pressed white uniform opened the plate glass lobby door. His hands were covered with white cotton gloves and he wore a white English bobby-style hat. He bowed slightly as the women passed. Sarah thought Singapore was like a fairy tale brought to life.

The Bistro was a pleasant restaurant with small round tables and red and white checked tablecloths. Sarah toyed absently with the glass of wine in her hands. Before she could decide how to broach the subject, Chris spoke.

"Do you have much experience with servants? You'll need at least three live-ins for a house that size, plus a gardener and a pool boy. Since they won't be needed every day, you can share. Most of the Trans Oil crowd uses the same two men. There should be no problem adding you to their list."

Sarah smiled more to herself than to Chris. If everyone else had help, she would as well. Appearances were important to the Parkers. They would expect their son to live at the same level as the other Trans Oil expats.

"Three? Why so many?"

"Ah Soon, a housekeeper who also cleans, and a cook."

"I love to cook. I won't need help in the kitchen."

Chris shook her head and smiled. "What about when you entertain? Entertaining is done on a lavish scale. You'll be glad for a cook the first time you try to have twenty or thirty people over for the evening. By the way, do you play bridge?"

Sarah was caught off guard at the abrupt change of topic. "Not very well. Why?"

"Several of us play on Thursday afternoon. We're always looking for a new member. If you play, you'll definitely need help in the kitchen. It's virtually impossible to host four or five tables of bridge, prepare lunch, and be anything but exhausted," Chris said conspiratorially.

Sarah reveled in the warmth and friendliness of her tone. After the lonesome days in Harare, it would be nice to have a friend. Sarah wrote down the names Chris suggested. Even if she never called them, Sarah didn't want to hurt Chris's feelings.

When Chris returned her to the Goodwood, Sarah raced into their suite, eager to tell Barney about her day. She practically threw herself into his arms. "Hello, love. Where's Trey?"

"Sleeping."

"Oh, Barney," she pouted. "He shouldn't still be napping. He'll never go to sleep tonight. I'd best wake him."

As Sarah turned toward Trey's room, Barney put out his arm to stop her. He took her hand and led her to the couch. "Trey had an accident. We've been at hospital. Doctor says there's no need to worry."

Sarah's stomach turned over. She'd enjoyed one afternoon and was being punished for her selfishness. "My poor baby. What happened?"

"Trey was in the wading pool. I couldn't have been sitting more than ten feet from him. He got out and ran. He slipped and fell, right in front of my eyes."

"I knew I shouldn't have gone out and left him with you. Barney, I warned you he has to be watched every second."

Barney took out his handkerchief and handed it to Sarah. "Don't cry, pretty Sarah. You know I'd never purposely hurt Trey."

Sarah sniffed back her tears. This wasn't going the way she planned. Earlier, she'd promised herself to give them a new start in Singapore. "I know how much you love Trey. How is he?"

"He has some cuts and bruises."

"And? I know there's something else."

"Sarah, it's nearly five o'clock and I haven't had a drink yet today. It wasn't my fault."

Sarah eyed the open soda bottle on the table. Perhaps she was being overly harsh. Accidents did happen. Trey could be a terror. She smiled and kissed her husband. "I know, love. Please tell me what else."

"He broke his arm. Doctor said not to worry. It's a clean break. He'll be in plaster for six weeks."

"My poor baby. Do you think it'd be okay if I peeked in on him?" she asked cautiously.

"Sure. I could use a nip of gin. Think I'll make myself a wee drink."

Trey woke as his mother walked into his room. He held up his arm. "Trey fall down."

Sarah sat on the bed and cradled him in her arms. "I see. Does it hurt?"

"No. Daddy and I went hospital. In a taxi. Daddy was scared. I wasn't."

"There's my brave boy," Sarah crooned softly. "You must be hungry after your big adventure. Shall I call room service? What would you like for dinner?"

"Chips."

Sarah smiled at Trey's self-satisfied grin. In Australia, Trey had discovered chips. They were the only things he wanted to eat. "Not for supper."

"Daddy let me have chips for lunch."

"I'm sure he did. Mummy's here now and she wants you to eat more than that. Shall I order prawns?" Fresh prawns had been a treat in Zimbabwe. She hoped he could be coaxed into eating them.

When she looked at the cast on his left arm, Sarah wanted to cry. His arm was covered from his hand to his elbow.

It took nearly two hours to feed and bathe Trey. By the time she finished reading Trey his second story, he was sound asleep.

When she returned to the living room it was obvious that Barney had been drinking heavily. She walked over to the couch, took the glass from his hands, and placed it on the table. "Chris suggested we hire their amah to care for Trey. What do you think?"

"That would be right. An amah's what we need. Good idea!"

Barney was enunciating too clearly, which meant he was drunk. Concerned that his behavior was the result of Trey's accident, Sarah ignored his drinking. There was no point in having a row. If she told him about the house, he'd know she didn't blame him.

"I saw the most wonderful house today, love. I can't wait to show it to you. I think I could do a lot with the place."

"I'm sure my father gave you a check to cover the work. If you need more, take it up with him."

"Barney, can't you pretend to be interested? I really want you to see it. It's for the three of us."

Before he could respond, there was a knock at the door. Barney crossed the room and opened the door. After tipping the waiter for the ice, he poured himself another drink. "What difference does it make what I want?"

She refused to let Barney shut her out as he'd done in the past. Steeling herself for a rebuff, she took the glass from his hands and placed it on the coffee table. "Barney, I want us to try again here. If you don't want me to use the money from your father, I won't."

"Then you'll whinge when you can't have the home of your dreams."

Sarah stood, hands on her hips, and glared. "You don't understand anything. I'd live in shanty with you and Trey, if only we could be a family."

Barney stood and walked towards Sarah. He held her in his arms. "Would you really, pretty Sarah? Would you live with me if I told you I don't want to stay with Trans Oil? That I want to move where no one knows who my father was?"

"Barney, I love you. I'd go anywhere you want. If you don't want to stay with Trans Oil, what do you want to do?"

"I don't know," he answered sadly. "If you care what I think of the house, call Chris for the address. We can look at it in the morning."

Chapter 6
TORY

Prairie View, North Dakota
Saturday, October 6, 1979

Tory had been about to leave for the American School when the doorbell sounded. She never had visitors. When she opened the door and saw the deliveryman holding a telegram, her heart pounded. Without thinking, she took money from her wallet, forgetting a tip wasn't expected. She had been so anxious to read the message that she failed to notice the man offer her the money back. She opened and read the message quickly.

This must be a joke, she thought. She slumped into a chair and reread the message slowly. It was from a lawyer in Prairie View. Her teacher and friend was dead. The funeral would be held once Tory got to Prairie View.

It can't be true, Tory thought. *I had a letter from Dora last week. She didn't say anything about being sick.*

Tory picked up her diary and reached for the telephone. Once she booked a flight, she called the lawyer to tell him her itinerary. Then she canceled her appointments for the next week.

She'd forgotten how cold North Dakota was. She pulled the collar of her navy blue stadium jacket up around her ears and readjusted her scarf to cover her mouth and nose. Even with three pair of socks over her stockings, her feet were freezing. She stood on at least nine inches of packed snow. Much as she wanted to, she refrained from stamping her feet. The wind picked up. She wished the minister would hurry through the service.

There were only four people at the gravesite: the minister, the gravedigger, Dora Martin's attorney, and Tory. Tory was surprised there wasn't a crowd. *Dora's been an institution in Prairie View for as long as I can remember. Where are her friends and students? Surely more people must want to bid her farewell. She only retired in June; she can't have been forgotten so quickly.*

Finally, the minister finished his homily and motioned to Tory and the attorney. It was time to toss a shovel of dirt over the casket. It was a strange custom. Tory wondered what it symbolized. Her duties done, she ran to the car for protection from the biting cold. Once inside, she rubbed her gloved hands together, trying to restore the circulation.

Jack Talbott leaned over, grabbed her hands, and moved them in front of the heater. "That should help. You're not accustomed to this weather, are you?"

Tory shook her head. "I've been living in the tropics. When I got your wire, I had to hunt for my winter coat and this old wool skirt. They're both from high school."

"I know where you've been. Dora was always telling me of your adventures. How long will you be staying?"

"I'll get a flight from Bismarck to the west coast later today. There are good connections to Singapore from there. I only came to say good-bye to Dora. There's no reason for me to hang around."

"Actually, there is. I'll explain when we get back to my office."

Tory felt a foreboding in the pit of her stomach and ignored it. Her imagination had been working overtime since she'd learned of Dora's death. It seemed impossible that only three days had passed since she got the telegram.

Back at his office, a cup of steaming coffee in his hands, Jack peered at Tory over the half-glasses he wore to read. "Dora told me so much about you I recognized you the minute you got off the plane. I'd like to hear how you and she came to be such fast friends. Would you mind indulging an old man and telling me the story?"

Tory heard the wistful tone in his voice and wondered if there had been strong feelings between Jack and Dora. Jack looked to be in his late sixties. It was possible. Yet, Tory thought Dora had held men in contempt.

There was an hour before she left for Bismarck, so she began, "Dora was my teacher when I lived here. Heck, she was everyone's teacher. There were only four rooms in the school. It started with Pygmalion. Do you remember the story?"

Jack leaned back in his chair and nodded.

"My real name's Eliza, Eliza Victoria. One day, about three weeks into the school year, Dora asked to see me after class. She told me there was a heroine named Eliza in a play and offered to loan me the book. That was a Friday. Monday morning, I couldn't wait to get to school and talk to her. I'd been transported into another world while I read. I couldn't believe Eliza could have changed so much she wasn't recognized. After that, Dora loaned me other books. We'd talk about them afterwards and discuss what they meant."

"You were her greatest success. Dora claimed all the years of teaching in Prairie View were worth it because she helped you reach your potential." Jack smiled at Tory.

Tory returned his grin. "Everything I am today I owe to Dora."

"I'm not sure I'd go that far. Dora loaned you books. What else?"

"She taught me about the world that existed away from here. I'm from a farm on the outskirts of town, as close to the back woods as you can get. Dora taught me table manners, how to analyze things rather than accept what was in front of me, to set goals for myself. At the time, it seemed she knew everything worth knowing. She corrected my speech, made me stand up straight. I always hunched over as a kid 'cause I was tall. When I was in my last year of school, she convinced me to apply to college. She said I owed it to myself to see the world. She even paid the application fees."

Tory brushed a tear from her cheek. "She was the first person who was nice to me. I still don't understand why she bothered." Tory pushed her hair behind her ears and cleared her throat. The memories hurt. "I must have been twelve when she came here. I have a friend with a thirteen-year-old. Alison's a nice kid, but I can't see myself spending a lot of time with her. Not the way Dora did with me."

"I think I can explain that," Jack offered. "I knew Dora in university. I was in law school at the time. We met in the library and dated off and on for two years. But, I was young and foolish. I married a woman who had a wonderful laugh and not a brain in her head. I couldn't see that at the time."

Jack poured himself another cup of coffee and continued. "One day I met Dora again, quite accidentally, in the supermarket. We'd both been living in Iowa City for years -- Dora, teaching in the high school, and me, a fledgling lawyer. My marriage was a mockery by then. I'm embarrassed to say I let Dora think I was divorced. We had an affair that lasted nearly ten years. When Dora found out I was married, she left Iowa City at the end of the school term."

Tory was speechless. This wasn't her beloved teacher, mentor and friend. Dora would never have sullied herself in a tawdry affair.

Jack hung his head. "I'm not proud of what I did. I know now that I prevented Dora from meeting other men because I was too selfish to give her up and too much of a coward to ask my wife for a divorce. By the time I realized what I'd lost it was too late. Dora was gone, and I was left with a woman who relished in her position as 'Mrs. Lawyer.'

"My wife died twelve years ago and I set out to find Dora. It took two years, but eventually I found her. At first, she'd have nothing to do with me. Not that I blamed her. But, I sold my practice in Iowa City and moved here anyway. In time, Dora softened and we became friends again."

"I don't believe you," Tory shouted. "Dora never said anything about you to me."

"You were a child when you lived here."

"We've been in touch all the time I've been gone."

"Did you tell Dora everything you did?"

"Well, no. But..."

"Dora knew the influence she had on you. She felt if she told you, it would lessen her in your eyes, or worse, give you ideas. Her biggest fear was that you'd fall for the first boy who sent you flowers. That's what she did. She always saw you as the vulnerable little girl she first met. She was concerned you'd be too naive to separate true gold from fool's gold."

Tory shook her long hair so that it whipped across her face and laughed. "She needn't have worried. I've never met a man who sent me flowers. Anyway, Dora taught me never to count on anyone but myself. Over the years I've become quite practiced at protecting myself from wolves. Even the ones who wear sheep's clothing."

"A little too good, perhaps?"

Tory was puzzled by the question. Much as she didn't want to believe Jack's tale, he knew too much about Dora and her. "What do you mean?"

"Dora found out she was dying three months ago. She was afraid you'd learned her lessons too well. She claimed you'd built a wall around your heart so no one would hurt you again. Although she understood why you felt it necessary, your behavior saddened her. Especially since she helped you manufacture your fortress. How old are you now? Thirty-five?"

"I'll be thirty-six in two months."

Tory leaned back and thought. *None of this is real. It's a bad dream. Soon, the alarm will go off and I'll wake up.* She closed her eyes and opened them quickly. *Damn it! Jack's still here and I'm still cold.*

"What are you thinking?" he asked.

"I don't want to hear any more. If Dora knew she was dying, why didn't she tell me? Hell, if you knew about me, why didn't you? I would have come back here for her. She must have known that." Tears in her eyes, Tory pleaded, "Please tell me she knew I'd come back for her."

Jack reached his hand across the desk and took Tory's hand in his. "Dora and I discussed it. Argued is probably more apt a description. She didn't want you to watch her die. It was her last request that you not be contacted until she passed on. Even though I disagreed, I'd never have gone against Dora's wishes."

"Why tell me now?"

"We have to discuss Dora's will. I hoped if you understood the past, it would be easier. You see I'd like a favor from you. I'm getting ahead of myself."

Jack looked up and Tory saw how red and puffy his eyes were. There were dark circles beneath them. Jack looked more distraught by Dora's death than she. For Tory, it was too soon to feel anything. The logistics of getting from Asia to Prairie View had been all she could handle. The reality of Dora's death was neatly labeled in a box that she wouldn't open until she was home.

"Are you warm yet?" Jack asked. "Would you like another cup of coffee before I start?"

Tory shook her head. She never drank coffee. The cup Jack had given her was still full. She hadn't seen tea bags on the table with the instant coffee and electric teakettle, so she didn't mention her preference. It didn't matter what she drank; she wouldn't be warm until she got home.

Jack took a folder from the middle drawer of his desk and unfolded the pale blue backing of the legal document. "This is the Last Will and Testament of Dora Hannah Martin. I hereby bequeath all my earthly possessions to Eliza Victoria Winslow. These include whatever moneys I have at the Building and Loan Society, my house, and all its contents."

Tory gasped.

"You were very important to Dora. She wanted to make sure you were taken care of. She felt your career choice was precarious. Most of your work is freelance, isn't it?"

"Yes, but Dora taught me to save. I have more than enough to satisfy my needs."

"Dora wanted more than survival for you. There's a little over twenty-five thousand dollars in Dora's bank account. It may take several months for the courts to free the money. If you leave me the name of your bank and the account number, I'll have the funds wired into your account."

"That'd be great. Thanks."

"About Dora's house. Once you've had a chance to go through her things and take what you want, I'd like to buy the house. I have appraised values from three realtors. I hope I'm not being presumptuous."

"The last thing I need is a house in Prairie View. I'll never come back. You can have the house and all that's in it. It has meaning to you. All it would be for me is the repository of bad memories." She saw the stricken look on Jack's face and realized he'd misunderstood. "Not of Dora, but of this place." Her hands pointed towards the main street.

"You should go through the house. You'll probably want some of the mementos. I know you want to leave today, but I think you should stay for a day or two. Dora left you a letter. Why don't I drop you at her house? You can read the letter in private. I'll fetch you for dinner at six and we can talk."

Much as she wanted to be on her way, Tory smiled. "I'd like to see the house again. Some of my happiest times were spent there. I'd rather remember Dora there than in her coffin."

When she saw Jack smile, Tory knew her instincts were correct. Another day would cost her little, and she owed Dora so much.

As she opened the door to the house, the sachet that permeated the air struck her. Tears came to her eyes. The aroma brought back so many memories.

Slowly Tory walked to the gramophone. Her fingers caressed the copper horn where the sound came out. The sight reminded her of the Sunday afternoons she and Dora spent listening to symphonies and discussing books. Every piece of furniture evoked a memory of the past, which wasn't buried as deeply as she believed.

If she were going to confront the pain, she'd best get comfortable. She made a pot of tea. When the tea was ready, she went back to the living room, turned on the gramophone, lit the kindling that lay on the grate, and sat in the green Chippendale chair. Hands trembling, she opened the letter.

My Darling Little Girl:

If you're reading this letter I have passed on to a better world. Don't shed a tear for me. By now, Jack has told you of our love affair.

I came to Prairie View because I desperately needed a place where I could hide. Jack doesn't know this, but those last few months in Iowa City, I thought I was pregnant. It was a false alarm. Surprisingly, I was despondent when I found out. This dreary little town only added to my mood of utter despair. Yet, I deserved banishment for my affair.

Then I found you. You were a beacon amid the sea of uneducated faces that stared glumly at me that first morning. You were so eager for knowledge. I decided I would guide you in the way I would never be able to direct my own child.

Now that I'm dying, I worry that I passed along some fears that would have been best kept to myself. I know that I warned you to never let yourself depend on anyone. I was wrong! I was speaking from the hurt I felt.

Tory, this is not a remake of Great Expectations. (I know what you're thinking, as you sit with your tea in your favorite green chair and read my letter.)

Circumstances have changed my mind about many things. Jack and I have been together for ten years now. They've been the happiest days of my life. Please, child, don't close yourself off. Life is short. Don't squander your time. I know your childhood wasn't pleasant. It's time for you make peace with the past. You're no longer a child. You should see Prairie View and your youth for what they were -- short periods of time that had to be endured, so you could grow and appreciate what is in front of you.

I see such emotion in your work. There are nights now when I can't sleep. Jack and I spend the hours looking over your photographs. We cry, we laugh. What you feel is so apparent in your work. Open your heart and release the emotions you show in your photos.

I'd appreciate it if you'd stay with Jack for a week. My going will be hard for him, and you always have been good at comforting others.

Always remember that you carry within yourself the key to peace, my wish for you always.

Love,

Dora

Tory was sitting in the chair, the letter clenched in her hands, when Jack returned. She had no idea how long she'd sat there thinking. The fire had gone out and the room was cold. Her face was streaked with tears. She sniffed them back and wiped her face with the sleeve of her sweater.

She walked in a daze. As she opened the door, she gave Jack the practiced smile she used for cocktail parties. "Why don't you come in? I've been woolgathering all afternoon."

"I see you've read the letter."

Tory paled. "Do you know what Dora wrote?"

"If you mean have I read the letter, the answer is no. I can guess what was in it, though. I thought you might not want to go out for a meal, so I bought some groceries. If you like, I'll cook."

"I could do it," she offered.

"It would make me feel better to do something. From what Dora told me, you believe in kitchen gremlins."

Tory laughed at the reference to Dora's aborted attempts to teach her to cook. Tory insisted that there were kitchen gremlins that invaded the room when she tried to do anything more sophisticated than boil water. Even now, she only prepared quick, simple meals. She lacked the patience to spend hours on something that would be eaten in ten minutes.

"Come into the kitchen and keep me company, please. Why don't you tell me about where you live?"

"It's an area called Jurong."

"Why Singapore?"

Tory shrugged. "Why not? It's pretty. The people are wonderful. The little villages that first attracted me are disappearing quickly. Buildings that race each other to the sky are replacing them. It's sad in a way."

"Are you opposed to progress?"

"Yes and no. It depends on what you mean by progress. The Prime Minister's made a concerted effort to bring the country into the twentieth century overnight. He's done an incredible job. But I think something's being lost in the transition.

"Singapore has a nice climate, especially for the tropics. The rainy season isn't like the monsoons of India. For two or three months, you get a heavy downpour most afternoons. One minute, the sky opens, and then just as quickly, it shuts like the opening and closing of a camera shutter. Part of me loves Singapore and can't imagine living anywhere else."

"I thought you didn't like the way it was changing."

Tory laughed. "You don't miss a trick, do you? Periodically I consider moving. I always get cold feet. I have friends and an easier lifestyle than I could afford anywhere else. There's not a place I like more, even with the changes." Something had been nagging at Tory's mind since the funeral. "Why wasn't anyone at Dora's funeral?"

"Now who doesn't miss a trick? The folks around here didn't approve of their teacher and her lawyer friend spending so much time together. Didn't think it was wholesome."

Tory's eyes filled with sadness and she brushed away a tear. "I see nothing's changed around here. I guessed as much, but I needed confirmation. The townsfolk are pretty good at closing ranks. Why would you stay here?"

"I need to be close to Dora's memory. I can't imagine what life will be like on my own."

Tory reflected upon his words. The simple declaration said so much. "Dora's been the one constant in my life since I was twelve. Missing her would make it impossible for me to stay."

"And Dora wouldn't expect you to. She wanted you to find the happiness that eluded you here. Once we've finalized the papers, you should go back to your life."

After dinner, Jack left. Tory sat in a chair with her tea and cried. Who would she turn to for comfort now? She and Dora wrote each week. Tory saved each letter. So, it seemed, had Dora.

When she first moved to Singapore, Tory used to reread Dora's letters to get the courage to face another cold call. Who would fill that void now? Who would be there to comfort her at midnight when the fears took over?

Chapter 7
SARAH

Singapore
Thursday, October 25, 1979

The alarm clock rang for the second time. Barney had drunk too much the night before. He covered his head with a pillow. Sarah leaned over and whispered in his ear, "Time to get up."

"Call the office. Tell them I'm crook," he groaned.

Sarah frowned. Barney must go to work. He'd called in sick twice last week. He couldn't miss another day. Sarah was petrified if she let Barney stay home, he'd be fired. It was up to her. She must force him to go to work.

Quietly, she put on an aqua satin robe that matched her negligee. In the kitchen, she stooped down to the cabinets below the counter and took out the blender. A cicak jumped out and her heart raced. No matter how often she saw one, she couldn't adopt the attitude that the lizards brought good luck.

She took an egg, orange juice and ice from the refrigerator and put them in the blender. When the mixture was nice and frothy, she added a dram of vodka. It was enough alcohol to get Barney moving, yet not enough to get him drunk. She placed the liquid in an ice cream soda glass, the glass on a lace doily centered on a silver tray, an orchid to the right, and a straw to the left of the glass. Even this drink, which turned her stomach, must be artfully displayed for Sarah to be comfortable.

In only three weeks Barney was showing the signs of discontent that signaled the start of a binge. Sarah had hoped things would be different this time. Barney had sworn he'd only drink socially. What a joke that was. Sarah had never seen a place where social drinking was an everyday occurrence.

Barney's drinking might have brought them to Singapore, but Sarah had no intention of being forced away. She was surprised how much she liked Singapore. The island was picturesque. There were flowers everywhere. The faintest scent of orchids filled the air. More than that, she was starting to make friends. People who liked her as a person and not because of her husband's connections.

Sarah had been a lonely child. She couldn't invite friends to play at her house after school because her mother worked. It would be rude to accept invitations that she couldn't reciprocate, so she became a loner. Her mother insisted that the children were jealous of Sarah because she was so pretty. As she grew up, her mother had been her closest friend.

As she had in the past, Sarah found her greatest pleasure in the kitchen. She painstakingly prepared meals that looked so good on the plate, you were afraid to eat them. Barney seldom noticed her creations. After half a bottle of gin, she could have served sawdust, and he wouldn't taste the difference.

It had been past nine o'clock when he had stumbled home the night before. Their dinner sat congealed on the serving plates.

"You call this food?" he shouted. "I want dinner. Is that too much work for you, love?"

Sarah looked at the dining room table and shuddered. *Why didn't I ask the servants to put things away?*

"What can you expect when you don't ring to say you'll be late?" Sarah would not take the blame for dinner. It had been ready at 7:30, when Barney said he would be home.

"I was busy. I work, you know."

"In a bar?"

"No. Geoff and I stopped for a drink when we left the office."

"Geoff Melbourne?" she asked with a smile. "Is he here on a trip?"

"He's moved here. Guess he missed seeing your face, pretty Sarah. He always was sweet on you."

"Don't be silly. Geoff knows I only have eyes for you." Sarah's mind drifted to the happy days of New Zealand when she and Barney spent time with Geoff. Since he was a bachelor and curtailed Barney's drinking; Sarah had invited Geoff to dinner often. She knew Geoff had a crush on her, and he knew she knew. It was an innocent flirtation, nothing more. It felt good to have someone pay attention to her. *It'll be wonderful having Geoff here,* she thought. *He's so interested in doing things. Maybe he'll get Barney thinking more about working than drinking.*

Her gentle musings over, Sarah looked at Barney. He was sipping his drink through a straw. She closed her eyes, recalling the last time she'd seen Geoff.

Barney had gone to Christchurch on business. Geoff invited her to go sailing. He handled all the details, even arranging a babysitter for Trey. They spent the day on the water, talking about music. Geoff complimented her clothes, her hair, and the picnic lunch she brought. He noticed the things about her Barney ignored.

"Why do you stay with him?" Geoff asked.

She had no answer to the question. Much as she disliked his drinking and the way he ignored her, Sarah never considered leaving Barney. He was her husband.

When the shower started, Sarah shook her head to clear her mind. She had a million things to do today. Chris had invited her to play bridge and meet several of the wives. The prospect made Sarah anxious. She wanted to fit in, to feel that she belonged. If Barney stayed home, they'd have a row, and she wouldn't be at her best.

She slipped from the bed and knocked on the door the bathroom. She could hear Barney shaving. "Trey and I are going to have breakfast. Will you be joining us?"

"I'm running late. I'll kiss Trey good-bye before I leave."

So much for becoming a family, Sarah thought.

Over breakfast, she listened to Trey's stories of his adventure in the park with Ah Soon. She smiled lovingly at her son. His cast was still on his arm and Trey thought it a badge of honor.

"You're the only boy with a cast? Why is that fun?"

"'Cause it makes me special."

Sarah kissed the top of his head. "You're always special. Shall you and I go to the park this morning?"

"After lunch. Ah Soon takes me in the morning."

"Mummy's going out this afternoon."

"We can go when you come back."

Sarah shook her head. "I don't think so."

Trey pouted and Sarah tickled his chin. "Don't show me that droopy bottom lip. We'll go to the park tomorrow."

Later Sarah stood in her closet frowning. She wasn't certain what was worn to bridge. She chose a cotton sundress that could be worn with the nail lacquer she had on. The dress was a pale pink with large aqua flowers. The full skirt skimmed her knees and showed off her attractive legs. The tight-fitting bodice exposed just the slightest hint of cleavage. A pert aqua hat made the outfit perfect.

Her hands trembled when Sarah paid the taxi driver. The housekeeper let her in and showed her into the living room. For a moment, Sarah thought she was alone, and then she saw a woman sitting in a chair. Her white-blonde hair shone in the sunlight. She was a striking woman, tall and thin, with dark brown eyes and a tan that was not typical of people with her fair skin.

The woman jumped from her seat and held out her right hand. "I'm Tory Winslow. You must be Sarah Parker."

Sarah shook the outstretched hand and smiled tentatively. *Where's Chris?* she wondered.

"Chris said you were coming early. How do you like Lotus Land?"

"Lotus Land?" Sarah questioned.

"It's my pet name for Singapore."

"Why?"

"It fits." Tory shrugged. "Chris said you're interested in art. What type?"

"All of it, I guess." Sarah felt the color rise in her cheeks and wished she could stop it. She must be making a dreadful first impression.

"Have you seen any that you like here?"

"The Indian temples."

"You've probably been to Serangoon Road. It's Deepavali now. Have you been there at night to see the lights? It's worth the trip."

"Is that why there are garlands and decorations everywhere?"

Tory nodded. "It's the most important Hindu festival. The temples are so lit up; you think it's day, not night. Jasmine fills the air. Even little children stay up to celebrate. You should go."

"I'll mention it to my husband. He likes experiencing new places." Sarah was surprised that the lie came so easily to her lips. She never thought of herself as dishonest. It was important that she give the right impression of her and Barney. It wouldn't do for anyone to suspect how barren their home life was. "What did you call the festival?"

"Deepavali. If you like Indian art, you should go to Sri Mariammam Temple."

"Is it special?"

"It's a national monument. The entrance to the temple has a goporam, a multi-tiered tower of carved deities. The carvings are much more intricate than the temples of Little India. They're exquisite."

Sarah smiled. This was someone who knew Singapore. "Where should I look for wicker baskets? I need one for the kitchen."

"Try Arab Street."

Chris came into the living room and Sarah panicked. If Chris had asked Tory to come early, she wanted to spend time with her. Sarah was surprised when the two of them included her in their conversation. It made her less fearful of meeting the other women.

Sarah had read a bridge book the night before to refresh her memory of the rules of the game. Not that it mattered. Several women were more interested in gossiping than playing cards. Since they switched tables after each rubber, Sarah met everyone there.

"I can't believe Tory's here. What does Chris see in her?" Janet Adams asked the table.

There had been no mistaking the venom in Janet's tone. It startled Sarah; especially since she thought was Tory nice.

"Chris nurses the wounded," someone joked.

"She can do that at Mount Elizabeth. Why must we be subjected to that woman?"

"Janet, hush. You know how protective Chris is. Count your blessings that Tory hasn't been around much."

"I don't trust that woman," Janet sneered.

"Why?" Sarah asked. There must be an explanation for the hostility in the woman's voice. It was similar to the contempt Violet used in describing Tory. Why did women dislike her?

Janet frowned. "Wait 'til she works with your husband on a marketing campaign. You'll see what I mean. Phil comes home and all I hear is Tory this, Tory that. It's infuriating."

Sarah smiled knowingly. Janet was jealous. Men liked Sarah; perhaps they liked Tory as well. If so, it wouldn't affect Barney. There wasn't a woman who could capture Barney's attention for long.

Chapter 8
CHRIS

Singapore
Thursday, October 25, 1979

"Damn," Chris said as she hung up the phone.

"What's wrong?" Tory asked.

"Kev's working late. Again. It's the third time he's missed dinner this week." Chris sneered at Tory's smile. "It's not good news."

"Look on the bright side. We can take the munchkins out for fish-head curry."

Chris stared at Tory. What was Tory talking about? When Tory had called and suggested tennis, she said it was the only time she could spare. She never mentioned where she'd been for the past month or why she hadn't been in touch. "I thought you were busy. That's what you said when I suggested you stay for bridge."

Tory shrugged. Chris was irritated at her seeming indifference. She was like Kevin, only interested in work.

"I've been thinking. Bridge doesn't sound so bad after all."

Once again, she'd misread Tory's words. When would she learn it was impossible to figure out what went on in Tory's head? She was being accommodating. She was a good friend.

"You'll stay?"

Tory shrugged again. "What's going on at Trans Oil?"

"Damned if I know. You know Kevin doesn't talk about work. If you'd been in town, you'd know what was going on before me. Where have you been, anyway?"

"Here and there. I'm doing some work for the WWF. They're doing a campaign for preserves like Sepilok. Since they have no money, I'm slipping the travel in with paying trips."

"Sepilok, home to the orangutan no one's ever seen. Why do you donate your services?"

"For the same reason you volunteer at Mount Elizabeth. To repay a kindness."

Chris smiled at Tory's vague answer. She knew why she gave her time to the hospital. Singapore had been a great place for the Taylors and time was something Chris had in abundance. What about Tory? She worked. What debt was she repaying? There was no sense asking the question; it wouldn't be answered.

"There's someone I'd like you to meet today. Sarah Parker."

"Of the bigwig Parkers?"

Chris nodded and saw Tory grow rigid. "Don't hold it against Sarah. She married into the family. I think you'll like her."

"Why? The rest of them were nothing to write home about."

"She's artistic. And she loves it here."

Tory paused as if to say something and appeared to think better of it. She tossed a pillow at Chris. "I'd better shower."

Chris replaced the pillow and went for the stairs. While she dressed, she wondered what was going on with Tory. She seemed more noncommittal than usual. *I'd better make her my partner,* she thought. When Tory was in her reticent mood, she could be difficult to talk to. Several women would not be happy that she was at bridge.

When she came downstairs, Chris was surprised to hear laughter in the living room. Sarah and Tory were engrossed in a discussion of stores.

Sarah smiled when Chris came into the room. "Tory suggested I go to Arab Street for wicker baskets. Have you been there?"

"It's not like shopping on Orchard Road," Chris said.

"You could get the same thing at the Far East Shopping Plaza for ten times the cost," Tory answered. She turned to Sarah. "If you let yourself get past the dilapidated buildings and disheveled way the inventory's displayed, Arab Street's an adventure. I always find amazing treasures in the shophouses."

"Really?"

Since they were getting along, Chris went into the kitchen to check on lunch. Tory was doing her tour guide impression. It was the pose she adopted when her mind was a million miles away.

She came back into the room as Sarah asked, "Do you have a house nearby?"

Chris laughed. "Tory won't tell anyone where she lives."

"Don't you have parties?" Sarah asked.

Tory nodded. "At hotels. With my travel schedule, it's easier. I get to change the venue to match the costume of the evening."

"Costume?" Sarah said in a questioning tone.

Chris grinned. "Tory travels all over Asia. When she comes back with an unbelievable costume, she throws a party so she can show it off."

Tory shook her head vehemently. "I only dress for myself. It's you women who dress to outdo each other." She pointed at Sarah and Chris. "Can you honestly tell me you're comfortable in those dresses? But then you'd never consider testing the dress code of the bridge table."

"I like dresses," Sarah said. "They're cooler in the heat."

"And they show off how much money your husband makes. I dress for my mood. Costume parties let me camp it up. For one evening it doesn't matter whose husband is king of the mountain."

"And you remain the woman of mystery," Chris added.

"People hate being excluded from Tory's galas," Chris whispered to Sarah. "Please don't tell her. If she thought we enjoyed it, she might stop."

The doorbell sounded and several women came in together. Since this was Sarah's first foray into the Thursday bridge game, Chris introduced her to each woman.

She could see Tory asking questions and smiling. On the surface, she looked as if she were enjoying herself. Chris knew better. Tory was play-acting, like she did at her parties. The women would miss that Tory gave nothing of herself while they spoke. All they'd recall was having a pleasant conversation with the famous photographer. The deceit didn't concern Chris. It allowed the women to overlook the fact that Tory wore shorts.

Marc ran into the house as the last of the guests was leaving. The only people who remained were Sarah and Tory. Knowing it would embarrass Marc, Chris kissed him hello.

"Not so fast, kiddo," Tory called. "How's frog lab?"

Marc turned, his hand on the banister. "Aunt Tory! When did you get home?"

"Tuesday." She ran up to him and punched him in the arm. "I've had all I can take of the grownups. Let's go to your room where we can be alone." Tory followed Marc up the stairs, laughing.

Sarah turned, a puzzled frown on her face. "From what I heard, I wouldn't have expected her to like children."

Chris laughed. "She's always gotten on well with Marc and Alison. We met because of Marc."

"Today was wonderful. Thank you so much for inviting me. It was nice to meet some of the women."

Chris smiled to herself. Did Sarah always say the proper thing? She'd been seated with Janet Adams for the last rubber. Janet was anything but nice. She'd have been furious Tory was here. Then Chris remembered how few people Sarah must have met. Furnishing her house and overseeing the renovations must take up all her time. She already had good bearings about the island, though. After her first three weeks, Chris hadn't been able to tell one street from another.

"I called a cab for you. It should be soon. What did you think of Tory?"

Sarah frowned. "You were right about her artistic sense."

"But?"

"I know she's your friend. And I did like her; I wouldn't want you to think otherwise. Does she strike you as vague?"

Chris burst out laughing. Over the years, she'd heard several adjectives used to describe Tory. Vague had never been one of them. When she saw the hesitant look in Sarah's face, she smiled. "I didn't mean to laugh. I've heard her called opinionated, smug or sure of herself. Vague is new to me."

"She never answers a question. She'd made Arab Street sound so interesting, I suggested we go one afternoon."

"Now I get it. You asked for a commitment. That's not Tory's style. When she wakes up one morning with a yen to go to Arab Street, she'll call and see if you're free."

Sarah seemed to ponder Chris's response. "She works. No doubt it's difficult for her to make definite plans. I was being frightfully harsh and I shouldn't have been."

"Kevin's working late tonight. Tory and I are taking the children out to dinner. Would you like to join us?"

"Oh dear, I hope Barney's not working late again. He was out almost every night last week."

"Call him and see," Chris suggested. The thought that Barney was working late comforted her. Trans Oil must be planning a marketing campaign for a new product.

Sarah shook her head. "Even if he works late, I like to read Trey his bedtime stories."

"He can come."

Sarah and Chris turned to see that Tory had returned. When she saw that Sarah was as surprised as she, Chris wondered how Tory had slipped in so quietly.

Sarah shook her head. "He's only three. He needs to keep to a schedule. He's a terror to put to bed if he's overtired."

"It's something you wouldn't understand, Tory." Chris turned to Sarah. "I hear your taxi. Some other time. Tory's adventures into the unknown are fun, you're never sure where you'll end up."

Sarah smiled. "Next time. Yes, I'd like that."

When Sarah left, Chris led the way to the solarium.

Tory said, "Alison's at cheerleading tryouts. Laurel's mother will drop her off."

"Why don't we have a glass of wine?" Chris suggested.

Tory played with her wineglass. "Have you seen John Horton since Monica died?"

"What brought that up?" The question stunned Chris. John worked for one of the tobacco companies. He and his wife were on the fringes of their social circle. His wife had died two months before. Except for the memorial service, Chris hadn't seen or thought about John.

Tory shrugged. "He's lonely without Monica."

"You claim to like being alone."

"I'm accustomed to it. John and Monica celebrated their twenty-fifth anniversary last year. It must be difficult for him to be on his own. I thought you'd know how he was."

"Are you interested in John?" She knew the question was absurd, but so was Tory's interest. Neither of them had cared for Monica. Tory likened her to the Queen of Hearts from *Alice in Wonderland,* always anxious to take off someone's head. John was the antithesis. He was quiet and reserved. Chris couldn't recall having said more than ten words to him. She doubted Tory had said that much.

"Can't I ask a question without you building a love affair of it?"

Chapter 9
TORY

Singapore
Thursday, October 24, 1979

As Chris waved good-bye to Sarah, her smiled faded. Tory followed her into the kitchen. Without a word, Chris opened the refrigerator and took out a bottle of wine. While she fumbled in a drawer for the corkscrew, Tory reached into the cupboard for two glasses and went into the solarium.

Chris sank onto the couch and sighed. She poured herself a glass of wine, gulped half the glass down, and filled her glass again. The open bottle sat on the table. Tory helped herself.

"I'm tired. Mind if I pass on tonight?" Chris asked.

Tory nodded. Chris wouldn't benefit from an evening spent alone. Mentally Tory reviewed the events of the afternoon to determine the reason for Chris's mood. "What's wrong?"

"Are you working with Trans Oil on the new campaign?"

"This one's only been out four months. They don't change that quickly."

"Maybe it's a new product then," Chris said softly.

Tory shrugged. "Are you down 'cause Kevin's working late? Doesn't sound like you."

"Silly, isn't it?" Chris nibbled on her lower lip. "Kevin and I usually go away for my birthday. Just the two of us. He hasn't mentioned it this year. I think he forgot."

Damn, Chris's birthday is in two days. Tory slammed her fist into her thigh. Kevin wasn't the only one who'd forgotten.

"Maybe he's planning a surprise." She hoped her voice was convincing.

"You think so? Really?" Her eyes brightened and she smiled. "Has he told you?"

Tory smiled knowingly. "I never betray a confidence. Let's just say, I don't think you have anything to worry about." If Kevin hadn't scheduled a holiday, she'd see that he did. "Don't pass on tonight. It'll be fun."

Tory fumed at Kevin. *How can he hurt Chris like this*? Instead of the quick dinner she intended, she decided to give Chris the full flavor of Deepavali. She asked the taxi to drop them at the end of Serangoon Road, so they could walk through the crowds. The Indians wore new clothes; the women had wound flowers in their hair. Many carried oil lamps to the Sri Veeramakayama Temple. The smell of incense and jasmine filled the air. Colorful garlands of fresh flowers and twinkling lights decorated the windows of the worn shophouse. Tory hoped that the celebratory spirit would be contagious.

In the restaurant Marc and Alison argued over the singsong Indian music in the restaurant.

"Hush you two, or I'll get the fish eye."

Chris gasped. "What are you talking about?"

Tory grinned. "Fish-head curry. Remember?"

The children eyed the platters of food on the other tables. They watched transfixed as a large banana leaf was put down in front of them. Marc picked it up, turned it over. Absently, Chris patted his hand to get him to stop.

"Is this a place mat?" Alison asked.

Tory shook her head. "It's your plate."

Alison giggled. "If Marc's not careful he'll rip it to shreds."

"Where are the place settings, Aunt Tory? If the plate's here, shouldn't they be?"

"We'll eat with our fingers. The spices penetrate your skin. Tomorrow when you smell your hands, you'll remember what you ate."

"Daddy says only savages eat with their fingers."

Marc poked Alison in the ribs at her comment. Then he pointed to the platter the waitress carried. The fish head in the middle of the curried vegetables had captured his attention.

The waitress placed their meal in the center of the table. Tory shook her head when the young girl offered to serve them. She took a tablespoon and scooped rice into the center of each banana leaf. Carefully, she ladled the curry on top of the rice. Then she used the spoon on the fish head to dig out the flesh buried beneath the skin. She de-boned the fish head until all that remained was the eye. "This is the best part. Who wants it?"

"Does Anna Banana eat this?" Marc asked.

Tory shook her head. "Anna's a vegetarian."

The children gazed at the food, their uncertainty as to what to do next apparent. "Watch me," Tory said. With the first two fingers of her right hand, she dipped into the mixture of curry and rice. Her thumb guided the food toward her mouth and she stuck her tongue out. The children emulated her behavior. Chris stared at her food.

"You can have silverware if you want," Tory offered.

Chris shook her head. Tentatively, her fingers went into the rice, avoiding the sauce. Such reticence was odd for Chris. Typically she indulged in journeys into the fabric of the country with wide-eyed enthusiasm. Evenings such as tonight, when she and Tory were with the children were treats.

Something was bothering Chris. Kevin should have told Chris about his new job by now. Did Chris view the change in her birthday routine as a precursor? Usually Chris looked on the bright side of things. She was the one who showed others that circumstances weren't as bleak as they imagined. Her sunny disposition was so much a part of her. It was important to Tory that Chris be happy, especially now.

For the first time since she was twelve, Tory was alone. Without Dora, her safety net was gone. For years, Tory had deluded herself that she didn't need anyone. Suddenly she saw how wrong she'd been. She not only relied on Dora, she depended on Chris. If Chris were unhappy, her last safe harbor would disappear.

All the bromides Tory used to calm herself were failing. She tried taking on more work than she could comfortably handle. But wearing herself out didn't keep her from tossing and turning sleeplessly at night. Visiting Anna left her feeling empty. It shocked her to understand her attachment to the orangutan. Anna was Dora's alter ego. Tory spoke to Anna, pretending she was Dora.

Tory was in overload. One minute she was positive Dora's letter was wrong. It was the feeble attempt of a dying woman to make sense of her life. The next minute, she was equally as certain it was true. Closing off the world wasn't what she should do.

Her agitation was starting to affect her work. In the last week she'd dropped chemicals several times and even exposed a roll of film. As she always did when she felt overwhelmed, Tory called Chris. Being around Chris always lifted Tory's mood. Now Chris needed cheering up. Tory had to remedy the situation to make the world right again. But she wasn't certain what was bothering Chris.

She tried to order the day's events so she could figure it out. Chris had welcomed her without questioning her whereabouts for the past month. "Bridge is here today. Why don't you play?"

Tory had shaken her head. She was too agitated. There was no way she could concentrate on cards. "Can't. Tennis is all I can squeeze into my schedule. Maybe next time."

Seeing the hurt look on Chris's face, Tory had wondered if she should stay. When Chris got up to answer the phone, Tory had weighed the alternatives. Chris was as close as Tory allowed anyone. If she wanted Tory to play bridge, what was the harm? Then she had remembered the other women. Tory couldn't stand most expat wives.

They're spoiled brats, she thought. *An Asian family could live for a year on the allowances the expats get in a month. They're no better than parasites. If I play bridge, I'm liable to lose it the first time one of them whines about the prices at Cold Storage.*

Chris was different. She had interests of her own. Most people saw Chris as the woman behind the man. They missed that she was her own person. The effort she put into her garden showed her tenacity. There were other pretty gardens among the expats, the work of their gardener.

"Kevin's working late," Chris announced when she came back into the room. She was not pleased at the turn of events.

Tory had a flash of inspiration. An adventure would lift both their moods. "Let's take the munchkins for fish-head curry."

"Thought you were busy," Chris had said sarcastically.

Tory shrugged. The affectation was her equivalent to counting to ten. It gave her time to frame an answer. "I've reconsidered bridge. If you think the women won't be horrified by my presence, I'll stay."

Chris threw a pillow at her. "It's my house. If they don't like you're being here, they're welcome to leave."

Tory had clutched the pillow to her chest. *Chris can afford to be confident,* she had thought. *No one would dare leave her house.* Chris was a role model for many of the wives. She had it all - two children and a loving husband. Chris and Kevin were a legend. They were as much in love as when they met at thirteen.

"I've asked Sarah Parker to come early. She's artistic, like you. I doubt she'll be any more comfortable this afternoon than you."

"Why?"

"She's deceptive. At the start, all you see is the packaging. Then you notice the hesitancy."

"If you look, which most people don't." Tory stopped. Had she and Chris switched places? "When did you become philosophical?"

"I did sound like you, didn't I?" Chris tossed another pillow at Tory. "How does it feel when the shoe's on the other foot? When you're not the one with all the answers?"

The question surprised her. Had she perfected her act so well that no one could tell how frightened she was? It was an appealing thought. Maybe she wasn't as close to the edge as she thought. If appearances were all that mattered, she'd be fine.

Now, as Tory watched Chris pick at her food, she was certain Kevin's behavior was plaguing her friend. Her mind was not on the Indian restaurant. She barely noticed when they left and walked towards Orchard Road where it would be easy to find a taxi.

Tory was desperate to stop Chris's pain. If Chris felt better, she might, too. For the first time since Dora death, she had a place to focus her fury. She turned down Chris's invitation for a drink and went to Trans Oil.

She marched into Kevin's office and screamed, "How dare you?"

Kevin looked startled when he heard her voice. He looked up scowling. "When you called, I said I was busy." Kevin glanced at his watch.

"Your watch hasn't stopped. I called from the lobby. And I don't give a damn about your problems. We had a deal."

Kevin rubbed his eyes. They were red from too much reading and too little sleep. "I haven't made up my mind about the job."

"Bull. You decided before Jakarta. You promised you'd tell Chris and the time it would take."

"I'm still in marketing. I'm tying up loose ends so I can turn my desk over to Barney Parker."

"So? Your late hours concern the job. Tell her. Now."

"I never said I'd tell her before I switched."

"That's semantics."

"You should know. You're the master of that game."

Tory picked a cigarette out of the pack on his desk, lit it, and inhaled. "When do you plan to tell Chris?" she demanded.

"This weekend."

"Which is her birthday."

Kevin dropped his head to his chest. The rapid motion reminded Tory of a puppet's head flopping when the string moved.

"Damn!"

"You forgot? How could you? Call your travel agent, book a trip and tell Chris what's going on," she ordered.

"Or what, you'll tell her? This may surprise you, but events aren't controlled by your will. The trip will have to wait."

"Do it now. Chris needs you."

"'And I need her. Life's not that simple. You may get to make up the rules as you go, the rest of us aren't so lucky. We have to consider more than what we want. I'll tell Chris when the time's right, not when you think I should."

Tory recoiled. Kevin's sharp words stung. She wouldn't let him get the better of her. Clapping her hands in quiet applause, she smiled. "Nice performance. What's got you so riled up?"

"I used to think you were the most arrogant, unidirectional person in the world. I've met your match. He's still here. Why don't you let me introduce you? The two of you can match wits while I finish work and go home."

"Your new boss must be a bachelor. Trouble in paradise already. My, my."

Kevin closed his eyes and slumped in his chair. "I'm too tired for verbal gymnastics. If you insist on staying, can we talk about something else?"

Tory went to the coffee machine. She reached in her pocket for change and fed the machine. Angrily, she punched the button for black coffee. She slammed the cup on Kevin's desk.

She leaned back in her chair and put her legs out so they reached the wall. "We went to Little India tonight. To Banana Leaf Apollo. You'd've hated it."

Kevin gulped the coffee. "What exotic tidbit did you expose my family to?"

"Fish-head curry. Marc loved it. The food's served on banana leaves and you eat with your hands. If you'd come, we would have let you eat the eyeball. It's an honor."

Kevin held his stomach with one hand and put the other over his mouth.

"It cheered Chris up. She was mopey after your call."

"Point taken."

Tory slid her legs to the floor and stood. Slowly she walked over and kissed Kevin's cheek. "Don't stay too late."

"Excuse me, I thought you were alone."

Kevin paled. Tory turned to see who was at the door. She didn't recognize the man. He lowered his head to avoid hitting the top of the doorway when he entered the room. This action made her smile. She did the same thing. Many of the buildings in Singapore were constructed to an Asian height standard. If you were taller than five foot eight, you hit your head if you weren't careful.

Kevin walked around his desk. "This is my soon-to-be boss Geoff. Geoff, this is ..."

"Someone who's leaving," Tory laughed as she slipped by the man.

That night, Tory couldn't sleep. After two hours she went to the kitchen for a cup of tea. She sat in bed sipping the herbal brew while she thought.

Chris was upset because Kevin worked late. If one missed trip and a few late nights caused such distress, Dora had been wrong. There was no reason for Tory to open her heart. Relationships caused pain. Her childhood suffering had been more than enough to last a lifetime. There was no reason to seek more.

Damn, she thought as she turned out the light. *I learned your lessons well, Dora. Jack taught you to trust. Who'll do that for me?*

Chapter 10
CHRIS

Singapore
Thursday, November 22, 1979

Chris hummed to herself as she checked the floral arrangements. Today was Thanksgiving. She and Kevin planned a traditional dinner for thirty friends. Since it wasn't a holiday in Singapore, the men had to work. Instead of an afternoon meal, it would be an evening affair. She made minor adjustments to the flowers as she walked, a touch here, a turn there. Subtle alterations made all the difference and transformed the arrangements into showpieces.

Their children were away until Sunday. Marc was in Bangkok on a school trip to explore the alligator farms. He was at the stage where he was fascinated with creepy, crawly animals. The thought made Chris shiver. Alison was with her best friend Laurel. They'd spend the long weekend reading *Teen Magazine* and talking.

Chris loved her children. They had their own interests. They no longer needed an amah to oversee their every move. Alison was in the school band, on the debating team, and a cheerleader. Her activities kept her at school until dinner. Marc spent his afternoons with the swim team.

I have so much to be thankful for this year, she thought. *It's hard to believe I actually thought Kevin had forgotten my birthday.* The memory of the four-day weekend they spent at Tioman two weeks before was fresh in her mind.

Tioman was a relatively undeveloped island off the Malaysian coast. There was only one hotel and they'd had to wait until November for a room. The magical island was worth the delay. Their room overlooked the pristine beach. They sailed, snorkeled, and enjoyed a romantic interlude. The time alone had been a respite for both of them. While they walked hand in hand watching the red-orange sun descend in the sky, Kevin told her about his latest promotion. He said it would keep him busier than ever at work. Chris didn't mind. She loved her husband. He was excited about the opportunity to try something new.

She was lost in thought and failed to hear Kevin come up behind her. His arms slid around her waist and he kissed the back of her neck. She turned and kissed him eagerly.

Kevin smiled. "The house looks great, as usual. Is everything under control?"

Nodding, she took Kevin's hand and led him to the couch. A chilled pitcher of martinis sat on the coffee table. They always enjoyed one drink together before a party started. It would be the last time they would be alone until the evening ended.

Kevin took a box from his pocket. "Alison said you had a new dress. I hope this goes with it."

Kevin was in good spirits these days. He bought her silly little gifts to let her know he thought about her during the day. Last night he'd come home with a plastic alligator so Marc could show them what he studied.

Chris's hands trembled as she opened the package. This was a jewelry box, not a plastic toy. Inside was a triple strand pearl choker with a black opal and diamond clasp. If she turned the clasp to the front, it would complement her dress. The fabric was such a dark green that it looked black in certain lights. In contrast, the opal had green highlights that swirled through the black stone when light hit it.

Her dressmaker had agreed with Tory that the dark silk was dramatic. She had transformed the fabric into an off the shoulder, Grecian-style gown.

"Oh, Kev, it's gorgeous. How did you know? Help me put it on." She lifted her auburn curls off her neck and let him latch the necklace. At Sarah's suggestion, Chris had let her hair grow so it covered the back of her neck.

"Tory said you fell in love with it at Tako Mas, and that I'd be the brute of the century if I didn't buy it."

"Kev, it's beautiful. But you know you should never take anything Tory says literally. This is much too extravagant."

"Nothing's too good for my wife. Anyway, I have an ulterior motive." Kevin reached for Chris's hand and squeezed it gently. "Remember the new guy I mentioned? I asked Geoff Melbourne and a guest to join us tonight. Will there be enough food?" They laughed at his question. Their dinner parties were buffets, with enough food for three times the number of guests.

Kevin's invitation was surprising. Bachelors were never invited to their Thanksgiving dinner. It was the one party of the year for couples only. To date the only exception had been Tory. "But why? I thought you said he did nothing but work."

"I'll be working for Geoff. No sense getting off on the wrong foot, which we might if he missed the social event of the season. Might be a good way to introduce him to Tory. Besides, he knew Barney and Sarah in New Zealand."

Chris was confused. "But you said you asked him and a guest."

"He rooms with a guy from one of the breweries. Geoff asked if he could bring his roommate, and I didn't think it good politics to say no."

Chris smiled. It was so like Kevin to open their house to anyone with a tie to their guests. A friend of the Parkers might be what Sarah needed. The renovations on Sarah's house were nearly complete. Any other woman would have considered that to be a superhuman accomplishment and would have relaxed, but not Sarah. She was determined to finish decorating before Christmas. Each time Chris saw her, Sarah was obsessed with some detail.

Had she been less secure, Chris might have been jealous of Sarah. Unlike Tory, who was blind to the heads that turned when she walked into a room, Sarah enjoyed the reaction her entrance made.

Despite all Sarah had going for her, there was something that belied her polished image. Chris couldn't put her finger on what it was. One day Sarah would be bright and cheerful, the next time Chris saw her she'd be quiet, brooding almost. Her mood swings were similar to Tory's. At first Chris assumed it was part of the artistic temperament. Then she noticed how different Sarah became when she was with Barney. She clung to his arm, seldom leaving his side. When her husband was with her, Sarah lost interest in everything else.

Since Sarah had so many interests, her behavior was odd. Last week while they shopped for a dining room suite, Sarah had exhibited a keen knowledge of Oriental designs. She was learning to make batik, the Indonesian art of using wax to separate colors when dying cotton fabric. She even took a Chinese cooking class once a week.

Chris made a mental note to invite Sarah for lunch. She'd taken on a great deal in a short period of time. Her schedule might be overwhelming her. Barney was probably too busy getting his bearings on his new job for them to have much time alone. Chris would be able to explain that this was all part of the expatriate life.

At that moment, the doorbell rang and the evening started. Chris smiled as she and Kevin welcomed their guests. The men congregated in the living room to discuss business or politics. The women preferred the solarium.

Surprisingly, this year several of their guests had family or friends visiting, so there were many people Chris didn't recognize. She made it a point to introduce herself to the newcomers.

She went into the kitchen to check on the turkey. When she returned, she saw Tory. She thought Tory had forgotten the date. It would be typical of her. At times Tory went into hibernation, removing herself from the social scene. Chris hoped Tory wasn't about to withdraw into her cocoon. The holiday party season was starting. Who else could she to talk to afterwards if Tory wasn't at a party?

No matter what Chris might share with the wives, there was something special about her bond with Tory. With Tory, Chris could drop her public persona and say what was on her mind. Tory made her feel safe. No matter what she did or said, Tory would be there for her. Although Tory might lecture her that she was wrong, she didn't diminish what Chris felt.

Chris was modeling her new necklace for Tory when she heard a voice out of nowhere. "Tory! Luv. Is that really you?"

Tory's reaction was startling. Her hand slipped off the clasp. She paled visibly, even before she turned around. In slow motion Tory forced herself to face the man. When she did, Chris saw the trembling in her hands, which were clenched into fists behind her back.

The man was the first to break their silence. "I can't believe my eyes. Thought you'd be long gone from these parts by now, luv."

After what seemed an eternity, Tory gasped, "Timothy! I had no idea you were here."

"I came with a friend," he answered with a wink.

"Not tonight. I meant I never expected you to be back in Singapore. Is this a business trip?"

Chris guessed this was the man Tory had been in love with. Since Tory had never referred to him by name, it took a while to make the connection.

Chris expected Tory to make a sarcastic comment and turn away. Instead, she went into his arms. For the rest of the evening, Tory was seldom far from Tim's side. Tory looked happy. Her calm, cool demeanor was replaced by a softer, radiant look. The Tory with Tim was not the Tory who went into seclusion.

Chris wanted to help keep that look alive. She set out to find who Tim had come with and how long he'd be in town. She was delighted to discover he was Geoff's guest. If they shared an apartment, Tim wasn't married. Maybe he and Tory would pick up where they left off. Chris smiled at the prospect.

As the evening progressed, Chris questioned her initial assessment of the situation. Although Tim paid attention to Tory, he mentally undressed every woman at the party. It surprised Chris that Tory was oblivious to Tim's behavior. Tory was the last person Chris expected to be taken in by a charmer.

A voice interrupted Chris's thoughts. "I'd like to thank you for allowing me to join the festivities on such short notice."

Chris turned quickly. "You must be Geoff Melbourne. I'm glad you could come."

Geoff nodded towards Tim, who stood with his arm protectively flung over Tory's shoulders. "I hope you don't mind. Kevin said I could bring a guest."

Chris did mind. Tory was enamored of Tim. She could see it in the way she glowed when she looked at him. From what she'd seen, Chris knew Tim would hurt Tory. Again.

Chris looked up at Geoff. He was a handsome man with a warm smile. She could see why he reminded Kevin of Tory. There was something similar about their eyes. They shared a look of thinly veiled pain that contradicted the pleasant mask of civility they wore.

"Is that Tory Winslow?" Geoff asked.

Chris was startled by his question. "Yes. How did you know?"

"Tim and I shared a flat in Auckland. He often spoke of her. He said she was a creative genius. Claimed she could capture any emotion with her camera."

Geoff really was sweet. "She's a wonderful photographer," Chris agreed.

"There's no need be concerned. In a week or two, Tim will be on to other birds. He only arrived Tuesday. I wanted him to come tonight so he'd meet people. I hadn't expected him to find an old friend."

It was as if Geoff knew how concerned she was for Tory. "How did you know what I was thinking?"

"You frown whenever you look at the two of them. From the way Tim spoke, you've nothing to worry about. He needs adoration. The woman he described was not likely to give it to him."

Despite her concern, Chris smiled. "That's for damn sure! That's not Tory's style."

“I'm glad."

“Why?”

Geoff paused. "Because I've seen her work."

Before she could ask more, Geoff left. The next time she saw him he was talking to Tim. Spying Tory walking towards the bar, Chris headed in the same direction. "Are you enjoying yourself?" she asked sarcastically.

Tory nodded. "I'd forgotten how well we fit together. What's Tim doing here? I can't imagine Trans Oil expanding into the brewery business."

"He shares a flat with Kevin's new boss. He's here as well. But I'm sure you haven't noticed him. You've been too busy."

Tory laughed. "Tall guy, black hair, green eyes. Not bad, if you go for the good-looking type." Tory pointed to Chris's necklace. "Do you like it?"

"What's my necklace got to do with anything?"

"Kevin bought it to make you happy. Be happy for me. It's what you always say you want."

"Is Tim what you want?"

Tory shrugged. "I never thought so. Tonight, I'm not sure."

Chapter 11
SARAH

Singapore
Friday, November 23, 1979

Sarah woke with a start. The man who'd been with Tory at the Taylor's party the night before had invaded her dreams. There was something overtly sensual about him. When Tory spoke, he gazed at her as if she were the most fascinating woman he'd ever met. She was delighted for Tory, who spent so much time alone. There was no mistaking the lust in the man's eyes when he looked at Tory. Then again, Sarah saw him look at other women the same way.

Why couldn't she get him out of her mind? She'd been drawn to him all evening. No matter where she and Barney stood, she positioned herself so she could see the man out of the corner of her eye. She watched him flirt with Tory, who blushed.

She glanced at Barney's sleeping form and understood. He was the opposite of her husband. The man at the party offered rapt attention to Tory when she spoke. Barney held on to Sarah like she was a trophy. He didn't speak to her, although he spoke about her. He acted as if she were an acquisition, like a painting. He didn't treat her like a person.

Barney's drinking was becoming more pronounced each day. When he drank heavily in the past, Barney had shut Sarah out. Now he flew into rages. If Sarah asked what was bothering him, he picked a fight.

On several occasions she considered ringing Barney Senior. She kept putting it off. There was no reason to trouble the man. It was the combination of alcohol and gambling that caused their previous problems. With the heavy fines levied by the government, Barney would be afraid to gamble in Singapore. If the tax didn't deter him, fear of his picture in the newspaper would.

Sarah wondered about Singapore. Nothing was quite what it seemed on the surface. At her first bridge afternoon, she passed off Janet Adams' comments as those of a jealous wife. Now, she understood that gossip was how many wives passed the long, hot afternoons. Already, Sarah knew which husbands played around and which wives had lovers.

Sarah heard from a spiteful woman that Kevin Taylor had a roving eye. She didn't believe it. It was obvious Kevin and Chris loved each other. The Taylors intimidated her. They represented what she'd expected, and not received, from her marriage. After fifteen years of marriage, the Taylors longed for weekends away together. Chris returned from Tioman glowing. She actually blushed when Sarah asked what they'd done.

Sarah ached for Barney to look at her the way the man from last night looked at Tory. When they first met he had; when they lived in London as well. Things started to change in Hong Kong. It was the booze. She must divert his attention from his gin bottle. How?

She had it! She'd ring Geoff and invite him to dinner. Geoff lived for work. If anyone could interest Barney in Trans Oil, Geoff could. Since it was impossible to focus on work and drink excessively, Barney's drinking would lessen. Then Sarah could work on ways to rekindle her husband's desire.

Having Geoff over would be like old times. Geoff wouldn't ignore Sarah. He commented on the clothes she wore, how she styled her hair, the meals she prepared. In New Zealand, Barney had been the teeniest bit jealous of the attention Geoff paid Sarah. If he reacted the same way now, his drinking would stop. She'd have more than her dreams to keep her company.

She paused. Last night was the first time she'd seen Geoff since he moved to Singapore. He seemed different, distracted almost. When they danced in New Zealand, Geoff clutched her so close she could hear his heart beat. Last night, he held her like she was his sister.

She reached for the alarm clock before it went off. She was seeing problems where there were none. Geoff was preoccupied about work, nothing more.

At breakfast she suggested inviting Geoff to dinner.

"Lonely? Aren't I enough for you? Must you have Geoff follow you around like a lovesick puppy?"

The vehemence of Barney's reaction stunned her. "If I'm lonely, whose fault is it? You're never home."

"If you'd quit whinging at me to stop drinking, I might come home more. The other wives don't carry on about their husbands drinking the way you do."

"You don't hear what gets said at bridge."

Barney shoved his plate away. "I don't want this slop. Sarah, be a dear and make me one of those milkshake things. I like them better than this."

"No more fighting," Trey said.

The interruption kept Sarah from telling Barney why he preferred the milkshake to bacon and eggs. She reached for Trey's hand. "All right, sweetie. Mummy and Daddy are sorry. Aren't we, Barney?"

"Of course. Sarah, my milkshake please. I can't sit here all morning."

"Me too," Trey said.

Sarah was trapped. If she made an issue of Barney's request, they'd argue. If they argued, it would upset Trey. She didn't want to hurt her little boy. As it was he only saw his father on the few mornings Barney could drag himself to the breakfast table. It wasn't fair for Sarah to destroy what little time Trey had with his father. Reluctantly she went into the kitchen.

As soon as Barney left, Sarah called Trans Oil and asked for Geoff. "It was lovely to see you last night. Would you like to join us for dinner tonight?"

"I'm busy."

"Oh darn." Sarah pouted, then realized Geoff would miss the effect since he couldn't see her. "You have to eat, don't you?"

"I promised my roommate we'd grab something at the hawker stands."

"Roommate?" This was news. Was that what distracted Geoff last night? "What's her name?"

Geoff chuckled. "Tim. We shared a flat in Auckland. Seemed logical to do the same here."

"He can come too. It's easier to cook for four than three."

"Great. Tim never believed me when I raved about your cooking. Shall we bring wine?"

"That would be nice. Is seven too early?"

"That'll be fine. See you then."

She no sooner put the receiver down, and then the phone rang. Sarah was certain it was Barney calling to apologize. She was stunned to hear Tory's voice asking, "Are you going to the baseball game at Sentosa tomorrow?"

"I don't think we've been invited."

Tory laughed. "It's a Thanksgiving tradition. An attempt to keep the American spirit alive and well."

"What is baseball?"

"The American sport. The oil companies get together and rent the island for the day for the expats. I think it's supposed to be a consolation prize for working on what would be a holiday at home. There are always a ton of children around. I'm sure your son would enjoy himself."

"Barney's been so busy. I don't know if we're free."

"No one works the day of the ball game. Why don't I meet you at Jardine Steps at eleven a.m.?"

Sarah smiled. "We could pick you up if you liked."

"No. I'll meet you there. Sentosa is picturesque. Bring along your art supplies. I'll show you the best places to sketch."

Sarah put Tory's call out of her mind as she planned her menu. Dinner would be salmon mousse as a starter, prawns, lightly steamed broccoli and rice pilaf as the main course. Fruit and Stilton for dessert. She checked the wine rack to be certain the proper wines were in stock. There was no telling if Geoff's selection would go with the meal.

Barney was in a better mood when he got home from work. Either he'd forgotten their argument or chose to ignore it. He made no disparaging remarks when she told him Geoff was coming to dinner.

Barney was fixing a drink when the front bell sounded, so Sarah went to the door. Her heart pounded when she opened the door -- Geoff was standing next to the mystery man from the previous night. She wasn't certain how she felt at the prospect of having him so close. His presence in her dreams was disturbing enough.

The evening was a success. Geoff's presence tempered Barney's drinking. Geoff talked about a new business venture that Sarah had difficulty following. Surprisingly Barney was interested in Geoff's discussion.

When Sarah looked away from the two of them, Tim was looking at her. His stare was so intense she looked to see if she had a stain on her blouse. Satisfied that nothing was amiss, she looked up. Tim was still watching her.

He winked his right eye and grinned. "If I know Geoff, he'll babble like that all night. I've never seen anyone get so excited about work."

"What interests you?"

Tim smiled slyly. "I can't think of anything with a pretty woman like you in the room."

Sarah blushed. She felt herself pulled toward Tim like a magnet, powerless to stop her attraction. Barney and Geoff were so involved in their conversation that they'd forgotten Sarah and Tim were in the room. Sarah was flattered by Tim's attention. At the same time, it was disconcerting. No matter what she did, his eyes were on her. When she got up to check on dinner, he followed her with an offer of assistance.

Tim's comments were fraught with sexual innuendo. She found herself responding with similar undertones. There seemed no way to slow their growing attraction unless she stopped Geoff and Barney's discussion. Serving dinner earlier than planned was the perfect way to involve Geoff and Barney. Geoff never discussed business at the dinner table.

Over dinner Tim regaled them with stories of what he remembered about Singapore. Barney warmed to Tim immediately. The fact that he was a friend of Geoff's, and Australian, made him seem less a stranger. If that were not enough, he shared their mutual love of movies.

Geoff invited them over on Wednesday evening to go to the movies and have a late supper. "The films change that morning. I'll check the paper and ring everyone so we can decide what to see," he offered. "There's nothing on now but mush."

"Oh, I don't know about that," Tim answered as he helped himself to another glass of port. "Doctor Zhivago is at the Cathay. That is definitely the greatest movie of all time." The topic of movies kept them occupied for hours.

No matter how hard she tried to stop herself, she constantly found herself peeking at Tim. What was more disconcerting, he seemed to enjoy the attention. When he caught her eye, he'd give her a playful wink.

As Sarah crawled into bed, she felt guilty about the attention she'd paid Tim. To atone for her thoughts, Sarah reached over and rubbed Barney's back. Over the last few months, their sex life had dwindled to nothing. She couldn't abide the overpowering smell of gin that permeated his skin. Tonight, Barney had limited his drinking to wine, so his body odor wasn't as offensive.

When he turned and pulled her towards him, Sarah eagerly returned his embrace.

Chapter 12
TORY

Singapore
Thursday - Saturday, November 22 - 24, 1979

At first Tory thought she'd mistaken an Australian accent for Tim. As the man continued speaking, she realized that Tim was at the Taylors. Her first reaction was to run out the door. She had to force herself to turn and face him. When she did, the time since their parting disappeared. It was as if Tim had never left. The more time she spent with him on Thanksgiving, the easier it was to remember only the good times.

The years had been good to him. Before he'd been thin to the point of emaciation. He'd filled out without putting on excess weight. His easygoing, flirtatious manner was intact. When he put his arms around her, she knew she'd stay at the party. It had been eight years since a man held her. She hadn't realized how much she missed the sensation.

The day after the party he called and asked to escort her to the baseball game on Sentosa. At the time his call pleased her. Now, as she waited on the corner for him, she wasn't sure she wanted to get involved with Tim again. She carried two camera bodies and various lenses in a camera case. She held a tripod under her left arm. The equipment would keep Tim at bay, so she could decide what she wanted. Tim was still an expat. He'd leave Singapore again. Could she face that? Could she overcome the fears from her childhood? Tim had never been violent. Why did she equate love with pain? Intellectually she understood it was from her parents and older sisters' marriages. But that was in another world.

Tim laughed when he saw her paraphernalia. "Tory, luv. The companies have their own PR folks. There's no need for you to be taking pictures," he teased.

She shook her hair. "It's not what it looks like. A few years ago I took candid shots of Alison and Marc for Chris. She showed them around. Then everyone wanted pictures of their kids. It's become a tradition. The photos are my Christmas gifts."

"Well, I'm not helping lug the stuff. Geoff, if you're smart, you'll steer clear too."

At the mention of another name, she peered into the car. Someone was seated in the front passenger seat. Apparently Tim was as anxious as she. Good. They should take things slowly.

She walked toward the open window and halted. It was Kevin's new boss. Not to be deterred, she extended her right hand through the open window, shook his hand, and smiled. "Hi. I'm Tory Winslow. You needn't worry. I'm quite accustomed to handling my own equipment."

"Geoff Melbourne at your service." He gave her a mock salute. "Tim and I share a flat."

"Oh, Tory, you'll love it. We've the two top floors, complete with a swimming pool on the patio. It's on Grange Road. The view is not to be believed."

Tim sounded smug. Obviously he was pleased with himself. When they'd first met he worked on the factory floor. They were both barely making it. Tim had regaled Tory with stories of the penthouse apartment he'd live in when he struck it big.

"You always said you'd live in a posh place."

Tim looked in the rear view mirror and winked. "Geoff and I were buds in Auckland. We got transferred here about the same time. With our two housing allowances, we can swing the place. It's a damn sight better than being stuck out here in Jurong. When did you move? Does your monkey like living in a flat?"

Tory shifted uncomfortably in her seat. Quietly, she said, "Anna's not in Singapore now."

"Gee, luv, I'm sorry. I know how much you liked the chimp. Hard to imagine her liking a flat. Not that I can see you in one."

"You had a pet monkey?" Geoff asked.

"Orangutan actually. Anna Banana. I used to live out in the boonies. She sort of adopted me."

"I can understand you leaving your grass shack if Anna died. But why on earth would you move here? Jurong's downright depressing."

Tory so resented Tim's snobbery that she didn't bother to correct him. Jurong was the opposite of Sembawang. Instead of a village, it was semi-industrial. The few government-built housing complexes were for the working class. Her apartment building was small; only six families lived there. Tory liked the anonymity it provided. There was little chance of meeting people she did business with or saw socially.

"Because no one gives me a housing allowance," she parried neatly. "I'm part of what's known as the working class. Perhaps you've read about us?"

"And bloody good you are at it. I've seen your stuff over the years. You can't miss a Winslow original. Always thought by now you'd be married to a rich American and living in the lap of luxury with the requisite two-point-three children."

"And give up all this?" she asked, as they drove past several dilapidated buildings.

Tim parked at Jardine Steps where they walked towards the ferry. Tory halted at the gate. "I promised to meet someone here." On a whim, she'd invited Sarah to meet her. If her camera equipment didn't stop Tim, the presence of another couple might.

Tim took her by the shoulders and turned her to face him. "Well now, don't tell me there is someone in your life after all? And here I thought you'd been pining for me all this time."

She swatted at him. "You're still the same incorrigible brute, I see. Her name's Sarah Parker. She's new."

Geoff added, "I knew the Parkers in Auckland. Tim and I had dinner with them last night."

Geoff's accent confused her. It was neither Australian nor British, although there was something decidedly British about it. He looked vaguely familiar, yet not like anyone she knew. He was taller than she. His hair was so black it had blue highlights. His eyes were a green she'd only seen in the jungle.

Before she could ask where he was from, the Parkers arrived. Once the introductions were complete, they got on the ferry. Tim told them about Sentosa Island. "There's a playground, hiking and biking trails, even museums for shells, coral, and rocks. There're several stretches of beach. There's an aquarium, some caves." Tim paused and scratched his head. "And the best for last, the Butterfly Park. You can't do Sentosa without seeing that. If you're game, meet me back at the ferry at three o'clock."

The suggestion irritated Tory. It had been their favorite spot. Either Tim had forgotten its meaning or he no longer cared.

"Did you bring your art supplies, Sarah?" Tory asked. "The Butterfly Park is one of the areas I thought you'd like to sketch."

The Sarah on the ferry hardly seemed the same woman Tory met at Chris's house. That day she'd seemed alive and full of enthusiasm. Today she looked frightened. Tory tried to figure out why. She leaned against the side of the boat and stared through her camera. If people thought she was framing a photograph, they overlooked her behavior.

Sarah did not hang on Barney's every word. From that, Tory guessed that he didn't beat her. Battered women jumped when their husband spoke for fear of what might happen if they failed to respond quickly. For years Tory had jumped when her father even looked at something. It was safer.

Sarah finished Barney's sentences for him. It was as if she were afraid to let him say too much. *Maybe he drinks,* Tory thought. *If so, Singapore's not the place for them. Too bad, Sarah has promise. If the husband turns out to be a lush, they'll be gone in less than a year. Trans Oil won't tolerate their copybook being blotted. It won't matter who his father is.*

When they reached Sentosa, Tory turned to Sarah. "Do you want to see the wildflowers I mentioned yesterday? You might want to sketch them."

"I really should stay with Barney and Trey. Perhaps later. Where will you be?"

Tory shrugged. "I thought I'd go to the playground to get some shots of the kids before they're covered in dirt. I'll be back before the baseball game starts."

"Well, luv," Tim said as he plucked her chin, "we'll catch up with you then. Can't imagine anything more boring than watching you snap piccies of the kids."

The situation was ironic. Tory had invited Sarah to keep Tim from getting too close, and now he was going off with Sarah. Shrugging, Tory walked in the direction of the playground. She put her 400-mm lens on the tripod and focused on the children. Once she looked through the camera lens, nothing mattered but the photos. The only time she stopped was to change film. She was so involved in her work; she didn't hear Geoff come up next to her.

"Kevin said you liked hotdogs. I brought you one."

Tory looked quizzically at Geoff. He carried a tray with three hotdogs and every condiment.

"I wasn't sure what you liked on your hotdog," he explained.

"You like to be prepared for any eventuality, I see."

"It makes life run smoother. Pick your poison. Mind if I join you?"

Tory took the cardboard tray and put it on the grass. She sat down and shrugged. Why should Geoff want to spend time with her? He worked for Trans Oil. He should be with the expats. Unless the family setting of the baseball outing left him feeling uncomfortable.

"What have you seen so far?" she asked.

"Today, or since I arrived in Singapore?"

"Today, I guess. Has Tim shown you any of the wonders he was spouting off about on the ferry?"

Geoff smiled. "You know Tim. He's off meeting and greeting. I haven't seen him in hours. When does the baseball game start?"

Tory looked at her watch. "Five minutes ago. Why did they cook lunch so late?"

"They didn't. It took forever to find you. Do you plan to watch the game?"

"As soon as I pack my equipment. I can't resist the chance of getting shots of the men cavorting like teenagers. It will make the twisted ankles and strained ligaments seem worth it. Are you playing?"

"Thought I'd sit it out. Baseball's not my sport." Geoff watched Tory take her camera off the tripod. "Since we're going in the same direction, I wouldn't mind carrying some of your things."

Tory paused. Geoff was being accommodating and it bothered her. She wondered why. "Be careful. This stuff is my livelihood."

Geoff backed off. "I understand how important your equipment must be to you. I feel the same about my car."

Tory handed him the tripod. "Your car," she said as they walked. "Isn't it silly to worry about your car while you're in Singapore?"

"Not really. I had it shipped. It should arrive in a month."

The statement surprised her. Expats were given company cars. No one paid to ship a car. It was expensive. "Is it special?"

"I like tinkering with it. If I promise not to get in the way of your picture taking, will you explain the game?"

As they neared the bleachers Tory figured out why Geoff had sought her out. The stands were full of women and children. The men were either on the field or hanging around what served as the dugout. With her, Geoff wouldn't look out of place.

Tory looked for Tim. He stood with the Trans Oil team doling out equipment. It made her smile.

Instead of asking about the game, Geoff asked why she switched lenses. She explained the image she was striving to capture and how the lens would help. While she spoke, he took a piece of paper and diagramed what she said. The science behind the optics appealed to him. Tory easily slipped into her teacher role.

When the game ended and the beer keg was rolled on to the field, Tory groaned. "I'm not up to Noah's Ark. Think I'll go back to the playground."

"As you wish."

To get one more shot of Trey, Tory moved her equipment and focused on the bushes near where she'd last seen him. When she still couldn't find him, she took out her binoculars. Just as she caught sight of Trey, she thought she noticed a movement in the undergrowth. She adjusted the glasses and peered into the heavy mangrove vegetation. To her surprise, she saw Sarah and Tim walking together. Not certain she should believe her eyes, she turned the camera in their direction, added a two times tele-converter to the lens, and shot the remainder of the film.

In her eagerness to develop her film, Tory turned down an invitation for a drink at Tim's apartment. When Geoff asked if he might help her, she said no. She was so unsettled by what she thought she'd seen that she didn't realize how sharp her tone was.

She struggled through the developing process until all ten rolls were done. She examined each negative with a magnifying glass. Then she found it, twelve shots of Tim and Sarah. There was no mistaking what the photos showed. The two of them were closer than they should have been. She thought back to Thursday's party. At the time, she had ignored the eye contact between them.

For a minute she considered going to the celebratory party. She put the thought out of her mind. She was angry and hurt, conditions she never allowed people she did business with to see. A smiling face was the only one she showed the world.

Too agitated to sleep, she changed clothes and went to the disco at the Marco Polo. If she were dancing, she could momentarily erase her pain. Action always made Tory feel better. Maybe she'd meet someone who'd dance into the small hours of the morning without asking questions.

Before leaving, she checked her schedule for the next day. Her only obligation was brunch with Trans Oil's Managing Director. She couldn't miss it. Trans Oil gave her a great deal of business. At least she wouldn't run into Tim there.

Chapter 13
SARAH

Singapore
Saturday – Thursday, November 24 - December 11, 1979

"No, Trey, you can't have chips." Sarah sighed. Arguments about lunch were becoming a daily event.

Trey stamped his feet. "Chips. Chips. I want chips."

Sarah reached for his hand. Grasping it firmly, she picked him up and held him. "Mummy thinks you should eat something else."

Trey began kicking Sarah and crying.

"Shh," she whispered, as she rubbed her hand across his back in circles. "There's nothing to cry about, sweetie."

"Trey wants chips," he wailed.

Sarah hated the fuss Trey made. She couldn't control him. Any second, Ah Soon would come and take him away. When that happened, she felt useless. No wonder she couldn't control Barney's drinking, she couldn't cope with a three-year-old's temper tantrum. Trey was as stubborn as Barney when he wanted something. Sarah knew she should hold her ground and insist Trey eat healthy food. Yet, when he carried on, she gave in to stop his tears. For the hundredth time, she realized how right Chris had been about the amah. No matter how much Trey cried, Ah Soon didn't give in to his demands. It was reassuring to know that one member of their household was behaving properly.

Barney stumbled into the dining room and announced, "we're going to Sentosa today," in a churlish tone.

Sarah did her best to smile and mask her anger. "I know. Tory Winslow told me about it yesterday. Trey and I are looking forward to it."

"Where's my hip flask? I don't know how I'll get through the afternoon without a nip. It's the weekend. Time to relax and unwind."

She nuzzled her head against his arm. Perhaps if she interested him in sex, his mood would improve. To her surprise, Barney shoved her away.

"I'm not in the mood. Find my flask now."

"Find it yourself."

Sarah turned to leave the bedroom and Barney stopped her. "Do it."

Rather than argue, she went to the sideboard in the dining room and took the flask from the liquor cupboard. This did not bode well for the rest of the day. To calm herself, Sarah packed her sketchpad and charcoal. Tory said there were interesting things to sketch. It would give her something to do besides stay with Barney. In his current mood, he'd be cutting and sarcastic towards her.

When Barney saw the pad sticking out from her canvas carryall, he pulled it out. "Who's going to watch Trey? There won't be time for you to draw."

"Chris said some of the teenagers would mind the children. I'm not interested in watching a silly game."

"It's important you be there. I don't want you going off by yourself."

Sarah grit her teeth. "Fine. I told Tory we'd meet her and take the ferry. Shall I ring and cancel?"

"Why? I'd like to meet her. I've heard a lot about her."

Sarah looked up, surprised. "From who?"

"Kevin. He has photos of his children on his desk. She took them."

"I've never seen her work."

"It's good. Much better than the stuff you draw."

Barney's comment stung. Sarah left the room so he wouldn't see her sniff back her tears. She knew he'd purposely denigrated her drawings to hurt her. She couldn't imagine why. Tory made her living as a photographer. It was to be expected that her work was good.

She was confused when they got to Jardine Steps and Tory was with Geoff and Tim. Why had Tory invited Sarah to join her? And when had she met Geoff? None of it made sense. Had she not been concerned about Barney, she'd have asked Tory to explain.

The boat trip was torture. Tory was deep in thought. Geoff, too, was silent. Sarah held Trey up on the railing so he could see the water. She didn't want him to act up and upset Barney. Tim appeared to be the only one looking forward to the outing. He chatted about the things to do at Sentosa.

Sarah hadn't planned to go off with Tim. She'd taken Trey to the swings when he got bored with the baseball game. Trey cried each time that she said she was tired of pushing him. One of the other mothers had had the foresight to include her amah in the outing. She volunteered to keep Trey. Sarah made a wrong turn on the way back to the ball field and ran into Tim.

"You left before the game ended."

Sarah nodded. "Trey was restless. Who won?"

"Have I told you today how pretty you are? You're the best looking woman here, bar none."

"What about Tory? Aren't the two of you an item?"

Tim chuckled as he brushed a lock of hair from her face. "Tory and I are old friends. We go to things sometimes. What is it she calls Singapore?"

"Lotus Land."

"That, too. No, I was thinking of the other name." He stopped and thought. "I remember now. Noah's Ark."

"Why?" she asked.

"She claims expats exist in pairs. That they have to be in twos to survive."

Sarah laughed. It was an apt description. Until Geoff came to town, Tory was the only single expat Sarah had met.

Sarah and Tim walked. She asked again who won the game.

"Do you care? I don't. I'd rather discuss other things."

"Such as?"

"You. I think you're fascinating."

Sarah blushed. "You don't know anything about me," she murmured.

"I know you're a wonderful cook and beautifully dressed. Geoff says you're a whiz at decorating. I'm not surprised. You have exquisite taste."

Sarah beamed at Tim's compliments. Here was a man who appreciated the things she did. After the way Barney treated her that morning, it boosted her spirits.

Sarah shook her head to stop the memories. Her behavior with Tim was not acceptable, no matter how poorly her husband treated her. When she looked at her watch, she realized Chris would be here for lunch any minute. She better make sure lunch was under control.

It was a beautiful afternoon and they ate on the patio. Sarah steered the conversation to safe topics.

"What are you doing for Christmas?" Chris asked.

"Barney and I plan to spend the day with Trey, just the three of us. Trey's so interested in things this year. Last year he didn't understand what was going on." Sarah hoped Chris would believe her. She couldn't risk being invited to the Taylors. It would be intolerable to have to play-act being the happy family.

Chris smiled. "I remember when Marc and Alison were that age. You shouldn't miss those years. They grow up so fast."

Sarah heard the nostalgic tone. "Will Christmas be for family only or will Tory be there?"

"Christmas is for the family. Tory has an open invitation, but she never shows. I'm not sure where she spends the day."

Remembering Tory's description of their community, Sarah asked, "Do you think it's hard for her being here on her own? I could never do something so brave as to open my own business, not even in Sydney."

"Neither could I" Chris agreed.

"I noticed her dancing with Geoff's roommate at Janet Adams' party last week. Do you think they're seeing each other?"

"I'm not sure. Her cab pulled up to the house behind our car. I think she left alone."

Sarah was surprised. She assumed Chris and Tory told each other everything. "Don't you talk about things like that?"

Chris shook her head. "Tory doesn't talk about herself. We had lunch on Tuesday before she taught her class. I discussed things I'd heard at bridge the week before and she told me about her trip to Jakarta." Chris reached into her purse. "Oh, I nearly forgot. She suggested a place to find the samovar you want. I wrote the name down. It's on Arab Street."

Sarah smiled demurely. "I'm not comfortable there. Would you mind going with me?"

"Why not? It's more fun when you're with someone."

The first time Chris took her to a worn-down shophouse, Sarah was positive Chris had lost her mind. Then she looked around and saw that the shop had just what she was looking for. It was odd for Sarah to think of walking through a dusty shop with cement floors to look for an accent piece. Yet she found treasures in the most unusual places.

Today was no exception. They went through several stores on their way. The minute they were in the door, Sarah spied the samovar of her dreams lying next to a wicker basket. It was dirty and tarnished but would polish well. There were no dents or scratches to mar the intricate scrollwork. Purposely, she put the coffee urn down and picked up one of the baskets. There were reeds coming loose that could easily be mended. "How much?"

"Five dollars."

“Two dollars," she said firmly. Bargaining was part of the fun of shopping in Singapore. She and the owner went back and forth for several minutes until they settled on a price. As an apparent afterthought, Sarah picked up the samovar and brought it to the counter. "How much for this with the basket?"

“This is a very old piece. Cost many dollars."

Sarah shook her head and pouted. "It's filthy. I'll have to pay my maid extra to clean it."

“Twenty dollars."

"Not today." She turned and motioned Chris to move to the door. Sarah walked slowly; knowing the man would not want to lose both sales.

"How much you give me?" he asked.

Sarah grinned at Chris before she turned. "Eight dollars for the basket and the urn."

"Ten."

Sarah tapped her foot impatiently. "Please, don't waste my time. Eight is my best offer. Take it or leave it."

"Take," he said in a dejected tone.

As they walked towards the taxi queue, Sarah felt better than she had all day.

"You do that well," Chris said in an envious tone. "I hate haggling over prices."

"I think it's fun. What I don't understand is how those places stay in business. He can't have made any money on that transaction."

While they waited for a taxi, Sarah thought of showing her finds to Tim after she cleaned and polished it. Why was she thinking of him?

Chapter 14
CHRIS

Singapore
Monday, December 31, 1979

Chris frowned. Tory was carrying presents. "You won't be here for Christmas?"

Tory shook her head. "It's a family holiday."

"You're family."

Tory shrugged. "It means a lot to me that you think so, even if it's not true. I'm off to Calcutta for two weeks. With the American School closed, I've got time to work uninterrupted."

"Studying your mantra," Chris joked.

"An article on Mother Teresa."

"Will you be here for my New Year's Eve party?" Sarah asked.

"Don't worry. I won't ruin your night."

"What a horrible thing to say," Chris scoffed. "Sarah asked a simple question. You didn't have to bite her head off."

Chris remembered the conversation from two weeks before as she looked around the Parkers' house on New Year's Eve. Chris wished Tory had apologized. Instead she smirked at Sarah. If Sarah knew what the look or comment were about, she said nothing. The pleasant lunch Chris planned for her two closest friends had been ruined by one remark. Why did Tory do things like that?

Chris smiled. Sarah was glowing as she spoke to Geoff. *I guess having an old friend around has helped. She's really so young. I should remember that more often,* Chris chided herself. It was easy to forget that Sarah was a decade younger than the youngest of the wives in their group. The Parkers' house was as grand as the others.

Sarah's mad rush to complete her house before the holidays had been successful. The decor was a mixture of antiques they'd brought with them and Asian furniture and accents. The two styles blended harmoniously. Most people who tried this failed; Sarah made it look effortless.

Chris walked to a display table and picked up the samovar.

"Nice piece."

Chris turned. Tim stood admiring the brass urn in her hands. "Yes, it is. You should've seen it the day Sarah found it."

"She showed us that week. The four of us go to the flicks on Wednesdays."

"Four?"

"Geoff, Barney, Sarah, and me. The down under crowd sticks together."

"That's nice," she said absently. Chris didn't like the way Tim looked at her. It was as if he could see through her dress. She shivered involuntarily.

Tim put his arm across her shoulders. "Are you cold, luv?"

Suddenly, another male arm was across her shoulders. Chris relaxed at the smell of Kevin's aftershave. She snuggled against his chest. "I was chilly."

"You're standing under an air vent." Kevin moved them away from Tim. "Was he disturbing you?" he asked.

"Thanks for rescuing me. I have the oddest feeling when I'm too close to that man. Guess my imagination's working overtime."

Kevin laughed. "Leave the fantasy stuff to Tory. I called home. Alison just got off the phone with her."

"Is something wrong?"

"You're such a worrier. Tory's fine. She wished the munchkins happy new year. Said she'll call you in a few days."

"Are the children okay?"

Kevin turned Chris to face him. "Chrissy, there are two servants with them. The children will be fine. Let's enjoy tonight without worrying about disasters that never come to pass."

"I do worry, don't I?"

He kissed the top of her head. "Yes, you do. Have you seen the buffet table?"

Chris nodded. "Unbelievable, isn't it? Only Sarah could adorn the platters with orchids and not have the flowers look limp and lifeless in an hour. I wonder how she did it."

"Ask her. Is she getting on okay?"

Chris grinned. "Now who's the worrier? She seems calmer lately. How's Barney working out?"

Kevin rubbed his chin, his thinking pose. "It's been two months since he took over my desk. I still get calls from some of his customers. They haven't seen Barney since the day I introduced them. The institutional side of the business needs more attention than he's giving it."

"Barney's style may be different from yours."

"I don't know. He's out of the office most afternoons. I thought he was with clients. The PUB contract is up for renewal. We can't afford to lose it."

Chris beamed at her husband. Getting the Public Utility Board contract was a coup for Trans Oil. Kevin had been proud when he wrested it from the previous holder three years before. "I'm sure Barney understands the importance. Are you being overly critical because he isn't doing things the way you did?"

"Maybe." Kevin squeezed her hand. "I'm sure you're right. Let's go outside. There's something I've been meaning to discuss with you."

They stopped at the buffet table on their way. Outside it was clear and balmy, typical December weather. Small tables surrounded the pool. Chris waved to several friends who were enjoying the pleasant evening. Kevin chose a table away from the others.

Kevin cleared his throat, a signal that he was uneasy. "Chrissy, I'm not sure I can get away at Easter."

Chris paused, her fork in mid air. "We always go home for Easter. It's the one holiday the children spend with their cousins."

"It's not definite. Geoff said we might be negotiating in April. I thought I should mention it before you made plans."

"Tell him you have to take your leave then. We've done it for seven years. Our families expect it."

"I know," he said. He patted her hand gently.

"Kevin, I won't hear of it."

"Don't get upset. I'm sorry I said anything."

When he reached for her hand, she pulled it away. "I'm serious. Tell Geoff to schedule his negotiations another time."

"I'll talk to him, Chrissy. If Geoff can't be swayed, take the kids by yourself. I hate to think of the three of you missing out because I'm stuck at the office."

Chris considered his suggestion. Spending the Easter holidays in Singapore would seem odd. Perhaps she and the children would go home. The more she thought, the less she liked the idea. It wouldn't be the same. "Our families will think something's wrong if you're not with us."

"Maybe I can work something out with Geoff." Although he sounded positive, his face gave him away. Kevin knew he wouldn't get the time.

"I thought he was the negotiator."

Kevin nodded. "Usually. This is with the Singapore government. I'm more familiar with the bureaucracy than he is. He wants my input."

"And you like being needed."

"In Tioman, I said this job would keep me busy until we get the venture up and running. Start-ups take time."

Work was important to Kevin. Chris might not understand what the new undertaking was about, but she knew how pleased Kevin was to be involved. When he came home late at night he was physically tired and emotionally charged at the same time. One Easter was not worth getting upset over. "Would it help if I spoke to Geoff?" The minute the words were out of her mouth, she wished she had an erase button and could take them back.

"That was silly of me. Work's your domain. When will you know for sure?"

"Early February. If I can't make it..."

"We'll deal with it." She kissed him on the cheek. "It's nearly midnight. Let's go inside and join the countdown to the New Year. It's the start of another decade."

"I love you, Chrissy," Kevin whispered. He held her close as they walked into the house.

Chapter 15
TORY

Sabah, Malaysia
Wednesday, January 9, 1980

Tory woke to the sound of the phone. She looked at the time. *It's 5 a.m. who'd call now?* She reached out and pulled the receiver to her ear, knocking the phone to the floor in the process. "Hello," she whispered sleepily.

"The end is near."

As soon as she heard Halim's voice, Tory was wide-awake. "Is there time for me to get there?"

Halim sighed loudly. Tory could sense his frustration. For weeks, Halim had been begging her to say a final good-bye and leave it at that. Tory couldn't; she called every day.

"Well, is there?" she demanded.

"No one can say. It could be today. It might not be until tomorrow. She won't last the week, that's all I know."

"I'm coming."

"As you wish."

Tory paused to figure out the plane schedule.

"A car will be waiting for you at Sandakan."

Her pulse raced as she rode the taxi between Sandakan and Sepilok. There had to be enough time. Anna couldn't die alone. Tory had promised herself she'd be there. It was something she hadn't been allowed to do for Dora.

Halim met Tory as she walked through the park gate. Today, for the first time, they dispensed with their polite bantering.

Instead, Halim led Tory to the bed of twigs and underbrush where Anna slept. Tory stooped down and leaned over the orangutan.

"Hi, Kiddo," she whispered, as she patted the orangutan's hair.

Anna's eyes were glassy and swollen almost closed. Tory doubted she could see anything. Anna turned her head slightly at the sound of Tory's voice. Tory kissed Anna's high forehead. Hearing seemed to be only of Anna's senses that was unaffected by her illness. If she kept talking, Anna would know that she wasn't alone.

"Tim's back. Sometimes I get tired of being alone. Maybe we'll work it out this time."

Tory took a comb and worked on Anna's matted hair. "Did I tell you about Tim's roommate? He's not bad looking, but I think he's got an attitude problem. He takes things too seriously. Tim's easier to be around."

In the last two months Geoff Melbourne had called and asked Tory out several times. She always turned him down. At first she enjoyed his persistence; now it was embarrassing. On several occasions, after she told Geoff she was busy, she bumped into him at a disco she'd gone to alone. When she saw Geoff she'd turn and go to the other side of the room. She knew he'd seen her, yet he never came over. He stayed on his side of the room and left within the hour.

Tory couldn't explain her refusal to go out with Geoff. He was pleasant, hard-working, handsome -- traits that appealed to her. There was more to him than that. She wondered what secrets he hid beneath his cool exterior.

Tory smiled at the tired faces Anna made to her comments. Tory could read Anna's expressions. She was positive the orangutan understood what she was being told. Anna frowned and tried to purse her lips into a raspberry every time Tory mentioned Tim's name. Tory was certain Anna was evidencing her displeasure that Tim was back in Tory's life. *Not that he really is*, Tory reminded herself.

Tim and she might laugh and joke with one another like they used to, but it was different between them now. Eight years of separation had wrought so many changes. Tim was more outgoing and jovial than she remembered. Having achieved his financial dreams, he'd become complacent and self-centered.

Two nights before in Bugis Street, she had seen the lascivious looks he gave Sarah. Tory was tempted to pull her hand away from his, but it didn't seem worth the effort. Part of her desperately needed to feel connected to someone, even if it was a sham. Later that evening, they argued. "I'm not blind, you know. I saw you ogling Sarah. She's married, in case you've forgotten."

"Married or not, she knows how to treat a man."

"Are you insinuating that I don't?" She had wanted to slap the smug grin off Tim's face.

"If the shoe fits, luv."

He'd put his arm across her shoulder and she'd shrugged it away. "What do you want from me?"

"Something you can't give."

"What?"

"Going out with you isn't much different from being alone. Men want to feel important. You haven't a clue how to do that. You play with your bloody camera like the rest of us don't exist."

"I was taking pictures for my friends. How else can they make anyone understand how beautiful the transvestites are? I don't recall inviting you to go with us."

"Sarah did. Our movie night was canceled because of something at Trans Oil. Chris asked her along and Sarah asked me. Why didn't you suggest I join the group?"

Tory shrugged. It hadn't entered her mind. Bugis Street had been meant to cheer Chris up. She'd been in a blue mood when they played tennis that morning.

"I'll tell you why. You're so wrapped up in your work; you don't give a tinker's damn about anyone. Work's the only thing that matters to you."

"Fine. Don't bother seeing me home. I'll grab a taxi."

"Suit yourself. I'm not in the mood to drive to Jurong anyway."

She realized now what was wrong between them. She and Tim were going through the motions out of habit. They meant nothing to each other. Tory wasn't certain she even liked Tim any more.

Although she'd come back from Dora's funeral thinking she needed to open up, the opposite had occurred. She pulled back when anyone came too close. Lately she purposely avoided people. She couldn't understand why. Desperate to get away from her thoughts, she suggested a trip to Bugis Street, hoping the nightlife would cheer her up. Although it hadn't worked, it made her see how much she missed spending time with Chris. It was foolish to keep avoiding her best friend.

At tennis, for a fleeting moment, she'd considered telling Chris about Dora's death and how much it hurt. There was no point in burdening Chris with her problems. How could she explain being upset about the death of a woman she hadn't seen in years? The story would make no sense, unless Tory explained about her childhood.

She heard Halim calling. She cringed when she saw the syringe in his hand. "You're not going to kill her, are you?"

Halim looked horrified at her question. "Quinine. We think it eases the pain."

Tory picked up Anna and gently placed the orangutan on her lap. Tory felt Anna wince when Halim put the needle into her arm. "It's okay, baby," she whispered. "I'm here. I'll stay until you feel better."

Halim held up a small package. "I thought you might want some food. Nasi goreng. You usually like it." Halim was trying to understand what she was doing. No matter how much he disagreed with her actions, he wouldn't stop her.

Tory tried to smile. The Indonesian version of fried rice was one of her favorite foods. "Thanks, but no. I don't think I could eat anything."

"As you wish. I'll leave it. Perhaps later you'll find your stomach."

Tory smiled at Halim's words. She wondered if she had the same problem with idioms when she spoke Bahasa. "Find your stomach" was a literal translation, and yet, it was an apt description. She scribbled the phrase in her notepad so she could use it in an article.

Anna had fallen asleep. Tory rested her head against a banana tree and cradled Anna's body. It was cool in the shade. Tory pulled Anna close so she could share her warmth. Despite her best intentions, Tory felt tears in her eyes.

Slowly, more to herself than Anna, Tory began to recite things that she and Anna had done together. "Hey, kiddo, do you remember Sembawang? You used to swing along the branches and wave to the children. You liked it there, a ready-made audience for your silly antics.

"Do your friends pose for pictures the way you did? Do they know how to smile for the camera and make funny faces, or do they play the brat? You used to do that sometimes.

"Like the day you stole my camera. You took it away and exposed a whole roll of film when you opened the back."

Tory closed her eyes and remembered the day Anna, Tim and she took a picnic lunch to the shore to watch the fishing boats. Tim was leaving in two days. She planned a special day for them to say good-bye.

"Must that ape of yours come with us?" Tim demanded.

Tory ignored Tim's question. When they had gotten to the beach, she couldn't believe their luck. The scene was from a picture postcard. A palm tree swayed gently in the breeze. The orange sun was descending in the rich blue sky. She took out her camera.

"Pose for me, Tim. When you get home you can brag about your life in paradise."

Although he grumbled, Tim jumped up. He liked being photographed. Suddenly, Anna began prancing in front of the camera, blocking Tim. When he tried to move in front of her, Anna shoved him away.

Tim screamed, "Bloody ape. Get out of here, you nuisance." With that he pushed Anna so hard she fell.

Tory ran to Anna. "He didn't mean that. Let me take a few shots of Tim, then I'll take some of you."

She positioned Tim in front of a palm tree near an overturned fishing boat. The minute she set her camera on the tripod, Anna again danced in front of Tim. This time, Tory admitted that Anna's behavior was a bit too much. Reluctantly, she told Anna to go home.

When Tory and Tim returned to the klang, Anna had grabbed the camera, climbed to the top of the highest tree, opened the camera, took out the film, and dangled it in the sunlight.

"You were jealous, weren't you? You shouldn't have been. Tim was going home to Australia. I'd never have left with him. You should have known that. Tim isn't in it for the long haul."

Anna's eyes opened. Tory was positive she smiled. Anna sighed and closed her eyes. Tory thought she was asleep. When Halim came back several hours later, Tory's arms were cradling Anna's lifeless body.

Chapter 16
CHRIS

Singapore and Kuala Lumpur, Malaysia
Wednesday, March 12, 1980

When Chris looked at Alison, she had to bite the inside of her lip to keep from laughing. Her daughter's hands were on her hips, and she was so serious. At thirteen, Alison was straddling two worlds. She was obviously uncomfortable with her swings between them, yet she didn't belong in either place.

"Mother, please. You don't understand," Alison screamed.

Chris wanted to go over and hug Alison, but knew her daughter would stiffen if she did. "I do, honey. Believe me. Daddy's too busy to take his leave now."

Alison glared at her mother. "I heard him talking to you last night. Dad said it was fine with him if the three of us went home. If Daddy doesn't mind, why do you?"

"Alison, it's not polite to eavesdrop on your parents' conversations. That discussion took place in our bedroom. Haven't we warned you about listening in?" Chris was annoyed that Alison was listening at closed doors again. It was a habit she thought Alison had gotten over.

Alison hung her head. "It's the first time I've done it in years. Honest. But I had to. Don't you see? You don't understand at all. All the kids will be doing these neat things during the school holidays. Even Marc's doing something. And I'll be stuck in this dumb house. Big deal."

Chris tugged at Alison's hand and pulled her to the rattan sofa. Alison might want to think she was an adult, but at moments like this she made it painfully obvious she was still a little girl. Her arm around Alison's shoulders, Chris whispered. "I know you're disappointed. I am too. It wouldn't be fun if the three of us went home and Daddy stayed here. The family has much more fun when we do things together."

"When's the last time we did anything as a family?" Alison asked.

Chris was surprised to realize she couldn't recall. Kevin had been working so much; he didn't have the energy for family outings on weekends. If he wasn't at the office, he spent the weekend on a chaise lounge by the pool, sleeping, with the newspaper clutched in his hands.

"I know it's been a while, sweetie, but Daddy's been busy. Do you want to do something with me? Every time I ask, you and Marc make faces."

"It's not the same without Daddy."

Chris nodded. "I know. When Daddy's not so rushed, we'll go home together." Chris pushed Alison's long bangs out of her eyes.

Alison gave her a disgusted look and wriggled out of Chris's grasp. At the door, she turned and looked at her mother. "Could I go somewhere with Aunt Tory?"

Chris was surprised by the suggestion. When Tory left town, it was to work. Why would Alison want to go away with Tory? "Sweetie, if you want to go away, we could go together," Chris volunteered. Then she saw the look of abject horror on Alison's face. She almost burst out laughing. *Who am I kidding? The last thing a thirteen-year-old wants to do is spend a week with her mother*

"It's just that Tory knows so many really neat places."

"Tory? When did you drop the Aunt, young lady?"

Alison laughed. *"Aunt* Tory said I could. She was at the school last week. She showed us slides of these neat places she goes. She said I could go with her some time. She said it in front of the whole class. May I? Please?"

Chris considered Alison's request. It was not that she didn't trust Tory. Tory was wonderful with the children, even when they were younger. But the places Tory went could be dangerous. On the other hand, she didn't want to overprotect Alison. If she wanted to go, and Tory didn't mind, what was the harm?

"Let me talk to Daddy."

"Why? He doesn't care what I do."

"Alison, that's not true. How many times do I have to tell you your father's got a great deal of work?"

"Then why doesn't he hire someone to help him? That's what Laurel's father does."

Out of the mouths of babes. Why doesn't he indeed?" I'll speak to Tory and see where she's going. If it's not too outlandish, and if she doesn't mind, you may go."

That conversation had taken place three weeks ago. Now Chris was in a suite at the Kuala Lumpur Hilton, thoroughly exhausted. For the past ten days Alison, Tory, and she had explored Taman Negara. Their journey was a nightmare. Chris wondered how Tory did things like that on a regular basis.

The first leg of their trip had been by boat. It was the only part Chris enjoyed. After five hours of a relaxing, gentle rocking motion through pristine waters, they landed on a riverbank. Tory arranged for two Orang Asli guides to lead them through the labyrinth of the jungle. The guides had to cut a path for them. Chris had been worn out after the first day.

Tory insisted they dress in heavy clothes, which were unbearably hot in the sun. To make them even more uncomfortable, they carried backpacks complete with a sleeping bag, cooking utensils, and food.

The first two days in the jungle were the hardest. Every step they took seemed dangerous. If Chris looked at her feet to keep from tripping on an exposed tree root, a vine caught her in the eye. If she watched what was in front of her, she lost her footing in the thick underbrush.

For dinner they ate rice and fish, if they'd caught any. The sounds of a tiger killing his dinner punctuated their meal. To make matters worse, Tory told them ghost stories. The first night Chris was so tired she could have slept on a log. They set their sleeping bags on the damp, hard ground. It felt like sleeping on wet granite. In the morning, she woke stiff and cramped.

Tory woke them at four a.m. each morning so they could hear the gibbons and hopefully catch sight of a macaque or leaf monkey swinging through the branches.

Alison enjoyed herself thoroughly. Even when she saw a python on a tree stump, her face glowed. She spent one night in a dugout hole near a salt lick, on the outside chance of seeing a rhino or tapir during the night. She didn't seem disappointed when it was too dark to see more than their shadows.

Chris now sat in the living room of the suite with a glass of wine, her eyes half closed.

Tory walked in wearing a white, terry cloth robe, her hair wrapped in a towel. "Is Alison asleep?"

"No need to whisper. She'll sleep for a week. So will I. Do you do this often?"

Tory reached for the open bottle of wine, poured herself a glass, and took one of Chris's cigarettes. "Like that? No. If I'd been alone, I'd have spent some nights in a bunk house."

Chris's jaw dropped. "You mean I didn't have to suffer through that?"

"That was for Alison's benefit. She's betwixt and between at the moment. All her friends have boyfriends and she feels she's the only teenager in the world who's different. She needed an adventure. I gave her one."

Chris was horrified. "Have you seen her leech bites? Are those part of her adventure, as you call it?"

Tory laughed. "She met one leech. The bites are from mosquitoes."

Chris sat pensively. "Did you study zoology in school? All that talk about diverse ecosystems impressed the hell out of me."

"Don't I wish? I'm certified to teach English, if you can believe that."

Chris started to ask more and stopped. She had seen the *do not disturb* look in Tory's eyes. Then she asked, "How'd you know about the boyfriend business? Alison's never mentioned it to me."

"I'm at the school every week for my class. I hear things." Tory shrugged. "How could Alison tell you? You and Kevin met when you were her age. She feels left out. It's tough to be different at that age."

Though she knew she was asking for another polite rebuff, Chris asked, "Were you different at thirteen?"

Tory paused, her eyes on her wineglass. "I wasn't popular, if that's what you mean. The kids where I grew up weren't as mature as Alison and her friends think they are. Anyway, it didn't matter to me. I didn't want a boyfriend."

"Okay, so Alison had her little adventure. Why did you ask me to come along? She would have gone without me. In fact, that's what she wanted."

Tory nodded her head sagely. "And good old Kevin would've had a pink fit at the prospect. Can you see Kevin letting his little princess go out alone with Lady Tarzan? You needed to get away, too. You were getting a restless look. It's gone now."

Chris smiled. "What did you get from this?"

"I got to spend time with my best friend and her daughter."

"Tory!" Chris shouted. There was no way she'd accept such an ambiguous answer. "What did you get from this?"

Tory didn't answer.

Chris was surprised to see tears in her friend's eyes. "Why did you do this for us?" she asked softly.

"An old friend of mine died recently. It made me feel ... I don't know." Tory shrugged and stared at her glass. "I didn't want to be alone," she whispered.

Chris tried to figure out what she could do to make Tory feel better. Everything she said was met with silence. She felt utterly helpless. There was no way to comfort Tory. She claimed to hate emotional scenes.

Tory went into her bedroom. Chris sat and finished the bottle of wine. *Who died? And why didn't she tell me before this?*

She phoned Kevin. It was nearly eleven at night, and she was able to reach him at home. "We're back safe and sound, Kev."

"I'm glad. I miss you so much."

"I missed you, too."

"Did you have fun?"

"Alison enjoyed herself. She thinks she hung the moon."

'What about you? Did you enjoy your holiday?"

"It gave me time to think. Tory insisted on silence while we trekked through jungle.'"

“What did you think about?"

"Us. I hate the hours you're working, Kev."

"So do I. Don't worry; it'll be over soon. When are you coming home? The house feels so lonely without you."

"Tory promised Alison three days to explore KL. We'll be back Saturday, I guess."

"I have an idea. When's Marc due back?"

"Sunday."

"Leave Tory some money. Let Alison and her stay in KL. After their trip, I'm sure even the jungle woman will remain in the confines of the city. If you came home in the morning, we could have some time alone."

"Are you suggesting what I think you are?"

"Yes. I'll tell Geoff I have to take some time off. I miss my wife and want to spend four days with her."

"Kev, I love you."

"I love you too, Chris."

Chapter 17
TORY

Kuala Lumpur, Malaysia
Thursday, March 13, 1980

Tory sat by the pool at the Hilton watching Alison swim. Tory was surprised when Chris asked if she'd mind staying with Alison until Sunday. Why would she object? Alison was fun. Thirteen was such a great age. Life's in front of you. Alison hadn't had the chance to screw it up yet. *I wonder if that's what Dora felt when she was with me?*

Tory swam for a while. Now, she was wrapped in a terry cloth robe, letting the equatorial sun beat down on her. She'd been relieved when Alison suggested spending the day by the pool instead or going sightseeing. The trip through Taman Negara had been grueling. Tory needed to unwind.

For too much of their journey, her thoughts had been her only companion. She was irritated it had taken her four months to see through Tim. Dora had been wrong, being alone was right for Tory. Thinking about Dora made Tory feel alone. She hoped the bright sunlight would improve her disposition.

Everyone she knew was at odds with the world. She wondered if there was something in the air. Chris was furious with Kevin because they didn't go home for Easter. Sarah and her husband drifted further apart every time she saw them. Even Kevin seemed irritated at the time he spent on his job.

The night before she left, Tory had gone out with Geoff Melbourne. They met accidentally on Scotts Road and she couldn't think of a good reason to turn him down. They ate dinner at Pete's Place, the Hyatt's basement-level Italian restaurant, and talked for hours. It had been pleasant. Before she knew where the time went, it was past midnight. Since she had to be up early in the morning, she'd insisted Geoff put her in a cab. Although he offered to drive her home, she'd been adamant and, ultimately, he acquiesced.

Geoff's parting comment had been odd. "I'll call you before too many moons go by." It took her a while to understand he planned to start calling her again. She wasn't sure she wanted him to. His rooming with Tim made her uneasy. Tory was doing her best to avoid Tim, and she was afraid Tim had asked Geoff to keep an eye on her.

Something was going on between Tim and Sarah. After the night in Bugis Street, Tory stopped ignoring it. Coupled with the insight that she didn't like Tim, she was skeptical of his friend.

Alison came out of the pool and wrapped herself in a towel. Tory watched Alison pick a strand of hair from behind her ear and start twirling it. Tory recognized the gesture as Alison's thinking pose.

Tory stretched her back. "I'm not sure how much longer I can do trips like that one. My muscles ache."

Alison laughed. "You're not old. Not like Mom and Dad."

"Alison, I'm only a year younger than your mother."

"Do you look younger because you're not married? I don't think marriage is all it's cracked up to be."

"Why?" Tory was curious.

"Mommy's always angry with Daddy lately. 'Cause he's never home. They fight about it a lot."

"How do you feel about the time your dad spends at work? Does it bother you?"

Alison twirled at her hair fiercely. "Marc hates it. Last month, Daddy missed the father and son dinner at school. Marc was the only seventh grader whose father didn't go. Daddy promised he'd be there and he forgot. Marc was really pissed. That's why he got to go snorkeling in Bali with Steven."

"Don't con me, Alison. I asked what you thought. All you've done is talk about Marc."

"Part of me hates it. I mean I know Daddy has to work and I understand that. It's just he's never home. Last month, I got sick at school. It was Tuesday, and Mom was at the hospital. Since Daddy's office is closer, I called him to pick me up. He didn't even listen to what I had to say. He yelled at me and told me never to bother him at work. I was awake when he came home, and he didn't even come into my room to see if I was okay. I think he doesn't like us any more."

There definitely was heightened activity at Trans Oil. The last two times Tory had been there, she'd looked for Kevin, thinking that they might have lunch. He'd not been in his office either time. When she'd asked his secretary when he'd be back, the woman avoided answering her question. At the time, Tory thought little of it. Now, she wondered.

"Are my parents getting a divorce? Is that why Daddy's never home? Is that why Mommy went home early?"

Tory reached across the table and took Alison's hand in hers. "I don't think so. Your mother went home early so she and your father could have time together. Sometimes adults need time without their children."

"Will you be teaching your class next year?"

Tory shook her head. "It's hard for me to arrange my schedule to be in town on the same day every week. I told the school to get someone else. Why?"

"Laurel says your class is really neat. I thought I'd take it next year."

"If you want to learn about photography, you don't have to wait for a class. I can teach you, starting right now."

Alison jumped out of her seat. "Would you? Really? Like you'd be my private tutor?"

"Sure. You stay here. I'll get us each a camera. Today's lesson will be how to work in the sun. It's something most people don't learn. Then they wonder why their holiday pictures look washed out."

Alison was an avid pupil. Tory showed her how to use various filters to preserve the color of the images she wanted to capture. Alison wanted to learn everything in one day.

Finally, Tory said, "Look, kiddo, I'm beat. What do you say we go inside and take a nap? I need one."

Alison agreed reluctantly.

When Tory woke and went into the living room of their suite, Alison had three camera bodies and all the lenses out of their cases. She was sitting on the floor surrounded by the equipment.

"What are you doing?" Tory asked. Although she understood Alison's fascination, Tory was irritated Alison would use her things without permission.

"I was trying to get the feel of things. Some of the lenses are heavy."

Tory nodded. "And they're not toys. Since you have all this stuff out, I'll show you the drudgework. It all has to be cleaned every time it's used."

Gently, Alison followed Tory's example and poured tiny drops of cleaning solution on a lens, rubbing it softly with chemically-treated paper. "Are you angry I took your equipment out without asking?"

"You were curious. I understand that. Just remember, this stuff is my livelihood."

"Did you always want to be a photographer?"

"I wanted to be a writer. The photography was an afterthought."

"What do you mean?"

"When I was in the Peace Corps, I wrote long letters about everything I saw and what I felt. So that my ... so people would understand, I sent snapshots. I had this old friend who'd been my teacher. She sent some of my letters to a magazine. They were published, along with the photographs. I still have the articles. The pictures are atrocious."

"If they weren't good, why'd the magazine use them?"

"Although they weren't technically good, they depicted my mood."

"I always think of you as photographer. You always have your camera with you. Remember the day Mommy, Marc and I met you? You had your camera with you then. If you're a writer, wouldn't you have a pad in your hands?"

Tory laughed. When she saw the hurt look on Alison's face, she moved closer to her and squeezed her shoulder. "I wasn't laughing at you, I was laughing at what you said."

"What's the difference?" Alison asked belligerently.

"If I were laughing at you, it would mean I thought what you asked was silly. I don't. It made me think. Alison, I'm what's called a photo-journalist. I write about things and take pictures, so that even if people don't understand it from my words, they can see it in my photos."

"But why do you always have your camera with you?"

"I can remember what I see well enough to write about it. But, if I see the perfect photo and I don't have my camera, it may not be there when I get back. You brought up the day at Cold Storage. Remember when Marc pulled the can in the bottom of the pile and the whole display came tumbling down around him?"

Alison giggled. "Mommy loves that picture. She says it's Marc to a tee."

Tory nodded. "If I hadn't had my camera, your mother wouldn't have the picture."

Alison appeared to consider the answer. "When I grow up, I'm going to be just like you and travel the world. I'm not getting married."

"You keep saying that, Alison. Why?"

"The boys in my class are such babies. Laurel's changed since she got a boyfriend. All she cares about is what he thinks. She doesn't want to do anything anymore. I want to be like you."

Tory shook her head. "If you want a career, do it your way. Don't ever follow someone else."

"You sound like Mom. Can you believe she actually asks Marc and me if we'd jump off the Brooklyn Bridge if our friends did? It's a silly question."

"All you mother wants is for you to do what's right for you. That's important. It's something many people don't learn until it's too late. You can never know what's going on in someone else's life unless you're attached to their hip. Sometimes things aren't what they appear to be."

"Like Mommy and Daddy aren't getting a divorce, even though they fight so much and Daddy's never home?"

"Right."

"Laurel's dad is being transferred at the end of the term. She's going to boarding school next year. Do you think my parents would let me go too?"

"Do you want to go because Laurel's going, or because you want to?"

"I'm not sure. Marc's a cretin. I wouldn't mind getting away from him. I'd miss Mom, though."

"Why don't you think about it some more, then talk to your parents?"

"I doubt Daddy would even know I was gone."

"Alison, have you told your mother what you're afraid of? She's the one you should be talking to."

"I can't talk to Mom. She worries about everything. If I told her what I thought, she'd get upset. Anyway, you said I was wrong."

"I know. But you don't believe me."

"Are you sure they're not?"

"Alison, your mother loves your father. Divorce is the last thing on her mind. She wouldn't've been so eager to go home and spend a long weekend with your father, if she didn't love him. And he wouldn't've suggested it, if he didn't love her."

"I've heard about them falling in love. How could Mommy see anything in Daddy when he was my age? The boys in my class are idiots."

"I don't know, sweetie. Maybe she saw something underneath his silly behavior."

"Maybe. Tell me a story. I'll start it. Once upon a time, an orangutan named Anna Banana..."

"No, Alison. I can't tell you an orangutan story today. Let's get something to eat. I'm starving."

Alison stood up, walked closer to Tory, and put her head on Tory's shoulder. "Anna was real, wasn't she? Mommy always said she was a story you made up for Marc and me, but we knew she was real. Did she die? Is that why you're so sad?"

Tory kissed Alison's cheek. "Yes, she was real and yes, she died. I can't talk about Anna now because it hurts too much."

"Mommy says it's good to talk about what hurts you. That way, you feel better faster. She says if you keep something inside, it only makes it hurt worse."

"Chris is right. But sometimes, when something hurts you very much, you have to put it in a box that you hide away until the pain stops. Anna's death is like that. I can't face it now, so I'm saving my memories until they don't hurt so much."

"What you need is a boyfriend. That would make you feel better. I know who'd be good for you -- the new guy Geoff who Daddy works for. He's gorgeous."

"Alison, you truly are your mother's daughter."

"Because I want you to be happy and I don't think you are?"

Tory jumped up and reached for her purse. "When did you get so smart?"

"Since I grew up when no one was looking."

Chapter 18
SARAH

Singapore
Wednesday, March 19, 1980

Life with Barney was horrible and getting worse every day. Sarah had hoped that she and Barney could make their marriage work here, and once again she'd been disappointed. They went through the motions, called each other "dear" and "love", but it was a lie. Barney was drinking too much. His moods were becoming more and more erratic. For no apparent reason, he'd change from euphoria to depression in a matter of seconds. He still went to work each morning. Sarah had been thankful for that small semblance of normality, until Geoff shattered her illusions.

He invited her to dinner on a night when Barney was out with a customer. While they sipped sherry, she asked, "What's keeping Barney so busy at work?"

Geoff stared at her blankly. "Barney's doing the bare minimum to keep himself employed. Anyone but him would've been sacked by now."

Sarah's heart raced. "What do you mean? Barney's never home. He tells me he's with clients all afternoon and into the evening."

Geoff shook his head sadly. "Where do you think he is?"

"There is a track in Malaysia," she said slowly, not wanting to think about the possibility.

Geoff nodded. "There are also betting parlors in the seedy part of town."

"At least he isn't on a losing streak." There hadn't been a creditor pounding on the door since they moved to Singapore. She'd been spared the embarrassment of ringing Barney Senior for financial help.

She considered facing Barney with the information Geoff gave her, and decided against it. It would only lead to a row. For the last few months, Sarah had tried to ignore her attraction to Tim. He was the reason she got out of bed to face her otherwise dreary existence. As Barney's drinking increased, Sarah became leery of too much involvement with her friends. She hated sitting through lunch, waiting for someone to mention Barney's drinking.

At the last two parties Barney had tripped and broken things as he lurched about drunkenly. Both times she'd run to him, laughed, kissed his cheek, called him a bull in a china shop, and prayed no one noticed his unfocused eyes. The next morning she went bought what he broke and had it gift wrapped and sent to the home of the hosts. So far luck was on their side; Barney only knocked over bric-a-brac items that were easily found. What would happen when he broke something irreplaceable?

The only pleasure she had Tim. He was an accepted fourth in their weekly dinner and movie outings, even if Geoff was out of town. Her happiness centered on Wednesday nights. She and Tim saw one movie while Geoff and Barney went to another. Barney didn't mind. He and Geoff liked horror movies and she couldn't stand them. She and Tim enjoyed films with subtitles that had meaning and could be discussed for hours afterwards. Barney hated going to a movie where he had to think.

At the movies she and Tim could be together with no one the wiser to the growing attraction between them. He warned her that they would have to be very careful. "Tory has the eyes of a hawk. She sees what everyone else misses. And she turns up in the least expected places."

If she and Tim laughed and talked on Wednesday nights, no one thought anything of it. They were simply discussing a movie. Since Barney drank until he could barely see and Geoff could only talk about work, what choice did they have? Neither

Geoff nor Barney made an attempt to include Sarah or Tim in their interests.

Each week Sarah prepared a simple tasteful meal to be eaten cold when they returned. When they were alone, Barney barely touched his food. Their constant bickering often caused her to lose her appetite as well. She had the best-fed servants in Singapore.

Sarah had done all the things that her mother told her would keep a man happy and contented. Her culinary skills were second to none. Her house was tasteful and elegant. Even after a baby, she wore a size 7. Sarah felt betrayed that the lessons she learned were useless. Why hadn't she studied art? At least then she'd have something for herself. As it was, all she knew how to be was be a wife, which was the last thing her husband wanted.

Wednesday nights Sarah reveled in being the center of attention. Geoff and Tim knew she was alive. Geoff's devotion was such a fact of life it made Barney brag about having a wife other men coveted. The bragging hurt. It was obvious she was nothing more to him than a toy his parents had bought and paid for.

For Sarah's twenty-fifth birthday, Geoff bought her four port glasses. They were Waterford crystal, in the Colleen pattern she loved. "Oh Geoff, they're lovely," she cried. Tim bought her a port decanter in the same pattern. Their two friends remembered her birthday, but her husband forgot. That night, she cried herself to sleep, after Barney passed out in bed.

Her birthday had been a week ago, and Barney still hadn't bought her a gift. The gifts from Geoff and Tim were displayed in a place of honor on the sideboard. He never seemed to notice them. Sarah blamed Barney for her attraction to Tim. If Barney were a proper husband, she wouldn't need anyone else.

When Sarah asked Barney if they could buy her a car, he laughed. "What for, love? To shop and play bridge? Take a taxi or have one of the wives fetch you."

"I'm the only wife who can't use her husband's car and driver during the day."

"Tory doesn't have a car and she has a job. If she can do that, surely you can survive scabbing lifts now and then."

Sarah pouted. "I'd really like my own car."

"Do you have any idea how high car taxes are? The government is doing all they can to avoid the traffic congestion of Jakarta and Bangkok."

"Well, why can't I use your car?"

"I'm in Marketing. I need the car to see my customers."

No matter what she said or did, she and Barney had a row. If she made dinner, he didn't come home on time. If she decided not to cook, he came home looking for a meal. She couldn't win.

With Tim it was different. There was chemistry between them. Even from across the room, she felt desired when he looked at her. At parties, she was consumed with jealousy if Tim danced with Tory.

"Not to worry," Tim would whisper when they danced. "Tory's a friend, nothing more. Remember, luv, I'm a bachelor. I'm expected to pay attention to all the lovely ladies."

Tim was right. The knowledge didn't make it easier to watch him with Tory. There was a special bond between the two of them, shared life experiences that she didn't have. It worried her. How long would Tim settle for their fleeting embraces when he had a single woman so readily available?

It was important to keep up appearances, especially in their world. But Sarah needed something more. There was a pervasive sense of emptiness inside her that needed to be filled. Wednesday nights were no longer enough. It was unbearable to spend six nights with only a drunken husband for company.

As they waited for the movie to begin, she told Tim how she felt. "Tim, I want so much more than holding your hand at the movies."

"Do you, luv? And here I thought you were enjoying making me suffer. I go home on Wednesday night and take a cold shower."

"These last few months of short-lived touches and whispered words aren't enough. I've racked my brain trying to figure out where we can be alone."

"Any ideas?"

"My house is out. Trey and Ah Soon are there. There's too much of a chance we'd meet someone if we went to a hotel."

"What about my flat?"

"Geoff lives there," she reminded Tim.

"Ah, but good old Geoff never comes home before eight o'clock."

"It's hard for me to slip away at night."

"I know, luv," he said, kissing her check. "I've got it. You play bridge on Thursday. Right?"

Sarah nodded, not understanding what Tim meant.

"There it is, then. After bridge, ask Chris to drop you at Cold Storage to do your marketing. Once she's out of sight, take a cab to Grange Road and meet me at the flat. Later, you can take a cab to Cold Storage and ring Barney to pick you up on his way home."

"But, we finish bridge at three o'clock. You're still at work."

"One of the glories of being in management is I can make my own hours. Not to worry. I can slip out of the office without causing a fuss."

Sarah smiled. Soon she'd have Wednesday nights and Thursday afternoons to look forward to.

The time Sarah had with Tim was precious. They shared many interests. Tim loved art, and appreciated the little things that she did to bring beauty into her world. He noticed the deft way she used splashes of color to complement the black lacquer furniture.

More important, they talked to one another. They discussed their hopes and dreams. They made plans for the future. Their conversations were never of Barney; he didn't exist when they were together. Sarah could tell Tim anything and know he'd understand exactly what she meant.

Tim never pressured her to leave Barney and go off with him. She was not ready to make that decision. Not yet, at least.

Chapter 19
CHRIS

Singapore
Thursday, May 8, 1980

The phone rang just as Chris was leaving for her Thursday bridge game. She let the housekeeper pick it up and headed for the front door. "Missy," the housekeeper called, "the school wants you."

Chris grabbed the phone. "May I help you?" she asked nervously.

"Mrs. Taylor, this is Mr. Ames. We just caught Marc smoking. We're suspending him. Would you please come and pick him up?"

"Suspending him for smoking? Isn't that a tad severe?"

"If this were his first offense, I'd agree with you. But, as you know from the notes we sent home, this is Marc's fourth infraction. We can't issue an on-campus suspension this time. Marc is being suspended for a week."

"I've never gotten a note."

"I'm looking at three notes that you supposedly wrote. If they aren't yours, you might want to find out who wrote them."

"I'll be right there." Chris was agitated as she hung up the phone. Nothing Mr. Ames said made sense.

This isn't like Marc at all. I can understand Marc experimenting with cigarettes, she thought, *I still smoke. But I know I've never seen a note. Maybe he showed the notes to*

Kevin. No one can read Kev's cat scratching. Mr. Ames probably thinks I wrote the notes because he can't read Kevin's signature.

When Chris got to the American School, she went directly to Mr. Ames' office. Peter Ames was Marc's science teacher and his favorite teacher, at least until now.

"I think we have a little problem brewing with Marc. It's nothing too serious, but it's best to catch these things early."

"Of course," Chris agreed. "What happened?"

"Since the Easter break, Marc's been a different lad. I noticed it the first day he came back. Initially I thought he was in high spirits after his holiday. Now it's getting worse. Marc's mind is not on his schoolwork."

Chris was confused. Marc's last report card had been the same as his others, B's and C's. He was not a brilliant student. His teachers all said Marc could do better. Since he did his assignments and wasn't a disciplinary problem, she and Kevin thought it best to leave Marc alone. Alison was only a year ahead of him and a straight A student. Sometimes the teachers made unfair comparisons between the two of them.

"Are his grades getting worse?"

"No. He's become a cut-up in class, tossing paper airplanes through the air, comes in late, leaves before the bell. He hasn't turned in a homework assignment in two weeks. I've checked with Marc's other teachers, and he's the same in their classes. Mrs. Taylor, I hate to pry, but is there a problem at home? If so, that might explain the change in Marc."

"Marc missed going back to the States on leave. My husband and I thought it would be better if we postponed our leave until the family could go away together."

"That could be it. The change in plans may have upset Marc more than either you or your husband thought."

Chris wondered. Marc was no different at home. He and Alison squabbled about little things, but they always bickered. It was similar to the bantering between Kevin and Tory. It didn't mean anything.

"What about Alison? Has she changed?" Mr. Ames taught science to both seventh and eighth grades. Alison was in his class.

"Now, that's the odd thing. Alison was morose before the break. Since she's been back, she's been the happy little girl we remember. Did Marc and Alison spend their break together?"

"No. Alison and I went to Taman Negara. Marc went snorkeling with Steven Adams. Phil couldn't get away either, so Janet took the boys to Bali by herself."

"Is it possible that, since he's busy, your husband hasn't had much time for Marc?"

"Kevin hasn't had time for anyone. It's not just Marc."

Peter Ames frowned. "Boys of Marc's age need a male role model. I think Marc could use some attention from his father. Would it be possible for your husband to come to the school? I tried his office and couldn't reach him."

"Kevin's always in meetings. I'll speak to him this evening. Would you please explain about this smoking business? I've never heard of it until today."

Peter Ames handed Chris a manila folder with Marc's name on the outside. She read the papers slowly. Apparently Marc had been under on-campus suspension for the past three weeks. With each new infraction, there was a note, supposedly from Chris, which stated the family was aware of the Marc's behavior and would handle the matter at home. Marc had forged Chris's handwriting. The writing and style were so typical of Chris; she could see why the school believed she'd written them.

"Whew. He's been a holy terror, hasn't he?"

"I take it you didn't write the notes?"

"Right. Where is Marc right now?"

"He's in an empty classroom. We wanted to separate the boys. Since you've always been so interested in your children, I thought I'd start with you."

"How long is Marc suspended for?"

"It should be two weeks now that I know the notes are forgeries. Why don't you and your husband discuss it and let me know? The smoking is one week. That's the minimum the school will accept. If you and your husband think you can reach Marc, we'll let him back after that. I'll see that his lessons are sent home with Alison."

Chris stood and shook Peter Ames' hand. "Thank you. I'm sure Marc will be back in a week. I doubt he's going to enjoy being home with me."

"Good luck. As I said, Marc's basically a good kid. He needs a little attention right now."

Chris went to the room number she'd been given. Marc was staring out the window, a bored look on his face.

"Pick up your books. We're going home."

"It's no big deal, Mom. Don't sweat it."

"I'll be the judge of that, young man. I'd like some quiet in the car while I think."

"Sure. Hate to think Suradmin might hear something."

Chris was furious at his sarcastic tone. *Does he really think I give a damn what the driver hears? I need time to think. I'm not ready for this.* Chris saw the defiant look on Marc's face and wanted to slap him. He looked as if he thought the entire incident was funny.

When they got home, she sent Marc to his room while she called Kevin. When his secretary said he was at a meeting, she told the girl to get him and tell him there was a family emergency. Chris was on her third cigarette before Kevin called back.

"Has something happened to one of the children?"

"Marc's been caught smoking."

"Chris, he's twelve. All boys his age experiment. If that's all this is about, I've got work to do."

"Don't you dare hang up on me, Kevin. It's more than smoking. I've spent the better part of the afternoon with Peter Ames. From the sounds of it, smoking is just the tip of the iceberg."

"Chrissy, I'm busy. Can't you handle it? Tell Marc he's grounded for the weekend."

"Kevin," she screamed. "Your son has just been suspended for two weeks. 'I'm busy' are not the words I want to hear from you right now."

"Well, they're the only words I have at the moment. I'll be home by eight. We can talk about it then."

Kevin hung up. Chris began to pace the room. She wanted to run upstairs and pummel Marc, but knew it would only make her feel worse. It was nearly four. Alison would be home from cheerleading practice in less than an hour. Chris wanted a glass of wine, but decided against it. She'd need her wits about her to talk intelligently to Marc. It was obvious Kevin had little interest in what was happening.

She made a plate of sandwiches, poured two glasses of milk, and carried them on a tray to Marc's room. She knocked at the door. Marc didn't answer. She set the tray down and knocked more forcefully.

"Come in, if that's what you want. It's not like I could stop you."

Chris's stomach lurched. It was there again in Marc's voice, the belligerent tone he used when angry or frightened. *What's bothering him? More importantly, will he tell me? Marc's always been closer to Kev than me.*

Chris opened the door carefully, balancing the tray on her hip. "I brought some sandwiches. I thought we could talk about what's bothering you."

Marc grabbed a sandwich and shoved it in his mouth. When he finished, he leaned back on his bed, his hands folded behind his head, his legs out straight. The nonchalant pose made him look like he hadn't a care in the world. "There's nothing bothering me. I got caught smoking. Big deal! You smoke. Dad smokes. What's the federal case?"

"We're adults. There are things adults can do that children can't. You know that."

"Oh brother, here we go again. Look, I'll save you the trouble. If my friends were jumping off the Brooklyn Bridge, I probably would go with them. You can spare me the lecture."

It took all of her self-control to keep from slapping Marc. She had never been angrier with him in her life. At the same time, she could see the pain in his face. "Why don't you tell me about it?"

"There's nothing to tell. When we were in Bali, Steven's mom let us smoke. If we could do it in front of her, what's the difference if we do it at school? Isn't it hypocritical to hide things?"

He's got me there. Janet let them smoke. I can't believe it. "Did Mrs. Adams say why she let the two of you smoke?"

"She said she'd rather Steven do things in front of her than behind her back. She let us have wine at dinner too. It was neat. Not like you and Dad, who wait until Alison and I are in our rooms. Like we wouldn't know the two of you drink if we didn't see it."

"So your behavior is perfectly acceptable because you weren't being a hypocrite? What about the school's rule against smoking? What about the notes you forged? If you thought your behavior was so above-board, why did you make up the notes? Why didn't you explain to your father or me what happened?"

"No one can tell Dad anything. He's never here."

"I'm always here when you get home from school. Why didn't you tell me?"

"'Cause you get so hysterical about stuff. You'd make a big thing out of it, just like you're doing now. Did you call Dad? Is he coming home for dinner?"

"That's what you want, isn't it?"

"If Dad really cared, he'd be here. If he stays at work, then Alison's wrong, as usual. I never should've listened to her. But she Tory said so, and Tory never lies."

"What are you talking about, Marc? What did Tory tell Alison?"

"Alison and I decided you and Dad were getting a divorce. That was why Daddy's never home anymore. Alison asked Tory, and she said no."

"Oh, baby," Chris cried, as she pulled him towards her. "Is that what this is all about? Do you miss your father that much?"

"I'm not a baby. I want Daddy."

Chris kissed the top of Marc's forehead and whispered in his ear. "We all do. Why didn't you or Alison tell me what you thought? Your father and I aren't getting a divorce."

"Then why isn't he home any more? And he isn't. You know that as well as me. I want to go home. I don't like it here any more."

"It's going to be all right. I'll talk to Daddy tonight. This weekend, we'll sit down and the four of us will talk about things. Will that make you feel better?"

"Yeah. Are you sure Dad'll be here? It seems like I haven't seen him in years."

"I'm sure. Now, I want you to stay in your room until Dad gets home and think about the trouble you're in."

When Kevin arrived home after nine, Chris was waiting for him. "Kev, you've got to spend more time with the kids. They think there's something wrong because you're never home."

Kevin dropped his briefcase in the foyer and loosened his tie. "Can't you give me five seconds of peace before you jump on me, Chrissy? I'm beat. Can't this wait until tomorrow?"

"What's going to be different tomorrow? You're always tired, Kevin. Either you sit down and talk to me right now, or I'm taking the children and going home."

"Well I want a drink. Can I interest you in a martini?"

"Damn you, Kevin. Listen to me. Your son's been suspended from school, and all you can think about is having a drink."

Kevin ignored Chris and went to the bar. Slowly, he took the ingredients to the kitchen and made a pitcher of martinis. He carried the pitcher and two glasses to the rattan sofa, poured a drink, which he finished in one swallow, and closed his eyes. It was nearly five minutes before he opened his eyes. "Okay, so what's the federal case about sneaking a cigarette or two? Your brother Mike and I did it often enough."

"It's more than that. Marc thinks you don't care about him because you're never home. Apparently Alison feels the same way."

"What about you, Chris? Have you all forgotten the only reason you're able to go off on your little jaunts is because I work? It's what I do. It's the way we can afford to live like this."

"Kevin, you're never home and it's starting to affect the children. Can't you spend more time here? What's so important that you're never home?"

"I'm on a special project. It's taking up all my energy. Can't you handle a little thing like smoking without making a federal case about it?"

"Kev, the kids miss you."

"And I miss them. Do you think I enjoy working fifteen hours a day? It's hell. But, I do it so my kids can have the advantages I never had."

Chris stood and screamed at Kevin. "And your kids would rather have their father home. Doesn't that tell you something?"

"Yeah, you're not living up to your half of the bargain. You're supposed to keep the kids under control. Look, Chrissy," Kevin said as he reached for her hand, "I'm not happy about the amount of time I spend away from home, but I have no choice. It could be worse, you know."

"How?"

"I could be the one traveling to Greece all the time instead of Geoff. He and I agreed that I'd handle things in S'pore and he'd travel, so I could be home at night. Sorry, but that's the best I can offer. If you want to take the kids home for the summer, you'll have to do it on your own. I can't get away."

"What's this special project about?"

"It doesn't matter. It's an idea of Geoff's."

"Can't you arrange to spend more time here on weekends? I promised Marc the four of us would talk this weekend."

"I wish you wouldn't commit my time without consulting me first. When is this family pow-wow supposed to be?"

"I said this weekend, nothing more specific. Why?"

"Geoff should be back tomorrow afternoon. I'll try to see him then or Saturday morning. I'll block out the rest of the weekend. Will that suffice?"

"Kevin, I think Marc needs more than one weekend."

"You know what? So do I. But that's all I've got right now. Maybe later I can steal a long weekend and we'll go to Tioman or Penang. Chrissy, this isn't what I want any more than you, but I'm committed. Geoff warned me this project would take all my time. I hadn't thought he meant it quite so literally."

"What about Marc?"

"I'll see him in the morning before I go to work. I'm too tired right now. Can we just leave it alone? After you sleep on it, you'll see you're making more of the incident than necessary."

Chapter 20
SARAH

Singapore
Thursday, May 8,1980

What's taking Janet so long? She said she only had a few things to pick up. Sarah fumed as she pretended to be fascinated with the ingredients in a can of stewed tomatoes. *Why wasn't Chris at bridge? It's not like her to miss a Thursday.*

For weeks Sarah's ruse had worked perfectly. Chris dropped Sarah in front of Cold Storage every Thursday and went home. Since Chris hadn't been at bridge today, Sarah asked Janet Adams for a lift to the supermarket.

"Good idea. I need some odds and ends. I don't mind waiting. I could run you home when you finish."

"Oh, no," Sarah laughed to mask her fear, "I take forever when I market. Anyway, Barney likes to meet me. It's a time for the two of us."

"Well, I'll just check on you when I'm done."

That had been forty-five minutes ago and Sarah could still see Janet thumping melons to check their ripeness. *I wonder if she suspects something? That's ridiculous. No one would find anything odd about my shopping. They know I love to cook.*

Absently Sarah put the tin of tomatoes in her cart and walked down the aisle. She'd leave the shopping cart full of groceries with the manager while she went home for her wallet. She was sure the man would suspect she wasn't so forgetful. Not that it mattered. She'd tip him lavishly for watching her groceries.

"Well, Sarah, I'm through. Should I wait?"

"No, Janet. Go home. I'll probably be another hour."

"There's not that much of a selection. How can it take you so long?"

"I'm still not that familiar with the brands. I have to read all the labels so I can be sure I get exactly what I want."

Once Janet left the store, Sarah laughed in relief. *I am getting what I want. Unfortunately, it's not sold at Cold Storage.* She took out her compact and checked her makeup and hair. She dabbed perfume on the inside of her elbows and wrists and went to find the manager.

Geoff was out of town and Barney was having dinner with a client. There was no need to rush. She and Tim could take as much time as they wanted.

By the time Sarah got to Tim's flat, she was lightheaded with anticipation. Thursday afternoons were so far apart, and today, she had squandered some of their precious time in the supermarket. She knocked on the door to the penthouse cautiously.

Tim opened the door, a relieved look on his face. "I thought something happened. I've been so worried. I had no idea what to do. What took you so long?"

"Chris wasn't at bridge. Janet Adams decided to run into Cold Storage for some last-minute things and got to chatting with some people. I couldn't leave while she was there. Are you certain Geoff won't be back tonight?"

"As certain as one can ever be about Geoff. I rang his secretary today. He's not booked back until tomorrow. What's old Barney up to tonight?"

"Dinner with a client. He said he wouldn't be home until late." Sarah smiled seductively and reached for Tim's shirt. "The way I see it, we still have several hours together."

Tim nibbled the back of Sarah's neck as he led her to the bedroom. When they had satisfied their physical longings, Tim held Sarah in his arms and toyed with her hair. "I love the way you smell. I love the way you feel. Sarah, I love everything about you. How much longer can you punish me this way?"

"Punish you? I didn't think that's what I was doing." Sarah pouted. "Tim, you know I'd do anything for you. If you can find another time for us to be together, tell me." Sarah reached over and rubbed her fingers along Tim's wrinkled forehead.

"Why don't you leave Barney? You can't tell me that you love him. I wouldn't believe it even if you were to say the words."

"Oh Tim, you're the only man I love. Surely you must know that."

He closed his eyes, and then opened them. "I know that. Sarah, I want so much more than what we have. The more time I spend with you, the more time I want. I never want you to leave. Isn't there some way we could go away together? I want nothing more than to wake up in the morning with you lying at my side."

"Oh, darling, I'd love that too. But how? Barney never leaves town. Where could I say I was going?"

"Think about it, luv. A friend of mine has a little beach cottage on Phuket, off the coast of Thailand. He offered to loan it to me any time I want. It sounds ideal. A little hideaway for the two of us."

Sarah closed her eyes and the thought of spending a long weekend away from Barney and their tomb of a house. How could she arrange it? Suddenly, an idea came to her. "I've got it. Book this place for two weeks from now."

"Are you sure?"

"Yes. There's a furniture store in Bangkok I've wanted to go to. I'll tell Barney I'm going there. He'll never notice."

"What if he suggests joining you?"

"He can't." Sarah grinned. "That's the weekend he and Geoff have meetings. I don't know why I didn't think of it sooner. Remember? Geoff said something about it before he left for Greece. Somebody's coming to town that weekend. Barney has to be there."

Tim kissed Sarah. "You are truly a little vixen and I love you." He reached under the sheet and caressed Sarah.

Sarah loved being with Tim. He was so responsive to her moods and he did the most incredible things to her body. He made her feel the way she always thought she was supposed to feel in bed. Tim knew when to be soft and gentle and when to use more force. It was as if he could read her mind. A weekend away would be good for both of them.

When Barney came home that evening, Sarah was seductive. She poured him a drink and offered him some hors d'oeuvres. When she knew he was relaxed, she brushed her hand along his arm. "Love, I was thinking, would you mind going to Bangkok in two weeks to look for that table and chair I want for the sitting room? One of the women at bridge today mentioned something she'd seen and it sounds perfect."

"I hate to shop. Can't you go with one of the wives?"

"We never go anywhere, just the two of us. It would be lovely. We could leave Thursday morning and come back Sunday. I'm sure Trey would be fine with Ah Soon." Sarah continued to rub Barney's arm and nuzzle her head against his face. "Please. It would mean so much to me."

"All right. When is it you want to go?"

"Two weeks from today. Oh, Barney, I'm so pleased. The sale ends that weekend. There's simply no time before then."

"Good. Now make me another drink, love."

The next morning when Barney called to say he had important meetings that weekend and couldn't get away, Sarah started to cry on the phone. "I was so looking forward to our little honeymoon."

"I know, dear. You've never been to Bangkok. Why don't you go without me?"

"Barney! The shopping trip was secondary. What I really wanted was some time with my husband."

"I know that, love, but I can't get away. My parents will be here in a month. You must have that suite finished for them. You'll simply have to go alone."

"Are you sure? You know I hate to travel by myself."

"You should be a bit more adventurous. Chris spent ten days in Taman Negara with Alison. If she could do that, I'm sure you can manage four days in Bangkok. You might ask Tory where to go sightseeing. I'm sure she knows everything there is to know about Bangkok."

"What a wonderful idea! Who knows, maybe she'll go with me."

"Now, that's what I like to hear, a smile in your voice. Why don't you ring Tory now?"

"Right you are. Bye, love."

I'm glad that's over with, she thought. *Ring Tory, indeed. She's the last person in the world I'd consider speaking to.* She rang the airlines to check on flights to Bangkok. If she were going to buy the perfect furniture in Bangkok, she'd better schedule the trip today. Barney was never home early on Fridays. She could use a little of Barney Senior's money to pay for the ticket. The money to furnish the house was nearly gone. Once she bought the final pieces for the sitting room, there'd be none left. That didn't concern Sarah. All that mattered was she'd have some much needed time with Tim.

Once Barney's parents left, if she was still head over heels in love with Tim, she'd come up with a more permanent solution to her dilemma. She deserved something for herself. The mere prospect of having Barney Senior and Violet as houseguests was dreadful. It would be impossible to hide Barney's drinking from them. *Maybe he'll be on his best behavior while they're here. Now, let's see, how can I guarantee they don't suspect a thing?*

A party. If she threw a party for her in-laws, she could control the atmosphere. They might be lulled into a false sense of security that things were going well. Sarah didn't have much time, but she could pull it off. She'd limit the guest list to Trans Oil people. No one from the company would dare say anything negative about Barney in front of his father. Once her in-laws saw how happy and content she and Barney were in Singapore, they'd return to Australia happy.

Chapter 21
TORY

Singapore
Friday, May 9, 1980

Tory lugged her suitcase and camera equipment to the taxi queue at Paya Lebar Airport. She inhaled the sweet mixture of sandalwood and orchids and knew that she was where she belonged. The Indonesian jungle, with its dank smell from rotting undergrowth, was pleasant for a while. Three weeks had been too long. Much as she liked the jungle, Singapore always made her feel that she was home again. The city was so thoroughly modern that it was antiseptic and sterile. It could be any major city in any country. There was nothing to remind you of where you were. Here, she lived in a large city, but anonymously, the way she liked, without having to worry what others felt.

She was so lost in thought that she was oblivious to the people exiting the terminal. She heard someone call her name and looked up. Geoff Melbourne stood grinning at her.

"Still carrying your camera, I see. Do you ever leave home without it?" he teased.

She was annoyed at his comment. Geoff was the last person she wanted to see. "I was working. Oh, I forgot, you probably don't recognize the word."

He shrugged. "Whatever. I've my car if you'd care for a lift. If you feel it will compromise you in some way, you needn't worry. I shan't be offended."

The taxi line was long. It would be at least half an hour before Tory got to the front of the queue. A ride would be faster. "Jurong's out of your way," she answered. If his offer had been made out of politeness, this would give him the perfect out.

To her surprise, Geoff bowed and reached for her suitcase. "Why don't we stop at Raffles for a Singapore Sling? Or is that something the working class doesn't do?"

Tory was irritated at his remark. He appeared to have a joke for all occasions. She ignored his barbed comment because she was not in the mood for verbal crossfire. While they drove, she glanced at his profile. His green eyes danced when he spoke. All in all, he was a good-looking man. If only he weren't so arrogant.

Raffles Hotel was a landmark. It boasted more dignitaries as guests than any other Singaporean hotel. It offered a panoramic view of the harbor and the islands off Singapore. Tory loved the neoclassical building with its high ceilings, intricately carved moldings, cornices and pillars, and marble floors. Uniformed doormen, floral displays and period-style armchairs on either side of the lobby welcomed the visitor. It reminded her of a bygone era.

While they sipped their drinks, she marveled over the early photos decorating the walls. "Have you ever really looked at them?" she asked. "It's incredible. Even in this heat the ladies are in ball gowns and gloves up to their elbows, and the men have on silly bow ties. It's like they're in jolly old England, and not in the middle of the tropics."

"Do you ever think about anything but photography?" he asked abruptly.

"Of course. I... Well..." Tory blushed. He was right. Since Anna's death, she'd thrown herself into work with a vengeance. It was her way of escaping from the emptiness she felt.

"Where've you been?" she asked politely. Since he was buying their drinks, Tory might as well talk to Geoff. Soon enough he'd drive her home and she would be free of him.

"Greece. I was reviewing contracts. And you?"

"Indonesia. I'm doing brochures about life in the oil camps for Trans Oil. You know, the kind of stuff they can give people to read while they make up their mind whether or not to accept the assignment."

"Why doesn't the PR department do that? Isn't that what we pay them for?"

Tory shook her head in disbelief. He wasn't serious, was he? "Because all PR types know how to write is humbug. If they described the camp, it'd sound like an ad for Club Med."

"How?"

Tory closed her eyes, leaned back in her chair and started to recite. "At once you'll be captivated by all the conveniences so readily available in this idyllic paradise. Like golf? There are three courses for your pleasure. Swimming's your sport, you say. Don't fret. We have four different pools to provide the perfect atmosphere to develop that backstroke. You prefer tennis? There are two courts in every sub-division. And, since the sun stays out 'til nearly nine o'clock, you'll never have the glare of artificial lighting." Tory was giggling so much she had to stop. When she opened her eyes, she saw Geoff was grinning as well.

"When you write, it's different?" he asked.

She nodded. "I love Asia. I see all its beauty. But I don't have any illusions about it. I write the truth, the good and the bad."

"I'm sure you do. No illusions for Ms. Winslow." His tone softer, he asked, "When did your mon ... your orangutan die?"

Tory looked startled. "How did you know about Anna?"

"Tim. He said you preferred her company to most humans'."

"In many ways, I guess I did. She was so fiercely independent and determined about what she wanted. There were no mixed signals from her. I always admired her honesty."

"Like you, I see."

Tory paused. "Sort of ... I never thought about it like that before."

"What else did you like about her?"

"She never minded my comings and goings the way most people do. If I went away for a week or a month, she was glad to see me when I returned. Even Chris gets huffy if I'm gone too long. It was hard for me to give Anna up."

"Why did you do it then?"

"In 1971 the government outlawed orangutans as pets. I ignored the law for nearly three years. I lived in a small village. My Malay neighbors were accustomed to seeing Anna with me. It would never have occurred to them to turn me in."

"Why did you get rid of her, then?"

"Expats discovered the area and started building weekend beach houses there. There was no way to keep Anna hidden and by then it was too late to donate her to the Zoological Gardens. Besides, I didn't want her to spend the rest of her life in a cage. The Malay government has a Nature Reserve on Sabah where they teach animals to survive in the wild again. I took Anna there. It seemed the right thing to do. At least in Sabah, she has her freedom. She's not peered at and poked by tourists like at the zoo."

"So she's alive, then? The way you spoke that day in the car, I presumed she was dead."

Tory shivered. "Anna died in my arms a few months ago."

Geoff looked at his watch. Tory assumed her story had bored him. Then she remembered it was Friday night. He probably had a date. Despite her initial misgivings, she was enjoying their talk.

"Do you realize you've been here for an hour without your camera? Are you going through withdrawal? I used to think the camera was part of your face, that you hid behind it to mask a deformity." As Geoff spoke, he pushed back a lock of hair that had fallen into her eyes. "You really are quite pretty, especially when you smile. You must smile more often."

Tory felt the base of her throat turn red. It had been a long time since anyone had complimented anything other than her work. "I had my camera with me at the airport because I'd been at work."

"It's more than that. No matter where you are, you have a camera. You had it the day we met. Remember?"

She thought for a second. When had they met? Sentosa. "I was taking photos for my friends that day," she said defensively.

"My point exactly. Everyone else was there to have fun. You kept your face pressed against a lens all day. Never said more than g'day to anyone. I've seen you in town. Your camera is always at your side. What are you hiding from?"

"Nothing," she answered angrily. Their pleasant interlude was obviously over. Geoff had reverted to the arrogant person she expected. "I really should go," Tory said. There was no way she'd allow Geoff to have his own version of the Spanish Inquisition at her expense.

Geoff smiled broadly. "I'm not surprised. I think you run whenever you don't like what you see. Your work has exceptional sensitivity. You have the ability to transport the reader to wherever you were -- the colors, the sights; even the smells come alive when you write. Your photos add to the experience. During the flight from Athens, I read your piece on the refugee camps in Thailand. When I finished, there were tears in my eyes. It made me think you were someone special. I see now I was mistaken."

Seething, Tory stood to leave, then, as quickly, slumped back in her chair. Something Geoff said had hit a nerve. No one had ever spoken to her like that and she didn't like it. Dora's letter had echoed the same sentiments. She was frightened to think that he might be right. “This is the land of Noah's Ark. My camera is my beau," she answered weakly.

“Why?”

"Why not?"

"For one thing, it's not polite to answer a question with a question. If you wish to change the subject, all you must do is say so."

"For a lot of reasons you'd never understand," she said through clenched teeth.

He smiled and reached for her hand, which had gripped the paper umbrella from her drink so tightly it was now shredded. "Why do you have such a chip on your shoulder?"

"It's part of my mystique. It makes the people who hire me think they're getting their monies worth." Before Geoff could respond, Tory attacked him. "Why do you have a fancy sports car?

Why don't you have a Trans Oil car and driver? I thought all expats got a car and driver when they got here."

"I saved for years to have the car of my dreams. I was not about to leave it in New Zealand because I moved. I work on the car to relax. Why must you always act as if expats are the enemy? If we are, why do you spend time with us? If I didn't like a group of people as much as you pretend, I'd certainly not waste my valuable time with them."

"You're here with me," she retorted with a smile. A small victory at last.

"Ah, but I like you, you see. You're the one who doesn't like me."

Geoff's answer caught her off guard. She had to think of what to say next. "You delight in making jokes at my expense."

Geoff threw his head back and laughed. "And that's all they are. Jokes." He smiled. "Your eyes change color when you're angry. Did you know that? There's obviously a great deal of passion inside you. Too bad it only surfaces in your work."

Although his tone sounded conciliatory, Tory was not easily placated. Geoff watched life like she did. "Humor is your camera."

Instead of angering Geoff, her remark made him laugh again. "Now we're getting somewhere. Have you plans for the evening? If not, would you care to have dinner with me?"

Tory was startled by his invitation. She'd been certain that by now he'd lost interest in her. It was fun matching wits with him, though. She accepted, with the proviso that she choose the location. Although Geoff was in a suit and tie, she was in shorts and she did not want to go to Jurong to change.

She selected Rasa Singapura, where they could eat from the hawker stands and visit the shops of the Handicraft Centre. It was an area little known to tourists since it was tucked behind the skyscrapers on Tanglin Road. Indian, Malay, and Chinese stalls intermingled to create a pan-Asiatic taste tour. They sampled various cuisines as they walked. Tory pointed out the differences between the artifacts displayed in the shop widows. She explained how to tell whether the wayang puppets were from Malaysia or Indonesia, the specific Indonesian island a piece of batik came from, and which Chinese province produced a carving or scroll. This was safe territory. She was comfortable in her role as a tour guide.

As they walked Geoff slipped his hand through hers. At first, she stiffened and pulled her hand back. Later, while they examined carvings, she stopped fighting his advances.

Since they were across from the Marco Polo Hotel, Geoff suggested they stop in for an Irish Coffee. The lobby-level bar was nearly full. The Irish Coffee it served was legendary, as were the beautiful Singaporean hostesses who wore skintight brown Chamsung dresses slit to their hips.

The hostess brought a carafe of coffee, a sterno burner, crystallized sugar, whipped cream, and whiskey on a serving cart. Watching the drink being made was part of the magic of the Marco Polo.

The hostesses were exquisite. Their lean bodies were perfectly suited to the old style Chinese dresses. When Tory looked up, she was surprised that Geoff's eyes were on her, instead of their hostess.

"Why're you staring at me?" she asked.

"I've already told you, I think you're pretty. When you're interested in something you lose that tough veneer you wear like armor. For a second or two I got a glimpse of a real person buried beneath your cynicism."

"Oh, please," she said with disgust. "I'm not some simpering piece of fluff who turns to jelly 'cause the moon's out or all the accouterments of romance are so obviously displayed."

"Have I accused you of that? You're a beautiful woman with everything going for you, yet you're miserable. You act like you're the only one in the world who was ever hurt by anyone."

How could she have been so foolish? She'd seen him at parties, leaning nonchalantly against a wall, observing. His eyes changed as he thought - clouding, clearing, but always moving. The intensity should have warned her. He drew conclusions from what he saw. That was why she rose to his bait earlier. He knew which buttons would get a reaction.

Geoff threw money on the table. He stormed to his car and drove her to Jurong without a word. As she got out of his car, he spat his words at her. "You live alone and you'll die the same way. It's such an incredible waste."

Tory was shaking as she put her key in the door. *Who does Geoff think he is anyway?* His last comment had elucidated her deepest fear.

The phone rang. She sniffed back her tears. "Hello", she whispered, confident the caller would mistake her hoarseness as the vestige of sleep, not tears. When she heard Geoff's voice, she was outraged. How dare he?

"I called because I realize I was out of line. I hadn't the right to say what I did."

"And I'm supposed to accept your apology? Just like that?"

"I've not apologized. I meant every word I said and you bloody well know it."

He was infuriating. "Well, if you're not apologizing, what exactly are you doing?"

"That should be patently obvious. I find you entertaining. Thought we might go to dinner tomorrow. Some place fancy where we dress up like big people and pretend we like each other. You're good at fabrication; you should enjoy the game. And you get a decent meal out of the arrangement."

She shook her head, as if that might make sense of their conversation. "And what do you get?" she asked contemptuously.

"A chance to see you again. I'll pick you up at 7:30. I'll book a table at Latour at the Shangri-La."

He hung up before she could say a word. Tory stared at the receiver in her hand. There was no way she would go out with him again.

Chapter 22
CHRIS

Singapore
Friday - Wednesday, May 9 - June 18, 1980

The Sunday after Marc's smoking incident, the family met in the solarium. Kevin started the discussion, "Marc, Alison, what's wrong?"

Alison glared at her father defiantly. "I didn't get caught smoking. Why am I here?"

"Because," Chris said, "you're upset."

Alison twirled a lock of her hair. "Did Tory tell you about KL? She said she wouldn't."

"No, dummy," Marc said as he shot his sister a dirty look. "I told Mom we think she and Dad are getting a divorce."

"Why bring me into it? I didn't do anything wrong," Alison whined.

"Enough. Your mother and I are not getting a divorce." Kevin's tone was harsh.

Chris rubbed his arm in what she hoped was a calming motion. "I'd like to know why you think there's something wrong. What makes you think your father and I aren't getting along?"

Marc and Alison looked at each other. Marc nodded to Alison and she took over the role of spokesperson. "Daddy's never home. When he is, you and he argue."

Kevin stared at the children, and then closed his eyes.

Chris was concerned at how upset the children were. It was obvious from their faces as they stared glumly at their father's closed eyes. "Kev, say something. Please."

Kevin opened his eyes. "I'm working on a startup venture for a new line of business. At the moment we're not sure we'll be able to pull it off. Since we can't guarantee success, our staffing is minimal. The job's taking up more time than I expected." He reached for Chris's hand. "Your mother and I aren't getting a divorce. She's not happy about the time I'm gone from home. Frankly, I don't like it either. But I gave my word."

Chris smiled and squeezed his hand. "Dad's right. I miss him when he's not here, and that makes me angry. What can we do to make the two of you feel better?"

"Look, I can't get home earlier at night. I need my papers with me when I'm on the phone and there's too much stuff for me to lug here."

Marc groaned. "Don't bother coming home if you're gonna lock yourself in your office and work."

Chris went to tap Marc's arm and Kevin stopped her. "Chris, he's right. So what you want is time when I'm home without work? Is that it?"

The children nodded eagerly and Chris's heart sank. She held her breath as she waited for Kevin to say something.

"If I got up earlier, I suppose we could have a family breakfast."

"We wouldn't mind getting up early, Dad. Not if we'd be together," Alison said excitedly.

"Okay. I'll make it a point to be here for breakfast each morning at 5:30. I'll also try to organize my schedule we can spend Sunday together."

Once the children left, Kevin put his elbows on the table and held his head. When he looked up at Chris, he frowned. "Were they as upset as they looked? I can't imagine either of them agreeing to breakfast at such an ungodly hour."

Chris looked at her husband questioningly. "Is that why you suggested it?"

He shook his head. "It's the only time I can fit in. With the time differences, I need to be at work at night. To compensate, I've been sleeping in mornings." He reached for her hand. "Bear with me, Chrissy. It won't be much longer. I'll try to save Sundays for you and the kids. I'm not promising, mind you. I don't want you throwing it up in my face if I don't manage it every week."

Two Saturdays later, Kevin was too tired to go to a party. The family was going to the Tiger Balm Gardens and out for chili-crabs the next day. Since the children were happier seeing more of Kevin, Chris didn't mind the crimp it put in their social calendar. Kevin was fast asleep and it was only 8:30 p.m. She called her brother Mike to see what was happening at home. Before they hung up, Mike's son Matthew asked to speak to Marc.

The next morning at breakfast, Marc announced, "I want to go to camp with Matthew. He and Kim are going to Maine for a month. The place sounds neat."

"I'd like to go, too," Alison added.

Chris gave Kevin a look that said the children wouldn't want to go away if he were more available. "Now, kids..."

Kevin interrupted. "Chrissy, it's not a bad idea. Let's call Mike and see what he thinks."

It had been settled in a matter of minutes. Marc and Alison would go to New York, stay with Mike and Patsy for a week to see the rest of their family, then go to camp for a month with their cousins. Patsy offered to keep the children for August. She and Mike had rented a house on Fire Island for the month. Alison and Marc were welcome to join them. Chris's mother would be there. Kevin's brother and his children would be, too. After his divorce, Kevin's brother had moved in with his mother, next door to Chris's mother and Mike and Patsy.

"It'll be good for them," Kevin had said. "You always complain they don't spend enough time with our families. This gives them a whole summer."

Several weeks later, as she waved good-bye to the bus carrying Marc and Alison to their plane, Chris cried. Paya Lebar Airport had not been built for jumbo jets. They were too large to come close to the terminal building; instead passengers took buses from the terminal to the plane.

Kevin pulled Chris towards him. His arm circling her waist, he waved with his other hand. "Don't worry," he whispered. "We won't leave 'til the plane takes off."

Chris nodded her head slowly. Saying good-bye to her children for the summer was real. For the past month, while she shopped and packed their clothes, it seemed like a game. As she watched them climb the stairs to the plane, she felt she and Kevin had made the wrong decision. The house would be empty without the children. *Maybe I'll fly home in August and go to Fire Island myself. I haven't seen Mom in a long time. Mike and Patsy will have their hands full with four teenagers.*

As the plane started its ascent, Kevin handed Chris his handkerchief. "I've never known you to have a tissue when you need one," he joked.

Kevin was right. Her purse was full to overflowing; yet she could never find anything in it. Kevin led her away from the plexiglas window.

She was surprised when he stopped at the canteen. "What?"

"You're upset. I have to go to the office when we get back to town. I thought maybe a cup of coffee would help."

Kevin was trying. Chris sniffed back her tears. He knew how much the children meant to her and how she'd miss them.

Kevin returned with two lukewarm, Styrofoam cups of coffee. "Chris, they'll be fine."

"It's such a long flight. Do you really think it's all right for them to travel by themselves?"

Kevin reached for Chris's hand. "It's a direct flight to JFK. Nothing can go wrong. You have to let them spread their wings, you know."

"I know. What will I do while they're gone?"

"What you do when they're here. You have your volunteer work and your friends. Why don't you call Tory for dinner?"

"She's out of town."

"Geoff says she's coming back this afternoon."

"Geoff?" Chris asked, her eyes wide with amazement. "When did that start?"

"Beats me. I said it was a shame Tory wouldn't be here to comfort you. Geoff grinned and said she was due back sometime this afternoon. He wasn't certain which flight. C'mon, finish your coffee. I have to get to work."

At home, Chris went into her garden. As she weeded, she thought. A summer with their cousins might cheer the children up. Laurel had left the week before. She wouldn't be returning to Singapore. Alison would have been morose with no best friend and two months off from school. Camp would teach Alison that when you made friends, you couldn't expect them to stay in the same place forever.

If Marc needed male bonding, Mike was Chris's second choice. Mike was great with his kids. Although Kevin had spent more time with the family recently, it was a forced closeness. Kevin's mind was on his special project, even when was with them.

Janet Adams was hosting a lunch today for Sarah's mother-in-law today. Chris used her volunteer work as an excuse to miss the event. She had little interest in seeing more of Violet. Despite her antipathy, she was hosting a lunch for Violet on Friday. It was the least Chris could do for Sarah. Sarah was having a big party Saturday night and insisted on doing the preparations herself. She needed the burden of entertaining her mother-in-law taken off her hands.

Since the Parkers were still VIPs, a party in their honor was a social obligation that couldn't be missed. Chris had turned down several invitations so she could spend time with her children. Chris was sick to death of the Parker Seniors. They had been in Singapore for three weeks. The woman was still a pretentious snob. Chris disliked her more with each passing day. If seeing so much of Violet weren't reason enough to avoid today's lunch, Chris felt that she spent too much time with the same people. Her life was too inbred. She saw the same women all the time. Her two afternoons at Mount Elizabeth didn't provide the sense of purpose they once had. Chris missed feeling her life mattered that she made a difference in some way.

Chris tried to reach Tory before she left for the hospital. There was no answer. *I wish she'd get an answering machine. Why does Geoff know her schedule? She's never mentioned a thing about him to me. Not that I've seen much of her since Malaysia. And that was three months ago.*

Either Tory was busy or she was avoiding Chris. It was impossible to know which. If Tory were seeing Geoff, that might explain her elusiveness. But Geoff was out of town a great deal as well. Chris couldn't imagine how the two of them found time to meet.

Before Chris left the hospital, she tried Tory again. Finally Tory answered the phone. "Where've you been?" Chris asked.

"Here, there, everywhere," Tory answered, in the lilting tone she used when pleased with life.

"What are you doing at this moment?"

"Talking to you."

"Tory!"

"Going through my mail. Why?"

"Kev's working late. I thought we could have dinner."

"Great. What time?"

"We'll pick you up in an hour, no, make it an hour and a half"

"We?" Tory asked cautiously.

"Suradmin. I have Kevin's car."

"Okay. See you then. Bye."

Chris smiled as she hung up. Tory sounded happy. Tory's good moods were contagious. She'd make silly comments about the people they knew and mimic them. Soon Chris would be laughing so hard she'd forget what had put her in a blue funk.

I wonder if she plans to play bridge tomorrow. Better yet, maybe she'll come to my lunch on Friday. I'd feel better if Tory were there. At least we could laugh about the whole thing afterwards.

Dinner was a simple meal: cold chicken, salad, French bread, and white wine. While they ate Tory told Chris about her recent forays into the jungle. She made the journeys sound like larks, side trips to break up the monotony of life in Singapore.

Having been in Taman Negara, Chris was sure it wasn't as much fun as Tory made out. She laughed at Tory's description of falling down the side of a hill and landing in a stream. She sounded more concerned about her camera equipment than herself.

"What's up with you and Geoff Melbourne? I thought you weren't in the market for a man?"

"I'm not." Tory shrugged. "I don't know. We bumped into each other a few times and had dinner."

Chris was intrigued. "Tell me."

Tory shrugged her shoulders again. "We've gone out, I don't know, maybe a dozen times. Sometimes it's just for a walk or a cup of coffee. Geoff's nice."

"That's it? He's nice?"

Tory smiled. "He's nice and we talk to each other. Nothing more."

"Is that why you haven't been around?"

"My schedule's been insane. Every assignment's been a long trip, two or three weeks at a clip. By the time I get home, all I want to do is not move for a day or two. By then I'm way behind and have to put my nose to the proverbial grindstone to meet a deadline. How are things with you?"

"The kids went to camp with their cousins. They left this morning."

"Oh, Chris, I wish I'd known. If it's any consolation, I'll be in town for the next two weeks."

"Great. How about coming to the lunch I'm having for Violet Parker Friday? I could use the moral support." Chris expected to be turned down.

Tory shifted in her seat. "Sure, if you want, but I don't think Mrs. Parker likes me. Last time she was here, she looked at me like I was poor white trash."

For the first time in weeks, Chris laughed. "I don't care for her either. But her husband is still important at Trans Oil and ..."

"And Kev works for Trans Oil," Tory finished.

"Don't you know it. Does Geoff work as much as Kev? Kevin's never home these days."

"I guess. He travels two weeks out of the month. I suppose he's tied up when he is here. I never thought about it."

"I thought you were seeing Tim. When did Geoff come into the picture?"

"Tim's the past." Tory paused and stared at the glass in her hands. "You can't go back. I should have known that."

"And Geoff? How does he fit into your life?"

"I'm not sure. For now, it's pleasant. He's different from most of the guys who end up here. He isn't looking for a permanent liaison, which suits me fine."

"But what do you feel?" Chris wanted Tory to be happy. Geoff might be the answer.

Tory shrugged. "I like him. At the moment, that's enough. Don't push me, Chris, just be happy for me."

"All right," she agreed reluctantly. "But, if anything starts to change, I want to know about it. I was shocked Kevin knew something before me."

Chapter 23
TORY

Indonesia and Singapore
Wednesday, June 18, 1980

Tory roamed the camp in Balikpapan, looking for something new to write about. Trans Oil planned to move a large contingent of families there in a few months. She wanted to see if there were any differences between this camp and the one in Sumatra.

When oil was discovered on the various Indonesian islands, oil companies constructed small towns in the center of the swampy land to house their workers. They cut down the lush vegetation and poured crude oil over it to kill off the thick underbrush. To complete the transformation they built houses, schools, churches, and office buildings. The roads were dirt, with oil poured on top once a month, to keep the foliage from coming back. Barbed wire fences to ward off the tigers surrounded the camps.

The houses were of two varieties -- California ranch or early Colonial. Each had a tin roof and screened-in front porch. Both styles were prefab structures, with a kitchen, dining room, living room, and three bedrooms. The walls were painted metal, usually pale yellow, which was supposed to be sunny and cheery. Instead the dull, washed-out color reminded Tory of traces of mustard found on a shirtsleeve three days after a meal.

If you stayed inside you could forget you were living practically on the equator. Once you went out to the front porch, the intense heat was an ever-present reminder. The houses were divided into small neighborhoods similar to the tract housing developments built in the United States after World War II.

Tory supposed the lifestyle could be pleasant for a brief period of time if you didn't mind living, eating, and working with the same people. Tory couldn't abide the thought of living in an oil camp. There was no privacy. She imagined any argument between a married couple would be known at the office before 7 a.m.

What she saw as the redeeming factor of the camp, the opportunity to be in the jungle, was missed by most of the inhabitants missed. The dark green vegetation grew abundantly and lawlessly. Torrential downpours that seemed like they'd never end came every afternoon at three o'clock. The rains were such a part of the day that Tory was oblivious to them. She kept a rain poncho in her camera case and pulled it over her head when the afternoon downpour started. Unlike most people who used this time for a siesta, Tory explored.

She would slip out the camp gate while the guards dozed. Their job was to keep strangers from entering, not residents from leaving. She would walk silently through the dense underbrush. The slimy animals didn't frighten her. Tigers seldom came too close to the fence. For three hours she made her way through the inviolable jungle and photographed primates.

With Anna gone, Tory's fascination with primates had increased. It was easier now to think about Anna and not feel a stabbing pain in her stomach. The ache was still there when she remembered Dora. Tory now understood why Dora had wanted to be alone with Jack Talbott in her final hours. She loved him.

Tory had emulated Dora since she was twelve. She'd followed her mentor's instructions blindly. Many of the things Dora taught her weren't true. Now, at thirty-six, Tory was trying to make sense of it all. She felt deceived. She'd built a wall around her heart so no man could hurt her. Cutting herself off from people hadn't protected her from pain. She wanted to reach out to people but had no idea how to start. She took a critical look at her life. It wasn't always a pretty picture.

While she analyzed her life, Tory withdrew. She needed to be alone to think. It was the only way she could make sense of everything. There were times she considered returning to Prairie View, so she could see the past more clearly.

She'd stopped avoiding Geoff Melbourne. He was impossible to ignore, if only because they frequented the same places. Geoff was pleasant. He challenged her when she retreated inside herself. His refusal to tolerate her behavior was done sympathetically. As she relaxed, they became friends. She never thought of it as more than that. They shared similar interests and dislikes. They took long walks to explore the outlying areas of Singapore.

Geoff enjoyed being outdoors as much as she. He never complained about the heat and humidity, and he welcomed the opportunity to traverse the narrow streets in the ethnic parts of town. He'd stopped making disparaging comments about the camera that was always at her side. Now he pointed out photo opportunities to her.

Today Tory explored the closest town to Trans Oil's camp. It was about twenty kilometers away, and only in the jungle would it be considered a town. It had two seedy-looking restaurants, a dentist who pulled teeth with pliers while a crowd watched, a pharmacy selling herbal cures, a general store carrying bits of everything, and several other stores selling Indonesian artifacts.

Tory got back to Singapore on Wednesday afternoon. Quickly she turned on her tapes. The music provided a soothing background while she unpacked and went through the mail that had accumulated in two weeks. The phone rang. She picked it up, expecting to hear Geoff's voice. She was surprised to hear Chris.

She'd purposely been avoiding Chris. Chris had the perfect life. She was happily married to a man she adored and had two charming children. Tory feared that seeing Chris would make her painfully aware of what was missing in her world.

The second she heard Chris's voice; Tory realized how much she missed her. Even though she hoped to see Geoff, Tory accepted Chris's dinner invitation. Before she began her soul-searching, she enjoyed spending time with Chris. It was silly to keep ignoring her. Chris wasn't responsible for the different paths their lives had taken. When Tory considered being married with two children, she laughed. It didn't matter what Dora had said. Tory was content with her life as it was.

Tory was surprised that Alison and Marc had gone back to the United States. Although she thought it a good idea for them to experience a world larger than Lotus Land, she knew how difficult it must have been for Chris to let them go. Chris was so protective of her children. She wanted to wrap them in cotton batting and protect them from harm. The children were growing up. It would be good for them to spend time in a more normal environment.

They sat in the solarium after dinner. Tory planned to leave once they finished the bottle of Chablis.

"Are you sure I did the right thing?" Chris asked.

Tory hated it when Chris looked for approval. She shrugged indifferently, her way to avoid the discussion. "Did they want to go?"

"It was Marc's idea."

"Well then, that should settle it. If it's what they wanted, I'm sure it's the right thing. You get island fever here. Why shouldn't they?"

"I hadn't thought of that. I was going insane before Taman Negara. I felt like everything was closing in on me."

Tory nodded. "And things have been better since you got back. Anyway, you and Kev could use some time alone."

"Don't I know it. Here it is, nearly half past nine and he's still not home. There are times . . ."

Chris stopped when she heard the front door open. "We're in the solarium, Kev," she called. "Tory's here with me. Did you get a lift back?"

"Yes, and I invited him in for a drink."

When Kevin walked in with Geoff, Tory started to flush. Since he hadn't called before she left Jurong, Tory hadn't expected to see Geoff tonight. This was the last place she wanted to come face to face with him. She didn't want Chris to make more of their friendship than there was. She searched his face to see if he was surprised. His startled look pleased her.

Kevin kissed Chris and gave Tory a peck on the cheek. "Long time no see. Where have you been hiding? Tory, you remember Geoff, don't you?"

Even had Chris not said Kevin knew she and Geoff were seeing each other, Kevin's self-satisfied grin would have given him away. Tory felt like a gawky teenager. She was tongue-tied. She stood stiffly and shook Geoff's hand.

"It's good to see you again," she offered with a smile.

Kevin seemed pleased with himself. "Can I interest anyone in a martini? Chris, are you ready to switch yet?"

Chris jumped up to help her husband. Tory and Geoff were left staring at one another. When Geoff touched Tory's arm, she realized she still had it outstretched from their handshake.

"Was your flight okay?" he asked solicitously.

She nodded.

"I'm glad. Do you need a lift home?" Geoff said softly.

Tory shook her head. "I'll call a cab."

"I don't mind. I had something to ask you, anyway. We can talk on the way."

"If you're sure it's not too much trouble. I know you have to be up early in the morning."

"Actually you'd be doing me a favor. I could use an excuse for a drive. It relaxes me."

Kevin carried a pitcher of martinis. "Why don't the two of you sit down? I swear you look like Chris and I asked you to walk across burning coals. This isn't Thimithi."

Tory smiled at Kevin's reference to the Hindu ritual. She tried to return to her place on the rattan chair, but Chris had taken that chair and Kevin the other. *Damn. They're going to force us to sit next to each other then watch like prying parents.* Tory smiled broadly as she sat next to Geoff on the couch. She wouldn't give Kevin or Chris the satisfaction of knowing how uncomfortable she was.

Since Geoff hadn't called this afternoon, Tory doubted he wanted to see her. His comment had been made for Chris and Kevin's benefit. Now, they'd have to endure a car ride. Geoff didn't look comfortable. She imagined he dreaded the long drive to Jurong.

When the pitcher of martinis was empty, Tory and Geoff left.

In the safety of Geoff's car, he leaned over and kissed her. "You were terribly quiet. Is something bothering you?"

Tory shrugged. Everything was bothering her and yet nothing was. "I was taken by surprise, that's all. I don't like giving Chris an inside track on my life. Before you know it, she'll be ordering wedding invitations."

"It's her way. Would you care to stop for coffee? And before you ask, I don't mind. It was my idea."

Tory had a good idea what she wanted, and it wasn't a cup of coffee. Since that was all Geoff offered, she accepted. They went to the Coffee Shop at the Marco Polo. She smiled when Geoff took her hands. She liked the feel of his hands. They didn't have the softness of a man who spent his life in an office. Then she remembered he worked on his car. For some reason, that pleased her. Maybe because her own hands showed the evidence of outdoor work.

They sat in a booth next to one another, close enough that Tory could feel the roughness of Geoff's Harris Tweed blazer. Next to her bare arms, the fabric pricked her skin. She shivered a little, and Geoff pulled her closer.

"Are you chilly?" he asked.

"The air conditioning's cold."

Geoff took off his jacket and put it around her shoulders. The silk lining still carried the warmth from his body. Geoff rubbed her arms, and she could feel the goose bumps start to subside.

"Warmer?"

Tory nodded.

"Good. Are you through shielding Tim?"

His question came from left field. "I don't," she said softly.

"Come on. I've seen you. You let Tim pretend he's interested in you at parties. He wants Sarah. You're a convenient ruse to keep Barney from guessing what's going on."

"I haven't been to a party in over four months." Tory reached for his hands. "I've needed time to think. I haven't given Tim a second glance since before Anna died. You're the only person I've seen lately. This afternoon I visited Chris for the first time since March. If I didn't make time for her, why would I waste time on Tim? Does it bother you to have competition for Sarah?"

"Competition? Sarah's my friend."

"That's not the way it looks to me."

"As you said, you haven't been at parties lately. I feel sorry for Sarah and the mess she and Barney have made of their marriage. But that's where my concern ends."

"Fine. I don't like Tim and you feel sorry for Sarah. Why are we discussing them?"

"Sarah and Barney are having a party Saturday night. I'd like you to go with me."

"No thanks. I'm not interested."

"If you come with me, I promise I'll only say hello to Sarah."

"I wouldn't want you to feel compelled to change your behavior on my account."

"It's too late. My mind's made up. Tory, I have to go. It would make me happy if you'd join me."

Tory bit her lower lip. So far she and Geoff had avoided being seen together. With their travel schedules, it was easy. She wasn't sure she was ready to change their relationship and appearing together in public would.

"If you wish, I'll ask Chris to stop production on the wedding invitations for at least a month."

Despite herself, Tory laughed. Geoff had the uncanny ability to turn anything into a joke. "Okay, but I want a six-month moratorium on the invitations. Anything less, and I'm staying home."

"Agreed," he whispered as he kissed her ear.

Chapter 24
SARAH

Singapore
Saturday, June 21, 1980

Thank goodness I had my weekend with Tim. I couldn't bear this ordeal without my memories. Sarah's mind raced as she worked in the kitchen. Their long weekend in Phuket had been wonderful. From Thursday morning until Sunday night, they were the only two people in the world. They walked on the beach, fell asleep in each other's arms, and enjoyed quiet dinners where they lingered over a glass of port and touched hands openly. Sarah relished every second of their idyllic holiday. Making love was everything she imagined. They fit together perfectly. Intuitively each knew how to please the other. It was as if they were destined for each other's arms from the day they were born.

There was never a cross word between them. They enjoyed the same things. Tim introduced Sarah to snorkeling. She enjoyed the sensation of the water encircling her body. Tim didn't think she was silly because she was afraid to get her face wet. Instead he showed her how to work with the equipment in a swimming pool, so she could overcome her anxiety. She was happy he'd coaxed her. The coral and fish were beautiful. Her only regret was she couldn't tell anyone what she'd seen.

Now that Violet and Barney Senior were in town, Sarah appreciated the calming influence of that weekend. Barney Senior spent time at Trans Oil, but Violet had to be entertained. Luckily the Trans Oil wives offered to host lunches for her. It took some of the burden off Sarah. She fretted that if she spent too much time alone with Violet, her mother-in-law would know something was wrong.

Barney was playing the dutiful husband and father. He curtailed his drinking and took his father to the office each day. Every night they had dinner *en famille,* either at home or at one of the restaurants in the posh hotels.

"What was that blonde hussy doing at Chris Taylor's lunch, Sarah? You don't spend time with her, do you?"

"Not if it can be avoided. She's Chris's friend. I didn't invite her to your farewell party tonight. The only person who's not from Trans Oil is Tim Hammond. He's Geoff's flat-mate. He goes to the movies with Barney and me on Wednesday nights. I thought it would be rude to exclude him." Sarah prayed her voice wouldn't betray her. She felt her heart pound at the mention of Tim's name.

"Of course, dear. If he's a friend of Barney's, he should be invited. I'm glad you've made friends here. You like Singapore, don't you?"

Sarah smiled a wry smile. "Yes, Mother Parker. I like it a great deal more than I expected I would."

"That's good. You look happy. Singapore must agree with you."

Sarah continued to chop vegetables and hum to herself. Tomorrow morning her in-laws would be gone, and Sarah's life could return to normal. With Violet and Barney Senior in town, there had been no way to see Tim. Sarah was desperate to see him again.

"Sarah, dear," Violet began, "you know I'd be the last person to interfere in your life."

Sarah turned, her heart pounding. "Yes?" she asked softly. *Was it possible Violet suspected something?*

"Do you think it wise for Trey to spend so much time with that strange woman? She seems too rigid to care for a young child."

"Trey adores Ah Soon. Chris suggested her. She used to work for the Taylors. Since you said Chris was the person to know,

I thought I should take her advice on an amah. If you think differently, of course, I'll discuss it with Barney."

Ah Soon was perfect for Trey. She had a set regime for Trey's day that even the presence of his grandparents could not alter. It was a pleasure for Sarah to leave her child in the care of such a guardian. Although Sarah knew it would sound ridiculous if she told anyone, she was frightened to be alone with her son. Trey needed constant supervision. She worried that Trey might get hurt while she fantasized about life with Tim. She hoped Violet wasn't going to make an issue of it. It would be nearly impossible to find someone as qualified as Ah Soon.

"No, dear heart. We always had a nanny for Barney. I was probably expecting to see the same thing. You know what I mean, a gray-haired lady with a starched white apron."

"She's not Mary Poppins, I'll admit, but she's so good with Trey. He's still too young to have friends, and I'm usually in such a rush. You have no idea what a social place Singapore is."

Violet smiled a self-satisfied grin. "If these last weeks have been any indication, I can only imagine. Are you certain I can't help? I hate to think of you doing all this work yourself."

"I love cooking. You know that. I wouldn't trust tonight's dinner to anyone. I want everything to be perfect for you and Father."

Sarah turned her head and saw the dreamy look on Violet's face. *She's probably congratulating herself again for choosing the perfect wife for Barney. If she only knew.*

Sarah was pleased Barney's parents thought everything was going well in Asia. She hoped they'd leave her alone for a while so she could think about what to do with her life. The trip with Tim had convinced Sarah that her marriage was a sham. She needed to figure out how to end things so she appeared to be the wronged party. She had an idea. Her in-laws' visit was the start of her master plan.

While they were here she and Barney would be the picture of marital bliss. In about a month, once Barney was drinking too much again, Sarah would ring Barney Senior in tears. It would be easier to leave Barney if she looked like the innocent victim who couldn't bear life with an alcoholic. Although they hated to admit it, Barney's parents knew their son drank too much. After they saw how hard she was trying, they'd believe she was faultless. They wouldn't know her affair with Tim started before the divorce.

The farewell party started at eight, with dinner to be served at ten. The party was in full force. Sarah walked among her guests with a contented smile on her face, playacting the role of the perfect hostess. Her in-laws were enjoying themselves. Nothing could spoil this evening.

When she saw Geoff walk into the living room with Tory on his arm, she nearly choked. Tory was the last person she expected to see. *How dare Geoff invite her without asking me,* she fumed. Sarah wanted to ask Tory to leave, but it would create a scene, which was the last thing she needed. By the time she got to Geoff, he and Tory were in the midst of a discussion with Barney Senior.

"Sarah, dear," Barney Senior said, "Tory here was just telling us the most marvelous story about Kalimantan."

"Hello, Tory. I didn't expect to see you." Sarah wore her prettiest smile and used her sweetest tone. It was imperative Barney Senior not sense her unhappiness with the turn of events.

Geoff moved his arm protectively across Tory's back. "I asked Barney if I could bring a guest. I hope it won't create an inconvenience."

"Oh, no," Sarah tittered. "The meal's a buffet. I'm always a little surprised when Tory comes to a party."

"I'm the proverbial bad penny," Tory laughed. "I'm forever turning up when I'm least expected."

"Well, I, for one, am glad you did," Barney Senior said as he beamed at Tory.

Sarah went off to see to her other guests. Tory's presence unnerved her. To calm herself, Sarah took a glass of champagne from a waiter and swallowed it without tasting it.

"I thought you said she wouldn't be here." Violet's soft tone did not mask her irritation.

"I didn't invite her. She came with Geoff," Sarah answered through clenched teeth.

"Are they seeing each other? She doesn't appear his sort. I always thought Geoff was a little bit taken with you."

Sarah wanted to scream. Instead she counted to ten before opening her mouth. "Tory does some work for Trans Oil. If she's been in the office recently, Geoff might have considered it polite to include her."

"Of course, dear. How silly of me. I'd forgotten she worked for us. You're quite right. She probably met Father at the office and it all was arranged there."

Sarah sighed. *Thank heavens that's resolved.* "Now, Mother, why don't we go chat with Chris and Kevin Taylor?"

Chapter 25
CHRIS

Singapore
Friday, July 4, 1980

"I swear Tory's the only happy woman I know," Chris murmured to Kevin, as he crept into bed. Chris had been lying in bed thinking. Kevin must have thought she was asleep, because he had tiptoed into the bedroom without turning on a light. She rolled on her side and looked at Kevin, anxious to talk about what was on her mind.

If he heard her whispered comment, Kevin ignored it. "Right. Night, Chrissy." Out of habit he moved to kiss her cheek, missed, didn't notice, and was out cold in a matter of seconds.

Chris was not certain what angered her more, that Kevin hadn't heard her or that he was asleep again. For the past few weeks, the only activity in their bed had been Kevin tugging the sheet to his side. Their romantic reunion after her Malaysian trip was a distant memory. Chris had anticipated that, with the children gone, she and Kevin would become closer. She was disappointed when Kevin spent more time at work.

They had argued about it that morning at breakfast. "If you were seeing another woman would you tell me?"

He threw his newspaper down in disgust. "I'm working. I don't have the energy to do more than that. I'm sorry."

"That's it. You're sorry? What about me? Where do I fit in your life?"

He reached for her hand.

Chris put them in her lap and glared at Kevin. "Well? The children are off in the States, now if only you could get your wife to disappear, your life would be perfect."

"Chrissy, I don't like the time I'm spending at work any more than you do. It'll end soon."

"You told me that three months ago. Nothing's changed. Can't you understand that I miss you?"

"And I miss you. Geoff thinks we've almost got the details ironed out. Once we do, I'll be around so much, you'll beg me to go on a business trip, so you can have some peace."

"Kevin, please. I want you here more."

"Chris, I don't have anything to give you right now. I wish I did, but I don't."

"Geoff makes time for Tory."

"A cup of tea once a week keeps Tory happy. She doesn't demand the time you do."

"I'm your wife. I have the right to count on more than stolen minutes."

Chris lay in bed, unable to sleep as she remembered their argument. She was hesitant to mention her fears to Tory. Tory hadn't managed her own love life all that effectively. Chris couldn't see herself having an affair, no matter how unhappy she was. It was different for men. They were exposed to younger women all day at work. What was worse, the women only saw the men at their best.

Why do I equate having a man in your life with happiness? I'm certainly not happy, and from the looks of it, Sarah isn't either. Sarah looked drawn and troubled. She frequently turned down invitations for lunch or shopping. When the Parkers went out socially, Sarah might smile and laugh but her face was strained. The one time Chris broached the subject, Sarah insisted she was fine and couldn't be happier.

It was obvious that Barney drank too much. On several occasions, she'd seen Sarah offer Barney her arm to lean on. Each time he shoved her away roughly. Sarah pretended to laugh the incidents off, but they weren't funny.

Chris got out of bed and went downstairs for a cigarette. There was no reason to stay in bed if all she did was toss and turn. She fell asleep on the couch in the solarium.

When she woke, Kevin had left for the office. The fact he'd gone without even a good-bye exacerbated her mood. While she sipped orange juice, she read his note.

Chrissy-
Won't be home for dinner or the party.
I'll see you on the weekend.
Love,
Kev

Well, damn him. Just because he isn't going, doesn't mean I can't go. Chris was tired of staying in because Kevin was too tired to go out. She didn't have Tory's courage; she couldn't walk into a party alone. She thought it over and called John Horton. Ever since the day last October, when Tory asked if she knew how John was getting along, Chris had spoken to John once a week. She kept suggesting he get out socially. He said he couldn't face the looks of tea and sympathy. Perhaps, if he thought he was doing her a favor, he'd go. It would be good for each of them.

The courage she felt earlier in the day disappeared as Chris dressed. To buoy her flagging spirits, she wore the dark green dress she'd worn on Thanksgiving. The color was magnificent against her alabaster skin. The thin silk clung to her body sensually. Her short cap of auburn curls looked lighter against the dark hues of the dress. She liked the image she presented when she saw her reflection in the mirror. She put her pearl choker on, trying not to think about when Kevin had given it to her.

The minute she and John were inside the house, Chris calmed down. These were her friends. There was no reason to be anxious. Out of the comer of her eye, she saw Barney's unsteady gait. He was drunk. Chris walked in the opposite direction. There was no need to further embarrass Sarah.

The room was too small for the crowd. The combination of the various perfumes and floral arrangements was cloying to the point of nausea. She went to the patio for a cigarette, hoping to block out the offensive scents. She overheard snatches of conversations around her. She wasn't in the mood to make polite conversation. When she stepped off the patio and onto the lawn, she sighed in relief that she'd gotten away.

"Ghastly, isn't it?"

The voice startled her and she looked up to be certain the comment had been addressed to her. When she saw John, she smiled. "It is a bit much tonight. There must be a hundred people here."

"At least," he agreed. "Why don't you tell me why you asked me to escort you tonight? Where's Kevin?"

"Working," she said.

"And you're lonely without him?"

She took a cigarette from the pack John extended. "Why don't we walk through the gardens?"

John followed Chris as they wound their way through the half-acre garden.

"Was your marriage happy?" she asked. The question was direct enough to break the ice. It was a ploy she'd seen Tory use on more than one occasion.

"You played bridge with Monica every week. Surely you heard all there was to tell."

Chris clutched her chest and pretended great insult. "Is that what you men think we ladies do at bridge? Gossip? Good heavens, no."

"Well then, what do you ladies do while we men are slaving away in our concrete jungle? Monica always came home from bridge with the most marvelous tales of who was doing what to whom."

"She didn't get them from me."

"You never struck me as the gossiping type. You're always so protective of Kevin, which brings us back to my first question. Why did you ask me to escort you this evening?"

Chris paused. She was afraid of sounding like a pampered expat wife. At the same time, she wanted to be heard. There had to be more to life than she'd been feeling for the last few days. "I think Kevin's having an affair."

"Why?"

"He's never home. He claims he's at work. But..."

"You can't see how it's possible. Is he part of Trans Oil's new venture?"

Chris's jaw dropped. Kevin insisted the venture was highly confidential. "Yes. How did you know what's going on at Trans Oil? I'm not even sure what it's all about."

John smiled. "Singapore has a well-developed rumor mill. We all know Trans Oil plans a coup of some kind. We're anxiously waiting to see what it is."

Chris picked a rose off a nearby bush. "You sound like Tory."

"Tory survives by being alert to what goes on in Lotus Land. Have you spoken to her about what you feel?"

Chris shook her head. "I'm not up to one of her lectures. She can be so certain about things."

"Your friend is a very wise woman, about everyone but herself. She sees patterns in others, which cause them harm, yet she ignores the same patterns in herself. I imagine she would lecture you if you suggested Kevin were having an affair. That wouldn't mean she was wrong."

"You work in the real world. Is it possible to spend twelve hours working every day?"

John nodded. "I moved to Singapore to open the office for my company. The first year was brutal. I didn't appreciate how hard my hours were for Monica. The brass ring was the only thing on my mind. That, and getting enough sleep." John shook his head sadly. "It practically destroyed our marriage."

"Was it worth it? The time you spent working. Do you regret it?"

"I regret many things." He smiled sadly. "I felt more alive that year than I have since. I wish I'd been able to include Monica in what was happening. But at the time, I didn't see how."

Chris nodded. She heard the pain in John's voice. "Which gets back to my question. Were you and Monica happy?"

John shook his head. "It's an old tale. I wanted children, Monica didn't. I wanted to return to Kentucky once I proved myself here. By then Monica was content to remain here forever. I owed her for the hell I put her through our first year. So we stayed, drifting further apart each year." John brought Chris's hand to his lips. "'Thank you, my dear. I needed to get some things off my chest tonight. Don't worry about Kevin. Understand this is something he has to do for himself."

Chris could tell they were about to revert to their superficial party faces. She wanted no part of the charade. John had opened up to her more tonight than Kevin had in months. "Not so fast, you must be thirsty. I am. The least you could do is have a glass of champagne with me."

Gallantly, John offered Chris his arm. It was late and the house was not so crowded. Suddenly there was a crash followed by the sound of splintering glass. They ran into the living room and saw Barney on the floor with the remnants of a glass door shattered around him. He was bleeding, his right arm turned at an awkward angle. Sarah was crying hysterically, and Tim had his arm around her.

Before Chris could offer her assistance, Geoff took control of the situation. He wrapped Barney's arm in cloth dinner napkins from the buffet table and sent Sarah for towels. When Geoff was satisfied that the tourniquet had stopped the bleeding, he brushed the loose glass from Barney's clothes with a towel and half-carried him to the car, ordering Tim to follow with Sarah.

After the four left, the room was abuzz as everyone tried to reconstruct what had happened. No one was certain. They remembered Sarah, Barney, Geoff and Tim talking before the incident. No one recalled loud voices or a disagreement.

Despite the heat, Chris was cold. This had never happened before. Everyone had a night when they drank a bit too much. But to walk through a glass door was incomprehensible. From the angle of Barney's arm, Chris guessed it was broken in at least two places. The gin in his system might act as an anesthesia temporarily, but soon he'd be in pain.

The tension in the air was broken when someone said, "That must be what they mean by the phrase blind drunk."

"Poor Sarah," Chris said to John. "I'd die if Kevin ever made a spectacle of himself like that."

"I'm sure Barney will be equally chagrined by his clumsiness," he offered chivalrously. "Would you care for a nightcap?"

Chris smiled gratefully. Barney's fall had ended the party atmosphere and Chris was eager to leave. If they stayed, she'd be forced to listen to people gossiping about Barney's behavior. His accident would be fodder for the gossip mill for weeks. She was saddened by the knowledge that her world was so small and inbred that Barney's accident would be the high point of the evening.

Kevin was asleep when she got home, the sheet already pulled to his side of the bed.

In the morning, when Chris started to tell him about Barney's accident, Kevin glared at her. "Do you have to pass judgment on the Parkers? Barney has a tough enough time living up to people's expectations, what with who his father is. It's not helpful to have his supposed friends talk behind his back."

Chris stared at Kevin in disbelief. "I'm not gossiping and you know it. I guess I expected you'd be interested."

Kevin threw his newspaper to the floor angrily. "I'm tired, bone tired. This new job is sapping all my strength. All I ask is some peace and quiet on the weekends. Is that so much?"

She felt as if he had slapped her. She couldn't have been angrier with him if he had. She stormed out of the solarium, and ran up the stairs to the bedroom in tears.

Chapter 26
SARAH

Singapore
Thursday, July 10, 1980

Sarah heard Barney's plaintive call and wondered how much more she could endure. Barney had stayed in hospital for two days. He'd been home now for nearly a week. His cuts were healing nicely, his arm was safely sheltered in plaster, but nothing improved his disposition. All he did was whinge and carry on like a child. Sarah tried to divert his attention, but they had little to talk about. Outside of drinking and gambling, Barney had no interests.

Geoff was out of town. Sarah and Tim suggested the three of them go on their Wednesday movie outing anyway. Barney refused. When he suggested Sarah and Tim go to the movies without him the previous night, they had. Today Barney was hell-bent on making Sarah pay for her decision. For the tenth time she reminded herself it had been his idea. She'd known at the time that it was a mistake to leave Barney alone for the evening. But she'd not had a second alone with Tim in a week.

They went to Tim's flat, knowing they could tell Barney about the film, since they'd each seen it before. Barney paid so little attention; he wouldn't remember he'd seen *A Man and A Woman* in Auckland.

Barney's accident had been so silly. She wanted to leave the party and Barney was adamant they stay until the bitter end. When Geoff arrived, Sarah went to him to plead her case. She'd been certain Barney would listen to Geoff. Instead he turned away, angry and drunk, and walked into the door.

Chris came over each morning and played nurse. She claimed she missed feeling useful. Barney loved the attention Chris gave him. After she left, he complained bitterly that Sarah was not as skillful. They fought about her inability to satisfy his needs the night before, loud piercing voices hurling nasty words at each other. They'd said hateful things. Unhappy as she was in her marriage, Sarah regretted some of what she'd said. The more Barney berated her, the less inclined she was to apologize.

Barney slept alone in their bedroom. With the cast on his arm, he had difficulty finding a comfortable position. The only way he could rest was to prop up his arm with so many pillows that there was no room left in the bed for Sarah. She was glad to be in the guest bedroom.

Best go see what he wants, she thought. Chris had left a few minutes earlier. She braced herself for a barrage of criticism. "Hello, love. What can I do for you?" she asked in her sweetest voice.

"I need something to drink. How about making lemonade? Like you used to make in the summer when we went to the Bay of Islands with Geoff."

Sarah smiled. "Of course. Can I get you anything else? Would you care for something to eat? How about a book to read?"

Barney groaned at her suggestions. "I hurt too much to read. Why won't the doctor give me something for the pain?"

Because you drink too much, she thought bitterly. In the hospital, the doctor had told Sarah to keep Barney from drinking.

"His body needs to mend. It will take all his strength to do so. Keep him away from alcohol for at least two weeks," the doctor ordered Sarah.

Like I have any control. Why does everyone think I'm responsible for Barney? First his parents, now his doctor. Even my friends are avoiding me because of him. After she saw Barney fill his hip flask at the liquor cabinet, she refused to give him pain pills.

"Life's unfair," she cried as she opened the refrigerator. She wasn't the one who fell through the door, yet she was being ostracized. Earlier in the morning, Janet Adams rang and suggested Sarah give a miss to the Thursday bridge game.

She wasn't in the mood to make fresh lemonade. She wanted to relish the memories of last night in Tim's arms. Since they had had time, their lovemaking had been slow and tender. Such a change from Barney, who came in three minutes and often fell asleep on top of her.

Her memories were so vivid; she could almost smell Tim's clean scent against the strong bleach the laundry used on his sheets. If she closed her eyes, she could reconstruct his room. The position of his king-sized bed, the photos on the wall, even the teak bureau, were clear in her mind.

As she carried the iced pitcher with lemonade, she heard laughter coming from the bedroom, which surprised her. She was stunned to see Tory engrossed in a tale that had Barney in stitches. Sarah hadn't heard the doorbell. She wondered how Tory had gotten into the house. Tory might breeze into Chris's house as if she owned the place, but Sarah couldn't conceive of her doing the same thing here.

Although Tory visited Barney daily, in the past he'd ignored her attempts to cheer him as steadfastly as he ignored Sarah's own. Sarah placed the pitcher and sterling silver tray on the night table and smiled tentatively. Tory wasn't her favorite person. She was always afraid Tory knew more than she should.

"Let me get another glass. Would you like lemonade? It's fresh. I just made it."

"If it's not too much trouble."

"No trouble at all," Sarah replied, happy for a reason to leave the room. The sight of the bedroom she shared with Barney was too much after her poignant recollections of Tim.

In the kitchen, she leaned against the refrigerator to catch her breath. Her heart pounded and her hands trembled. For weeks, she had experienced attacks where she couldn't seem to get enough air. They were always precipitated by an encounter with her husband. It was stress, no doubt. But they were happening several times a day now. If the symptoms persisted, she'd see a doctor.

When she returned to the bedroom, she saw Tory seated on the side of the bed showing Barney a small object resembling a calculator. He was looking at it with interest, which was absurd since he detested anything to do with figures.

"See, you push this button and the race starts. You can play against the computer. When the race is finished, you get to see who won. Here, you try it." Tory thrust the game in Barney's left hand.

"I'm not left-handed," he wailed in his most peevish tone.

"So learn," Tory answered. She took the game and put it in her left hand. "I'm not left-handed either, but I can do it. See." She smiled triumphantly and put the game on Barney's chest, well within his grasp.

Barney ignored Tory and sipped his drink through a straw while Sarah held the glass. When he had enough, he shoved the glass to the side with his chin. "It would taste much better with some gin. Sarah, please be a dear and add a little splash of gin."

"Don't," Tory ordered.

Sarah stood still in shock. *Who does Tory think she is? This isn't her house. If I give Barney a drink, maybe he'll sleep for an hour and I can get some rest.* Her head throbbed. If Barney slept, perhaps she could as well.

"That stuff will kill you one day," Tory continued, oblivious to Sarah's anger. "The heat and humidity of the tropics are hard on your body. Alcohol dehydrates you. What you should drink are pitchers of soothing drinks like this lemonade. In the long run, they'll help you feel better faster."

Sarah was indignant. She was so irritated at what she saw as Tory's reprimand, she failed to see that Tory was telling Barney what no one else would.

"I've seen you drink," Sarah snapped. Her head hurt so much she could barely see. There was no way she'd be civil to this woman for another minute.

Tory shrugged indifferently. "Sure, but in moderation. Never when I'm sick."

"I'm not crook. My arm's broken, that's all," Barney whined.

"It's just a bit longer. Why don't you and I see what we can do with this game? If you want, both of us can play. I'll show you how. Let's see who wins. Okay?"

To Sarah's amazement, Barney picked up the game and inspected it carefully. *Lovely, one more person Barney listens to. How come he never cares what I say? Why is he always so nice to other people?*

Tory turned to smile at Sarah, as if to include her in the scene. "You look exhausted. If you want to grab some shut-eye, I'll stay with Barney for an hour."

Sarah's head was in agony. "Maybe I will close my eyes for a few minutes."

Like she was watching a movie of what was going on around her, Sarah saw Tory slip off the bed, lead her to the guest room, ease her onto the divan, and shut the rattan blinds. "That should help," Tory offered.

Sarah slept until the phone rang, disturbing the blanket of silence enveloping her. As she opened her eyes, she no longer felt the excruciating pain that nearly blinded her earlier. To her delight, Tim was on the phone.

"How's it going, luv?" he asked solicitously. "How's my star nurse?"

"As well as can be expected," she sighed.

"Is he being a beast again?"

"Timothy, you have no idea. I don't know how much more of this I can stand. I just had a lie-down. I thought I'd perish if I didn't get away."

"Hmm." Tim understood what she felt. She could tell that from the soothing tone of his voice. "The natives excluded you from bridge, I see. I rushed to my flat this afternoon, hoping against hope that you'd show up. I was so disappointed not to see you."

"Oh, Tim, I'm sorry."

"Not to worry. It's not your fault. I've a suggestion, though. Why don't you invite me for dinner? We can touch toes under the table. It's not much, I know. But at the moment, it's all I can offer a beautiful damsel in distress."

Sarah agreed immediately. Anything was better than another evening spent cosseting Barney. Her breath got short and her chest constricted at the mere thought of another battle.

"Calm down," she ordered herself. Sarah practiced some ballet movements to relax before she fixed her hair and put on fresh lipstick.

When she got to the bedroom, Barney was head to head with Tory and they were in gales of laughter. Sarah tiptoed into the room, not wanting to break the mood.

"What's so funny?" she asked.

Barney looked up and grinned. "I'm beating the socks off Tory."

"I never was good at games," Tory explained. She glanced at her watch and jumped off the bed. "Gee, it's late. I've got to dash."

Tory's presence gave Sarah an inspiration. "Please don't. Tim just rang. He's coming for dinner. If you stay, we can have a foursome. Maybe we can play a board game later."

Sarah turned to Barney and smiled. "Would you like that, love? We could have dinner in the dining room and enjoy a quiet evening with our friends. I'm sure Tim would appreciate it if we asked Tory to stay. I think he's sweet on her."

"Sure," he answered absently, as he eyed the game in his hand. "C'mon Tory, let's play again. Sarah will be in the kitchen for hours and I'll be bored. If you stay, I won't have to be alone."

Barney was manipulating Tory. Since it fit in so well with her own plans, Sarah didn't mind. If Tory were there, Tim could stay after dinner. At least she could hear Tim's voice and talk to him again. It was a better idea than the three of them spending the evening together. She and Tim would have to watch their step with Tory in the house. That would be easy. They were well schooled in masking their feelings.

At first Tory refused and Sarah's heart raced. *Tory must stay*, she raged silently. *She simply must*. Sarah had no idea how to change Tory's mind. Tory lived by a set of rules only she understood. It was impossible to decide what button to push to make her agree. It was a strange predicament for Sarah, who was accustomed to knowing how to play people so they did what she wanted. While Sarah considered the matter, Barney convinced Tory to stay.

When Tory offered to help Sarah in the kitchen, she turned her down. "You could be much more help if you'd occupy Barney," she whispered conspiratorially.

Since Barney had difficulty manipulating a fork, she prepared finger foods: crudités, shrimp, satay (skewers of beef and chicken marinated in peanut sauce), and deviled eggs.

Tim was charming. His presence soothed Sarah's frazzled nerves. When it came time to clear the table, he jumped up to offer his assistance.

Tory got up as well, but Barney pulled her back to her chair. "Let's play the racing game again."

Sarah let Tim carry the platters to the kitchen. Sarah wrapped the leftovers and hummed to herself while Tim started the coffee. Once they finished their mundane chores, they flew into each other's arms and kissed.

Tim broke off their embrace. "Coffee's done, luv. Can't be too careful. I'll carry the coffee. Can you can manage the fruit?"

For a brief period in the kitchen, Sarah felt as if she were married to Tim. He helped her put things away, got cups and saucers from the cupboards, and opened the drawers for a cheese knife. He knew just what to do. He was the opposite of Barney, who could barely get himself a glass of water unassisted even when his arm wasn't in plaster.

Chapter 27
TORY

Singapore
Saturday, August 9, 1980

Tory smiled as the plane made its descent. Nearly three weeks in Kuala Terengganu made her long for the cleanliness and order of Singapore. More than that, she missed Geoff. It was an odd feeling. There were times, during other trips, when she missed the Taylors. Other than them, she never thought about the people from her other world when she worked.

The more time they spent together, the more Tory liked Geoff. She never intended him to be more than a friend, yet he was an important part of her life. Sometimes Geoff called in the early evening and suggested they meet for a walk or a cup of coffee. Tory liked that they could be alone together and not need the stimulation of a party to enjoy themselves. Without meaning to she started looking forward to seeing Geoff.

She was lost in her reverie and barely noticed the Customs Inspector go through her camera case. She stood impassively as he took the cap off a lens and peered through the wrong end, his fingers leaving oily smudges on the mirror.

She walked into the small arrival hall. Out of the corner of her eye she saw Geoff among the waiting faces along the roped-off area. She hurried to get to him.

"This is a surprise," she said.

Geoff kissed her. "Good or bad?"

"Good." She dropped her suitcase and put her arms around his neck. "Very good," she whispered.

Geoff picked up her suitcase and led her to his car. "Kevin and I were knackered. I suggested we take the weekend off."

"Chris will like that. Kev's hours are bugging her, especially with the munchkins at camp."

"Only Chris?"

Tory laughed. "I like Kev. But I don't miss him."

“That wasn't what I meant.”

Tory stopped walking abruptly, and looked at Geoff, her hands on her hips. "You want me to say I missed you?" she asked in a joking tone.

"Now why would I want that? I drive to the back of beyond to meet your plane. I'm a driver, nothing more."

"I missed you," she giggled. She kissed him, and then stood smiling. "Does that convince you?"

He shook his head. "I suppose that's the most I can expect in a car park. Would you care to stop at Rasa Singapura for dinner?"

Geoff was obviously exhausted. He had the chalky pallor of someone released from a sick-bed. “You look as beat as I feel. If you're serious about taking the weekend off, we could make a day of it tomorrow."

Geoff gave her a mock salute as he put her suitcase in the car. "As you wish."

Neither spoke while Geoff drove. Tory wondered if Geoff was upset that she didn't want to see him tonight. Geoff had never met her plane before. Coming so close after her realization that she missed him, his presence unnerved her. She wanted time to put the pieces together. Were they about to propel their relationship to a new level? Did she want that? Up to this point, the most Geoff had done was hold her hand or kiss her.

"What would you like to do tomorrow?" she asked.

"Why don't you decide? There's no doubt an arcane festival only you know of."

"How early can you be up?"

"Whenever. I'll take advantage of being home early, and go to bed before Tim gets in."

"Have you ever watched the sun rise from Mount Faber? It overlooks Keppel Harbor. You can see Sentosa and the smaller Singaporean and Indonesian islands. At first the water's cloaked in fog. Then the sky turns orange that gets paler and paler, until it's translucent."

"Your wish is my command. Tomorrow I shall be your humble servant."

She laughed at Geoff's cockney accent. He could make the simplest conversations humorous. She wondered if it was his way to avoid intimacy. Geoff had many subterfuges to dance around things that made him uncomfortable. Since she was adept at the same behavior, she recognized it.

She kissed him good-bye at the door to her apartment building. "I'll be waiting for you at 6:30. Wear comfortable clothes."

The next morning, she came out of the building as his car pulled up in the morning. As she slid into the passenger seat, she leaned over to kiss him. "Good morning."

Geoff eyed the bag she carried. "What's that?"

"You'll see. You said I could plan today and I have. These are things we'll need."

Geoff drove to the World Trade Centre where they caught the cable car to the top of Mount Faber. Tory took a blanket and spread it on the grass to protect them from the dew. She handed Geoff a pair of binoculars and pointed. "If you look over there, you'll see the small islands come to life."

Tory was on her stomach, staring at the harbor that was shrouded in what looked like dense clouds. Watching the sun come up over the harbor was one of her special things. For a while Singapore reverted to its past when it was little more than a sleepy village. Once the sun came out the oil tankers, ferries, freighters, and fishing boats would be visible. The light dispelled the myth that Singapore was anything other than a bustling port. Tory had never shared the transformation with anyone. She wondered if Geoff would think it as fascinating as she.

Geoff was silent. She looked over to see if he'd fallen asleep. The binoculars were turned on the harbor and he looked pensive.

"See something interesting?"

"It never ceases to amaze me how busy the harbor is." He continued to watch for several minutes. Then he stood and reached for her hand. "Where to next?"

"How adventurous are you feeling?" There was more color to his face than yesterday. That didn't preclude his being tired. Tory had planned two different scenarios, depending on Geoff's mood.

"Deciding how much torture I can tolerate?" he joked. "Not to worry. I'm ready for anything."

"Drive to Orchard Road. We'll eat breakfast there."

"In a restaurant? That's hardly what I expected."

Tory smiled slowly. Let Geoff believe what he wanted. Part of the fun would be showing him another world close to the chic shopping district.

Geoff parked the car. She took his hand and led him to Emerald Hill Road. As they turned on to the side street, the skyscrapers and shopping arcades were replaced by old Malacca-style shophouses. The brightly painted houses were ornamented with elaborate plaster moldings, European tiles and woodcarvings. The Peranakan architecture was from the period before air-conditioning. The terraced buildings' half-doors, called pintu pagar, boasted elegantly carved panels to keep out prying eyes and allow ventilation. Tory pointed to the recurring motifs of dragons, fu dogs, crabs, deer, and roses.

"What do they symbolize?" Geoff asked.

"Good luck, longevity, happiness." She stopped abruptly. "How'd you know they weren't decorative flourishes?"

"They wouldn't interest you if they were. You need to understand the whys and wherefores of all that goes on around you. The superficial doesn't impress you."

"Are you saying I'm jaded?"

He shook his head. "Those details took time. The carving was done by hand. There had to be a reason to go to the effort."

They dawdled to examine the intricate handiwork. Tory explained the history of the area.

"We're going to Cuppage Road Market," she announced, as she opened a door. The floor was damp from the slap of wet fish on the white tiles. At 8 a.m. the market hummed with activity. There were over a hundred small stalls, each with a crowd around it. Fresh fish, meats, vegetables, and fruit abounded. The aromas mixed together, a pungent blend of fresh fish and sweet fruit.

Tory walked to her favorite fish seller. Geoff stood at her side, watching the frenzy of activity. Salesmen with their abacuses argued over each sale. "Is there anything you don't eat?" she asked.

He shook his head. Geoff stood, captivated by the sight of a cleaver slicing rapidly through an enormous fish. There was no need to challenge him. He was enjoying the experience.

"I take it you've never been to a wet market?"

"No. Hard to conceive of this being so close to where I live. I never knew it existed."

Tory moved between the stands swiftly. She tossed Geoff a honey mango to eat while they walked. "This should hold you until breakfast."

"And where will that be?"

"The East Coast."

It was too early for the park to be crowded. They barbecued breakfast over an open pit. The coconut trees moved gently in the breeze. Tory luxuriated in the picturesque scene. After they ate, she lay back and closed her eyes. When something tickled her legs, she opened her eyes with a start. Geoff was brushing rough grass along her calves.

"Enjoy your nap?" he asked.

Tory flushed. She hadn't intended to fall asleep. "I'm sorry."

"Why? You were peaceful. You seldom look like that when you're awake. Why are you so guarded? Why must you keep me at bay?"

"Is that what I do?"

Geoff nodded. "What frightens you so? There must be a reason."

Tory jumped to her feet. "Time for a bike ride."

Geoff reached for her hand. "Please, Tory," he said softly. "I'll never hurt you intentionally. You must know that. Why must you hide behind activity?"

"Why do you have to ask so many questions? Can't you enjoy the scenery and relax?"

When she didn't answer, he dropped her hand and glared. "If I wanted a tour guide for the day, I would have hired one. I fancy spending time with you. But you've built an impregnable wall around yourself so no one can get close." When she still didn't speak, Geoff busied himself with packing the blanket and spices.

She watched his angry motions. This was not what she wanted. "Geoff," she said, her voice nearly a whisper, "be patient with me. Please. I'm trying."

"Trying is right. If we can't get past this point, there's no need to continue."

"I know," she said sadly. "I wish I could open up the way you want. It's not as simple as you make it out to be. I missed you when I was away. That's new territory for me. And it's frightening. Can't you understand?"

Geoff put his arm across her back, pulling her to his chest. "How can I understand when you refuse to explain?"

Tory didn't want Geoff to leave. If Geoff needed to hear about her past, she would tell him. "Walk with me, please. What do you want to know?"

"About you. All anyone knows is what's contained in the biographical sketches accompanying your articles."

Tory chuckled. "Ms. Winslow has made her home in Singapore for thirteen years. She travels extensively throughout Asia. Her work is varied, ranging from studies of nature preserves to the ravages of civil war."

"Where were you before Singapore? Where did you grow up?"

Tory's voice faltered. "North Dakota. On a farm. I'm the fifth of seven children. I had two older brothers and two older sisters, and a younger brother and sister."

"Had?"

Tory shrugged. "Still have, I guess. I haven't spoken to my family in years. I left home when I was sixteen."

"Why?"

"My father and I had a fight. He threw me out of the house." Tory tried to get her hand out of Geoff's and he tightened his grasp. "My father tossed me away like I was nothing more than an empty sack. No, that's not right, he would've saved a burlap bag. His own daughter didn't mean that much to him."

Geoff put his arm around her shoulders and Tory shrugged it off. "Are you happy? You know something about me. Does it make you feel important?"

"No," he whispered. "I shan't ask more questions." He reached for her hand. "I apologize."

Tory ran to the barbecue area. She shoved her things into her canvas bag. Geoff's reaction was what she always feared. Knowing about her past would make him turn away. Expats lived in a fairy tale world. They'd assume her father had a valid reason for his actions.

"Where shall we go next?" Geoff asked. "Do you still wish to go cycling?"

Tory looked at him quizzically. "I thought ..."

"That I'd take you home? No. I only wish I could say something to make what happened hurt less. But I can't."

"What were you apologizing for?"

"For making you relive something so painful. I should have respected your privacy."

Tory forced herself to smile. Geoff was not turning his back on her. "I couldn't ride a bike now. Do you mind?"

He shook his head. "I've an idea. Why don't we drive along the coast?"

Tory agreed readily. She hadn't realized how emotionally draining remembering would be. She closed her eyes while they drove. She was awake, but not in the mood for conversation. Geoff deferred to her need for silence.

She opened her eyes when the car stopped. They were at the construction site for the new airport. "Changi," she said.

Geoff nodded. He turned to face her. "I'm sorry about earlier. I hadn't the right to push you. I shan't do that again."

"Maybe it was for the best." She reached for his hand. "Could we go back to town?"

"I understand. You want to be alone."

"No. I thought we'd go to Bukit Timah. Have you been there?"

Geoff shook his head.

Tory smiled. "It's a strip of unspoiled jungle. The hiking trails are tough, but the view at the top makes it worth the effort. It's one of the most peaceful places I've ever been."

Geoff kissed her before he put the car in gear.

Chapter 28
CHRIS

Singapore
Sunday, August 10, 1980

Chris rolled over in bed to grin seductively at Kevin. "I feel so decadent. We haven't spent an entire day in bed since before Alison was born."

He returned her smile. "I told you sending the kids to camp was a good idea. Are you still thinking of meeting them in Fire Island?"

"Not if there's a chance of another weekend like this. What happened to all your work?"

Kevin laughed. "Either Geoff is worn out or he has a hot date. Is Tory in town?"

Chris hadn't heard from Tory in three weeks. "I don't know. Last time I saw her, she was going to the east coast of Malaysia. I think she's working on something for one of your competitors."

Kevin reached over and pulled Chris on top of him. "Promise me you'll find out if she's with Geoff this weekend. If so, we may have found the way to slow Geoff down."

Chris got out of bed and reached for her robe, which had fallen on the floor. "I'm getting some juice and fruit. Want anything?"

Kevin jumped out of bed. "I'll meet you downstairs in a sec."

They ate in the solarium. Kevin thumbed through the Saturday edition of the *New Straits Times*. Chris didn't mind that his attention was diverted. It was the first time in over twenty-four hours he'd been interested in more than their mutual pleasure.

Kevin had been home when she got in Friday afternoon. He was exhausted and went to bed after dinner. Saturday they never left their bedroom. They were supposed to go to a party Saturday night. Chris still hadn't called to offer their apologies for missing the event.

"How does Barney fit into your group?" she asked. She'd been surprised to learn that Barney worked with Kevin. With the way he drank, she couldn't imagine Barney having much to offer.

Kevin shook his head. "I don't understand why Geoff puts up with him. Barney bungles anything we give him. Geoff won't consider letting him go or sending him back to Marketing. Anyway, I think Phil Adams would go for his jugular if Barney went back to the institutional desk."

"Is Barney the reason for your long hours?"

"No. Geoff takes on Barney's load most of the time."

"Why?" Chris asked.

"They were friends in New Zealand."

"You're friendly with Phil. I can't see you covering for him."

"I wouldn't. Geoff says Barney has problems at home. He says he'll give him 'til the end of year to sort himself out."

"Do all men do that?" Chris was stunned that the man Kevin described as focused only on business would care about someone else's problems. "It doesn't fit with your description of Geoff."

"I know. Geoff says Barney and Sarah were good to him when he was lonely. They included him in their lives, never made him feel he was in the way. He doesn't think they're happy here. Says they're different from when he knew them before."

"How?"

Kevin shrugged. "I didn't ask."

Chris shook her head in exasperation. It was so typical of Kevin to settle for snippets of information. "Sarah's changed in the last few months. She withdraws into herself the way Tory does. Do you think it has anything to do with Barney's drinking?"

Kevin reached for Chris's hands. "I don't know. I'm not certain what Geoff means half the time. We all know Barney drinks too much. His fall indicates as much. How's he getting on?"

"He's in a lot of pain. I suggested Sarah take him to the orthopedist we went to when Marc broke his ankle. A broken arm shouldn't hurt so much after a month."

"Did she?"

Chris shrugged. She hadn't been certain her words registered.

"What does Tory say about she and Geoff?" he asked.

Chris laughed. "This is an exact quote: 'We enjoy dancing together.'"

"Dancing?"

"Get close. Pull apart. I know it sounds silly, but that's what she said. What does Geoff say?"

"It's what he doesn't say. When Tory's out of town, he works more. There've been mornings he looks like he slept at the office. He's rescheduled some trips to Greece. Now that I think about it, it was so he'd be out of town when she was. Or here when she was."

Chris smiled. "That's nice. Tory could use a man in her life."

"Why? She doesn't need or want anyone. I can't see Geoff in a relationship either. Don't make more of this than there is."

"Why would he change his schedule to match hers if he weren't interested?"

"Tory can be fascinating. You know that." He squeezed Chris's hand. "I think her unavailability appeals to Geoff. I doubt he wants a commitment. It wouldn't surprised me if he were involved with a married woman."

"And how long would he get away with that?" Chris paused. Their island community was a constant source of gossip. If Geoff and Tory were seeing each other, she'd have heard something. To date she'd not heard as much as a whisper linking their names. "Are you sure they see each other?"

Kevin nodded. "A couple of times when he's run me home, we've stopped at Tory's apartment to pick her up while we were in

Jurong. Sharing the passenger seat in the Jaguar with Tory isn't something I'd forget readily."

Chris folded her arms on her chest. "Now I know why you work so late: the thrill of having a woman sit on your lap."

Kevin reached over and pulled Chris on to his lap. "This is more like it." He nestled Chris's head against his chest. "If I want a woman in my lap, you'd be my first choice. You know that. Want to try the kids? It's night in New York. They should be back from the beach."

"In a minute. Do you want me to go home and see them?"

"Only if you want to. You seem restless lately. Is something bothering you? Do you have island fever?"

Chris shook her head. She wasn't certain what was wrong with her. "I've been feeling out of sorts since the Parker Seniors were here."

"They came at the same time the kids left. Are you still upset we let them go?"

"No. They're enjoying themselves. I haven't heard them this happy in ages. I think this was the perfect summer for them to be away." Chris shrugged. "You know how quiet this place gets in July and August."

"Has missing your friends been this hard for you before? I don't remember you being so fidgety other summers."

Chris shook her head. "The children were here. I spent so much time ferrying them to their friends' houses or having their friends over, I didn't have time to think, much less be bored."

"Are you bored? Doesn't sound like you."

"I guess. I hate that this island is so male-dominated. Tory's the only woman I know with a job. The rest of us are here like part of the scenery. I live in a style most people can only fantasize about, and I'm unhappy. I feel terribly selfish."

"Raising children is a job," he kissed her head, "and one you do extremely well. I always thought you loved your life here. If you're not happy, why not use the time the kids are gone to do the things you can't do when they're here?"

"What are they? What is it I want? I don't know why I feel so blue all the time."

"Are you pregnant?"

Chris was startled at his suggestion, and then she remembered that depression had been the first signal that she was pregnant. "If so, it's an immaculate conception. In case you haven't noticed, you've not been interested in romance in months. Not since I came back early from Malaysia."

"Chris, I've been interested. I've also been exhausted. What about John Horton?"

Chris paled. John was her friend and confidante. There was nothing sexual between them. "How did you hear?" she asked fearfully.

"Geoff. He said he saw you with John the night of Barney's accident. He thought he'd tell me before I heard it from someone else."

"You've known for a month and never said a word? I can't believe it. If I thought you were fooling around, I'd jump on you the minute you walked through the door."

"I haven't known for a month. Geoff only told me Friday when he suggested we close shop for the weekend. Guess he thought I'd hear something, if I weren't too exhausted to go to the Adams' party. It's probably a good thing we were too busy to go out last night."

Chris stared at her husband. He was smiling. "Don't you think another man would be attracted to me?" she asked defiantly.

"Chrissy, I love you. I also know you. Very well. You could no more have an affair than I'd be comfortable eating at those hawker stands Tory takes the kids to. I feel bad you're getting something from John I can't give you."

Kevin was being so accepting. There was no reason for him to feel guilty. "John and I help each other with our gardens. It's nothing more than that."

Kevin kissed her cheek. "If I had any doubts, those would've been erased yesterday. What is John giving you that I can't?"

"Oh Kev, he lets me cry on his shoulder about your hours. He explains about business and reassures me you love me."

Kevin hung his head. "I'm sorry about the time this project is taking. I didn't realize Geoff was so literal when he said the project would be time-consuming." He reached for her hand. "We've got a day. What can I do to make it up to you?"

"Hold me." Chris sighed. "I don't know what's wrong with me. I'm starting to hate Singapore and our inbred community. Do you realize we see the same people all the time? I don't really like most of them."

"You've got island fever. Why don't you get away for a few days? I can fend for myself. I only come home to sleep most nights anyway. Maybe Sarah or Tory would like to go away."

How could Kevin be so understanding? For months all she'd done was rail about the time he spent at work. Yet, instead of making an issue of things, he wanted her to be happy. She rested her head against his chest. She was unhappy and he wanted to make it better for her. He was sweet. "I love you so much, Kev. Do you think a trip would help me?"

"Something's making you sad. All your talk about male-dominated worlds and an inbred community sounds more like Tory than you. You're probably bored with the kids away. Make the most of it. Go some place and have fun. I wish both of us could sneak away for a few days."

"So do I." She closed her eyes and thought about where she'd like to go. Over the years, she and Tory often took trips in January to overcome Chris's post-holiday blues. After their journey through Taman Negara, she wasn't certain she wanted to go anywhere with Tory. Sarah had looked so miserable on Friday. Maybe a trip would cheer her.

"What are you thinking?" Kevin asked.

"That you're the most wonderful man in the world."

He patted her rump gently. "I couldn't agree more. Then you won't mind getting off my lap. My legs are going numb. Let's call the kids before we go upstairs."

In their bedroom, Kevin asked, "Will you go away for a few days? I think it would make you feel better."

"I don't know. I'll see if Sarah's interested. Since Barney's accident, she's been excluded from things. Maybe she'd be cheered up getting away for a few days. She never leaves their house. I'm worried about her."

"You're sounding more like yourself already. The woman I fell in love always worried about making everyone else feel better. I'm surprised you don't want to go away with Tory. I thought the two of you traveled together well."

"We do. Tory's been acting strange lately, even for her. Something is on her mind. She won't talk about it, but it's tearing her apart. I don't know how to help her. I wish I did."

"Why don't you ask both Sarah and Tory? Sarah's presence would keep Tory away from places like Taman Negara. I think she spends too much time in the jungle."

Chris slid into bed and reached for Kevin's hand. "I declare a moratorium. No more discussions about our friends."

"What a wonderful idea."

Chapter 29
SARAH

Singapore
Monday, August 11, 1980

Sarah hadn't seen Tim in a month. It had been too difficult to arrange. More than that, Barney needed her. If half of what he said were true, he was in terrible pain. It worried Sarah. Except for Trey, she had no experience with broken bones. Trey's plaster hadn't bothered him until it itched.

For a month she waited on Barney hand and foot. She had hoped his recuperation would give them a chance to start over. If Barney were home and sober, there might be an opportunity for them to discover mutual interests. Things didn't turn out as she imagined. Barney was impervious to cheering up. The only time he left the bed was to go to the liquor cabinet. Suggesting a game or conversation was met with stony silence, or worse, a barrage of angry words.

She made his favorite foods and fed him. Barney whined like a petulant child. If Sarah came into the bedroom and asked if he needed anything, Barney yelled at her to leave him alone. If she set lunch out by the pool, he couldn't be coaxed from his bed. If she took Trey to the park for an hour, Barney screamed that she'd been ignoring him. It didn't matter what Sarah did. She was always wrong.

She tried to understand what it must be like to hurt all the time. The closest she could imagine was the agony she felt when they fought. She wasn't sure it was a valid comparison. Were physical and emotional pains similar?

She carried a tray with skewers of satay, tiny sticky-rice cakes, which could be eaten by hand, sliced onions and cucumbers. Cautiously she opened the bedroom door with her foot. "Love, I brought lunch. Why don't we eat together?"

"I don't want food. I want my arm to stop hurting," he whined.

Sarah smiled as best she could. She hated it when Barney moaned. It usually preceded a flash of anger. "We're seeing a new doctor this afternoon. Perhaps he'll suss out why your arm hurts so much."

"I'm not going to the doctor," Barney roared. "You can get that idea out of your head this minute."

Sarah stood her ground. "You're going," she said firmly. "Chris was kind enough to ring doctor and schedule the appointment. We can't disappoint her."

Barney slapped the tray from Sarah's hands with his cast. "I said I wasn't hungry. Why don't you ever listen to me?"

Sarah kneeled down. Slowly she righted the serving tray and collected the fragments. She went into the bathroom, dampened a face cloth, and wiped up the mixture of peanut sauce and sticky rice. If she didn't get it up immediately, Barney might slip on the marble floor when he got up.

"Sarah, love, I've no intention of seeing another doctor. Now make me a drink like a good wife."

Sarah was on her hands and knees swabbing the floor. She looked up at her husband through her tears. "No. If you want a drink, make it yourself. We are going to the doctor if I must ring Geoff to carry you."

"Geoff? You think Geoff will come to your rescue? You're daft. The only woman Geoff cares for is Tory."

"Geoff most certainly would help me get you to doctor. He's as concerned as I that you're still in pain."

"And when did you find that out, pretty Sarah? Do you and he speak on the phone when I'm napping?"

"Geoff was here for dinner last night." Sarah stood. "Barney, if you don't get out of bed, I shall ring for an ambulance and have you taken to hospital. We must find out why your arm hurts. It's ridiculous that you're still in bed a month after you broke it."

"Maybe I like being in bed. Maybe I don't want to go to work. Did you ever think of that?"

"How long do you expect Trans Oil to put up with your behavior? Don't you worry that they'll give you the sack?"

Barney shook his head. "Good old Geoff wouldn't do that to me. He may not like that I'm home, but he'll not make an issue of it."

Sarah was puzzled. "What hold do you have on him? Why is he willing to cover for you?"

"Geoff was infatuated with you in New Zealand. He's embarrassed by how nice I was to him then, especially since I knew the way he felt."

"What?"

Barney laughed. "Geoff didn't like me; you were the one he wanted to be around. I liked watching him suffer. He wanted you and I had you. There was one thing Geoff's brains and hard work wouldn't get for him. It made me important. For the first time in my life, someone envied me."

Sarah paled. "What are you talking about?"

"All my life I've been compared to my father, and I've never measured up. Do you know what it's like to never be good enough? To know that no matter what you do, you'll always be an also-ran?"

Sarah wanted to believe it was the gin talking. At the same time she knew it was the truth. This was the most honest conversation they'd ever had. Perhaps it was the sign of a shift in their relationship. Sarah walked to the bed. Gingerly she sat down, careful not to disturb Barney. "Why do you stay at Trans Oil if it's so difficult for you? Wouldn't it be best if you worked for another company?"

"Doing what, pretty Sarah? What am I qualified to do? I'm no more skilled than you. We're a matched pair, the bride and groom on top of the wedding cake. With as little to offer. We're decorations."

"No, love. We're more than plastic statues. We're people. Real people. People with dreams, hopes, and fears."

"Pretty little Sarah. You believe the pabulum in the stories you read Trey. Real life isn't like that."

"It could be if we worked together. We could make more of our lives than we have."

"How much do you think anyone would pay for your supposed skills? What's the price of a nice meal or finding the perfect accent piece for a room? Not enough to live on."

"Barney, what do you want to do? What are you interested in?"

He hung his head. "Drinking. Gambling. Neither of which would keep you in dresses for a week," he said in disgust.

"Surely you must be interested in more than that."

Barney gave her a sardonic grin. "I like having you around to show the blokes I'm not the failure they think. Men like looking at you. They see you with me, and their opinion changes. There's more to me than meets the eye if I can keep you happy."

The more Barney spoke, the more Sarah's stomach twisted and turned. Barney didn't love her. She was a trophy. Although she often suspected as much, the confirmation was overwhelming. She put her hands over her ears to block out Barney's voice.

Barney grabbed her right hand and yanked it away roughly. "That's right, love. Cry. No one's here, I don't have to pretend I'm interested in you."

"Did you ever love me?"

He shook his head. "There's nothing to love. You're a shell with the right trimmings. You're the proper image of a wife, not too smart, no opinions of your own, and too comfortable in the lifestyle I provide to risk changing things."

Sarah ran into the bathroom, locking the door behind her. It was an automatic reaction, like washing a piece of fruit before giving it to Trey. She leaned against the marble countertop, shaking. Her body heaved with sobs. She couldn't stop the flow of tears. Usually crying helped her feel better. This time her tears didn't provide comfort. If anything, they worsened her mood. *And I was considering resuscitating our marriage. What a joke. It needs a funeral.*

She would take Barney to the doctor, get his arm taken care of, and then leave him. There was no reason to stay. She'd never discussed her son with Tim. Would he be willing to keep Trey? More than that, did he see Sarah as more than a decoration?

When she opened the door to the bedroom, she met Barney's belligerent stare. His mood no longer bothered her. "Get out of bed," she said as she opened his bureau. "We're taking you to doctor."

"No."

"Yes." Sarah walked to the telephone and picked it up. She dialed a number from memory. "Chris, I hate to bother you, but Barney refuses to see the doctor you recommended. Could you suggest an ambulance service, please?"

She jotted down the number while Chris spoke. As she hung up she glared at her husband. "Which shall it be? Ambulance or car?"

"Car," he said begrudgingly.

Sarah flipped through the pages of a magazine in the waiting room without seeing a word. She couldn't stop replaying Barney's hateful words in her mind. The scene repeated itself over and over until she thought she'd go crazy.

"Mrs. Parker, doctor will see you now."

In her haste to hear the prognosis, Sarah dropped the magazine on the floor and stepped on it as she followed the nurse. Barney sat in a chair in front of the doctor's desk. The doctor motioned for Sarah to take the chair next to her husband.

"You should have seen someone sooner. The arm isn't healing properly. It will have to be re-broken and set again. There's a fracture in the shoulder as well. Your husband will have to go into hospital."

"No," Barney screamed. "No hospital."

The doctor ignored him and turned to Sarah. "I can't force him. You do understand it's for the best, though. Why don't I leave the two of you to discuss the matter? After my next patient we'll talk again."

When the doctor left, Barney turned so his back faced Sarah.

"It's your life. I don't care what you do any longer," she said.

"Yes you do. You're miffed. It's a momentary thing. I'll not go to hospital."

"Fine."

"Where are the tears and pouting you're so good at? No tears left for your husband?"

"After the horrid things you said to me, what do you expect?"

"I'm sorry, pretty Sarah. It was the pain talking. You know I didn't mean what I said."

Sarah wondered what to believe. The pain from a broken shoulder might have distorted Barney's thinking. "I think you should go to hospital."

"Will you be here when I get out?"

Barney's uncertainty stunned Sarah. He must care for her if he was worried that she might leave him. "Of course, love. Trey and I will be waiting for you."

"I don't want to be in plaster for the rest of my life. Is Chris certain this doctor is good?"

Sarah nodded eagerly. "She's seen him work at Mount Elizabeth. He's the doctor she took Marc to when he broke his ankle. That should say something. Shall we ring Chris? Would that make you more comfortable?"

"Yes. Please ring Geoff as well. Ask them to meet us at hospital. I'll need courage to face this. I'm not certain I have enough of my own."

An hour later Sarah, Barney, and Chris sat with a doctor at Mount Elizabeth Hospital having the X-rays reviewed and the recommended surgery explained. All the medical jargon upset

Sarah. When she couldn't listen to any more, she went to Barney's room to unpack.

When Barney and Chris joined her, neither of them looked pleased, making Sarah's stomach lurch. She wasn't sure she could handle more bad news. "What is it?"

"Nothing, love," Barney said.

Just then Geoff rushed into the room, panting as if he'd run from the car park and up the two flights of stairs. "What's wrong? I came as soon as I could get away."

Sarah settled Barney in the bed and sat next to him.

Chris motioned for everyone to take a seat. "The night of the accident the hospital missed a hairline fracture in the shoulder. The arm hasn't healed properly since the shoulder wasn't in the right position. They operate in the morning. They'll put a pin in the shoulder to hold it in place, and re-break the arm so it can be set properly. The new cast will be different. Barney's arm will go out straight at his shoulder; his elbow will be bent upwards at a right angle. The cast will cover part of his chest."

Sarah was horrified. She couldn't blame Barney for the hateful things he said earlier. The pain must have been intolerable. She must be a horrible wife. What other explanation was there for ignoring Barney's suffering?

Chapter 30
SARAH

Singapore
Tuesday, August 12, 1980

Chris sat with Sarah during the surgery. Sarah was relieved when Geoff showed up. He wouldn't barrage her with meaningless conversation the way Chris did. He wouldn't try to divert her attention by giving her a guided tour of the hospital. Geoff was content to sit silently in Barney's room.

When Barney was wheeled into the room, he was still groggy from the anesthesia. After half an hour Geoff insisted on driving Sarah home. "Barney will sleep until morning. You and I need to have a talk."

"About what?"

"Barney and I spoke last night. He said the two of you had a row."

"Not to worry. Fighting is part of marriage."

Geoff continued. "He claims he said horrible things he didn't mean. He's worried you won't be here when he's ready to go home."

"It's not your problem, Geoff. It's ours."

Geoff nodded. "I know. This has been a traumatic experience for both of you. I think you should take a break. Go away for a few days and sort through what you want."

Sarah smiled. "Chris said the same thing. She suggested we go somewhere together. I'll tell you what I told her: I'm not interested. My place is with Barney."

Geoff shook his head. "Barney will be hospitalized for at least a week. The amah can care for Trey. You owe it to yourself to get away. You look awful."

"Thank you very much," she snapped.

Geoff stopped the car in the driveway. "I didn't mean that the way it came out. I'm concerned about you. Barney's being cared for. You're the one who needs a break. None of this must have been easy for you."

"What type of wife would I be if I left my husband now?"

"A brief holiday isn't the same as leaving him. I shall visit Barney every day. I promise."

"What can you offer him that I can't?"

"For one thing, I'll not allow him to hide from his job any longer. When his shoulder heals enough that his arm can go into a more traditional plaster, I shall insist he return to work."

"Do you think it will make any difference?"

"Staying home and feeling sorry for himself hasn't. Barney must occupy his mind. He is an adult you know."

Sarah laughed. "Was that meant to be funny? Barney's a little boy who plays dress-up. He's no more adult than Trey."

"Nor will he be if we let him wallow in self-pity. I don't know what Barney said to you and I don't care. He feels horrible about it, and so do you. Why not take a holiday with Chris and think about something else?"

"Think about what? I ignored Barney's pain. I thought he was pretending so I'd feel sorry for him. I don't deserve a holiday. I'm a sorry excuse for a wife."

Geoff looked at his watch. "As you wish. I must go. I have plans for the evening."

"Please don't leave me. I can't bear to be alone tonight."

Sarah watched Geoff consider her words. If he stayed, everything would be all right. If Geoff left, she might be tempted to ring Tim. That would be the worst thing she could do. Despite how angry she'd been at Barney, she was willing to forgive him. She'd give them one last chance to work things out. If they couldn't sort through their problems, she would leave him. Before then she and

Tim must discuss Trey. She must know how Tim felt about keeping Trey.

"Geoff, please don't leave me," she pleaded. "I'll make dinner."

"I can eat in a restaurant."

Sarah cried, hoping Geoff would acquiesce to stop the waterworks. She smiled when he got out of the car, opened the door for her and followed her into the house. Barney was wrong. Geoff still cared for her. It Barney was wrong about Geoff, it followed that he was wrong about everything.

She waited while Geoff used the phone. She looked at him carefully as he walked into the living room. "You look nice," she whispered softly. He wore gray trousers, a navy blazer, and a pale yellow Oxford cloth shirt open at the neck. A tie was stuffed in the left pocket of his blazer. It looked as if he had shaved before leaving the office. "I hope your date wasn't too cross at the change in plans."

Geoff looked at her strangely. "Not to worry. She's given me a rain check."

Sarah started to say more and Geoff interrupted. "You can stop the act now, Sarah. You've won whatever contest you imagine existed. My staying here was a judgment call. You must work things out. If my being here will help, there was no choice. Tory will understand."

"There was no contest," she argued.

"I know that. It's you who doesn't. Now sit down and think about things rationally. You and Barney can't continue as you've been. If you cannot resolve your differences, then you should separate."

"It's not an easy decision."

"Did I say it was? Barney must stop drinking. If you can't make that happen, find someone who can."

"How?"

"Speak with his parents. Perhaps they'll have a solution."

Sarah shook her head. "Barney's mother will tell me he's high-spirited. They'll not believe how out of control he is."

"You might be surprised what they'd believe. Have you ever tried telling them the truth?"

"What's the use," Sarah asked with a sigh. "Barney's father will do what he always does – have us transferred."

"Not this time," Geoff said emphatically. "He'll not be able to do that again."

Sarah paled. It was the same thing Barney Senior had told her in Sydney. "How do you know that?"

"Barney told me. Months ago. That's why I had him put in the new venture with me. He was mucking things up in Marketing. It was a matter of time before it caught up with him."

"Did you congratulate yourself for covering for him?"

"At the time it seemed the right thing to do. I see now that it wasn't. I expected he would find something of interest in the undertaking. I should have been more insistent that he carry himself. I'll not make that mistake again."

"You'll give him another chance?"

"Someone should. If I'm willing to do that for Barney, why can't you do the same for yourself? A holiday would do you good. If nothing else, it will give you the strength to face whatever's ahead."

Sarah considered his suggestion. It would be nice to get out of this tomb of a house. Sarah had never traveled with a woman. What would it be like? "What if Chris only offered to cheer me up? What if she doesn't want to go away?"

"Ring her and find out. I'll wait."

Sarah picked up the phone and dialed the Taylor's number. "Chris, it's Sarah. Were you serious about getting away for a few days?"

"Yes. Tory suggests we go to Penang. Are you joining us?"

"Tory's going?" Sarah asked. "Doesn't she have to work?"

"Apparently she thinks four days away from here would be fun. We're leaving Thursday morning. Can you let me know tomorrow? We need to make arrangements."

"Of course. Tomorrow morning." She hung the phone and glared at Geoff. "Tory's going."

"Good. She could use a break. She's been working too hard. A holiday will do her the world of good."

Sarah had expected Geoff to be irritated at her news. Why was he so accommodating? Tory must mean little to him if he was happy she was going away without him. "If Tory's going there's no reason for me to go as well."

Geoff shook his head vehemently. "All the arguments still apply. I can see where Tory might make you uncomfortable. It doesn't change anything. I'm sure the three of you would have a good time. Where are you going?"

"Penang," she said glumly. She would have to go. Geoff would give her no peace if she stayed home.

"I've heard it's very nice."

"Why did you say you could see where Tory might make me uneasy? Has she said something to you about me?"

"Tory and I seldom discuss the people we know. As for you and she, let's simply say you're opposites. When you look at the world you see beauty. You don't delve beneath the surface. You're content with appearance. Tory isn't. She wants to believe in fairy tales and happy endings, but all she knows are nightmares."

"Why?"

Geoff shrugged.

Once Geoff left, Sarah tried to make sense of everything. In less than twenty-four hours her emotions had run the gamut. She was worn out and not certain what she wanted."

She visited Barney in the morning. "How are you feeling, love?" Sarah asked, as she averted her eyes from the pulleys that held Barney's arm in the proper position. It looked like a torture device.

"Much better, Sarah. I'm so sorry about the things I said to you the say you took me to the doctor. Will you ever forgive me? I couldn't bear the thought of you're being cross with me."

Sarah ran to the bed and kissed him. "Of course. It was the pain talking. I know that."

"Doctor says I'll be here for a week. What will you do while I'm laid up?"

"Chris suggested that we go to Penang for a few days, but I'd feel horrid leaving you all alone."

"I think it's a fine idea. You could use a holiday. I'll not be good company when the pain pills wear off. Why don't you go?"

Sarah formed her words slowly. She didn't want to walk into a trap. "Barney, are you certain? I won't go if you need me here."

"No, love. A holiday's what you need. It will put a smile on your face. You look so drawn. Are you feeling all right?"

Sarah nodded. "I've a headache, that's all. Maybe a holiday is a good idea."

"Have you seen doctor about your headache? You mustn't ignore things, love. See what that did for me."

Sarah giggled. "I doubt they'll put my head in plaster for a few headaches. No doubt it's something foolish."

"Like worrying your pretty head about me. I admit I've been a beast. I insist that you go away with Chris. The rest will do wonders for you. Now when do you leave?"

"Tomorrow. I'm to ring Chris this morning and let her know what I've decided. Barney, Tory's going as well. I feel like an also-ran. Chris and Tory are so close I feel like I'll be in the way."

"That's ridiculous. Who wouldn't enjoy your company? If you take your art supplies you can sketch everything and show me when you come back. It shall give us something to share."

Sarah wasn't convinced. "Maybe I should wait until you're better and we can go together."

"Geoff won't give me any time off. He's told me as much. Says it's time I pulled my weight. I can't muck it up this time." He reached for Sarah's hand. "It would make me feel better if you went. You've given up all your activities with the wives since the accident. You deserve something nice for yourself."

"Geoff said the same thing last night."

"When did you see him?"

Sarah held her breath. She didn't want to start another row. "He came here to see you last night. We were both here when they wheeled you in after surgery. When the nurse said you'd sleep through the night, Geoff drove me home."

"Geoff's a good friend."

"You don't mind that he saw me home?"

"Why would I mind? It was a sporting thing for him to do. I'm pleased he was there to hold your hand. You're not very brave, are you?"

Sarah agreed. "Would you like me to be less timid? Would you prefer it if I were more like Tory?"

"Good heavens no. Tory doesn't need or want anyone or anything. I don't see why Geoff's attracted to her. She's so unyielding. No, love, I have what I want in you. Don't change."

Chapter 31
CHRIS

Singapore
Wednesday, August 13, 1980

The morning sun slipped through the rattan blinds into the solarium where Chris and Kevin were eating breakfast. Ever since their long weekend together, Kevin made time to have breakfast and dinner with her. "Did you mean what you said over the weekend?" she asked.

"Of course," Kevin agreed and then looked puzzled. "What in particular?"

"About my going away. I asked both Tory and Sarah. Tory's agreed. Sarah said she'd let me know this morning. She wants to speak to Barney first."

"Chris, you need to get away. For the last two days you've done nothing but obsess about the Parkers. The strain shows on your face. Geoff and I have enough to keep us up to our eyeballs in work. Where are you going?"

"Tory suggested Penang of all places."

Kevin reached for her hand. "You sound disappointed. You like Penang. Were you expecting Taman Negara or somewhere equally outrageous?"

"Penang isn't like Tory. It's too pedestrian."

"Maybe she's tired. Or remembers how you always rave about George Town."

Chris paused. It was possible but hardly likely. "Something's on her mind. And has been for months. She's retreating into her shell."

"She does that. It's nothing to worry about. Are you and she playing tennis today?"

"I don't know. Why?"

"Geoff called while you were in the shower. He said he had something to take care of and would be late getting into the office."

"And you want to know if it's business or pleasure. Wouldn't he say if it were business?"

"Not necessarily. Geoff's an odd duck."

Chris jumped up to answer the telephone. She came back to the table grinning. "That was Tory. Tennis is on. Geoff is dropping her off. Curiouser and curiouser."

"Why?"

"She sounds angry. Really angry. Even losing a job doesn't upset her this much."

"Have fun. I think I'll go into the office for sanctuary. See you tonight."

Chris thought about Tory's phone call while she waited. Her tightly controlled tone practically shouted tension. It wasn't typical of Tory. No matter what was going on, Tory usually appeared the picture of serenity. Tory had been changing recently. She no longer seemed so in control.

Halfway into their first set, after Tory had purposely aimed the ball at her several times, Chris waved her racquet above her head. "I surrender, I surrender," she called with a laugh. "You can stop your attack now."

Tory glared across the net, her racquet gripped tightly in her hands.

Chris walked towards her. "You're certainly out for blood this morning. Is it mine in particular or will any bloody form suffice?"

"I heard all the lectures I care to before I got here," Tory snapped.

Chris turned and walked towards the house. She had no idea why Tory was so upset. Likewise, she had no intention of bearing the brunt of her rage, especially if it was a physical assault.

Tory called out, "are you quitting? I thought you liked a tough game."

"I'm not a cat, I don't have nine lives," Chris yelled over her shoulder.

"What's that supposed to mean?"

Chris turned. Tory stood with her hands on her hips. Despite her tan her face was stark white. "Are you annoyed at me for something? If so, why not confront me instead of murdering me on the tennis court?"

"Why? You don't understand anything but the happy life family you have. You... Oh never..." Tory couldn't get her words out through her sobs.

Chris ran to her friend. "Have you and Geoff quarreled?"

"It depends on how you see things. Apparently he and I don't see them the same way. He's arrogant, unyielding, and uninterested in anything that smacks of compromise."

Chris chuckled at the irony. "You've just described yourself. Come inside and we'll talk about it. And don't think you can tell me to mind my own business. You've made it my business."

Tory slumped into the rattan chair and put her legs out on the coffee table. She closed her eyes and frowned. "Geoff told me both you and he think Sarah should come along on our jaunt. When I said I'd rather stay home than travel with her, he called me a spoiled brat."

Chris was happy to hear that Geoff didn't cut Tory much slack. It was time someone put a stop to her isolationist behavior. "Why would you stay home because of Sarah?"

"I don't like her."

"You don't like most people. What's Sarah ever done to you?"

"She's a simpering fool."

"Tory! What's gotten into you?"

Tory shrugged. "Nothing makes sense anymore. I feel like I went to bed one night understanding how life worked, and in the morning when I woke up the rules had changed. And no one will give me a copy."

"Then you need this trip as much as the rest of us. Did you know Barney's in the hospital again? You can imagine what Sarah's been going through. Sarah needs to get away."

Tory nodded, but didn't say a word.

"Did you see Geoff this weekend?"

"Sort of. He met me at the airport Friday night. Saturday morning we went for what I thought would be a pleasant day. Was I ever wrong."

"What happened?"

"Geoff can't leave things alone. He has to push and prod until I blurt out things I didn't mean to say."

"Like what?" Chris smiled when Tory said shrugged. "Why don't you tell me what's bugging you? Something's been on your mind for months. You haven't been yourself since Thanksgiving. That was before Geoff came into your life, so he's not at the root of the problem, he's merely a safe target."

"I told you in Malaysia – a good friend of mine died."

"Who? And why does it bother you?"

Tory jumped up. "It doesn't matter. Sorry about tennis. Are you certain Sarah's coming? I want to make the arrangements before I go back to Jurong."

"I'll call her." She paused, her hand on the telephone and looked at Tory. "Will it bother you if Sarah comes along?"

Tory shook her head. "Forget everything I've said. You're right. I need a break."

By the time Chris got off the phone, Tory was gone. At first Chris thought she'd gone upstairs to shower, and then she realized that Tory had left. *What's wrong with her? How can Tory still be upset about a death after so much time?* In all the time they'd known each other, Tory never mentioned being close to anyone. Was it someone from her family? If so, why wouldn't she just say so?

Chris went to her garden to think. As the trimmed her roses, she saw Tory in the gentle blooms. The rose was delicate, easily destroyed by too fierce a rain or a strong wind. Chris never worked in her rose beds without sturdy gloves. If she forgot them thorns pricked her. The thorns gave the flower the chance to survive. Tory was just the same. Why hadn't she noticed it before? Tory's caustic wit and standoffish behavior were her thorns. None but the brave dared come near Tory. Underneath her bristly exterior was a delicate flower that couldn't let anyone close.

Chris didn't know what to make of her sudden insight. Tory was hurting. Rather than reach out, she lashed out at anyone who came close. That must be what happened with Geoff. He came nearer than Tory could tolerate, so she stuck him with a thorn. Now he's withdrawn so he can stop bleeding.

Sarah was hurting as well. Her pain could be stopped more easily. Sarah blamed herself for Barney's hospitalization. She thought she was responsible because she'd ignored his complaints. Once Barney was better Sarah would see her behavior was ridiculous. Barney was an adult. He should have kept his appointment with the doctor. Sarah had been cooped up in the house too long. After a few days on the sunny beaches of Penang Sarah would see things rationally.

Chris wondered about her own mood. Was she still at odds with the world? The weekend with Kevin had been wonderful. For the first time in ages they talked about more than where the children were or their social calendar. She felt close to Kevin again. He missed her. That didn't stop him wanting his chance at what he saw as the brass ring. She understood how important it was to him.

She wanted to experience the same passion about something. The garden was a nice hobby, but that's all it was. It didn't fill the void in her life. She wanted to make a difference. Her recent experience with Barney's hospitalization helped focus her feelings. Finding the right doctor for the Parkers and explaining what he said to Sarah in simple terms gave her a purpose. Where would she get meaning from next? She knew one thing – she wanted to be more than the scenery.

There was no more time to think. In less than an hour she was due at the hospital. She hurried upstairs to change. At the hospital, Chris wondered why she'd bothered. All she did was fluff pillows, deliver magazines, and wheel patients to appointments. She was capable of so much more. There weren't enough nurses to care for the patients. It disturbed Chris to see a void she was barred from filling. The laws on work permits infuriated her. She wondered how Tory got around them. Much of her work was outside Singapore, yet several local companies hired her periodically. It might be a subject worth raising while they were on vacation. Perhaps Tory knew a loophole in the legislation.

At the end of her appointed three hours, Chris stuck her head into Barney's room to see how he was. He seemed to be in good spirits. Since he couldn't drink, his good mood surprised her. She'd expected him to be crawling the walls. "How're you doing?"

"Great. Great. I hear Sarah and you are off Penang for a long weekend. Sounds like a nice trip."

Chris nodded. "I'm sure it will be. Tory's coming as well."

"If anyone knows what to see there, she'd be the one." Barney looked around the room furtively. "Would you see that Sarah has a good time? It's been hard for her, what with my arm and all. She gets headaches. She needs this holiday more than she's willing to admit."

"Of course," Chris agreed. "We all want Sarah to be happy."

"Sarah's so beautiful and fragile. She's not strong. She needs to be shielded from the hard, cold realities of life. When things don't go well, it hurts her badly."

Barney sounded so loving and caring. Was this what Geoff meant by the way the Parkers were in New Zealand? "We'll see she has a wonderful time. Tory's managed to get reservations at Rasa Sayang in Batu Ferringhi. The hotel is right on the beach."

"It sounds perfect. Sarah likes beaches."

"We could stay there the entire time and not run out of things to do. There's snorkeling, sailing, sun bathing, wind surfing, and wonderful restaurants." Chris waved goodbye to Barney.

At home Chris hummed to herself as she packed. Her clothes were strewn across the bed as she decided what to take.

Kevin walked into the room and whistled at the mess. "How long will you be away? You have enough clothes out for a month."

Chris sat in the chaise lounge and frowned. "I can't make up my mind."

"Put wheels on the closet," Kevin suggested.

Chris laughed. Kevin enjoyed teasing her about how much she packed. "Silly, isn't it? Tory will have nothing but a carry-on and she'll look smashing."

"How hard can it be to throw khaki shorts and a safari shirt into a suitcase? That's all she ever wears." Kevin eased himself on to the chaise with Chris. "Geoff was with Tory this weekend. I think we've found the key to taking his mind off the office."

Chris shook her head. "I don't think so. Tory was hyper today. I've never seen her so agitated."

Kevin looked perplexed. "Something doesn't add up. I asked Geoff how his weekend was and he wore me out listening to the things they did. He sounded like he enjoyed himself."

"Tory was furious at Geoff when she got here."

Kevin smiled indulgently. "They were supposed to go to an art exhibit last night. He backed out at the last minute to stay with Sarah after the surgery."

"That explains why she doesn't want Sarah coming with us. Is it possible she's jealous?"

"Never happen. Not Tory."

Chapter 32
TORY

Penang, Malaysia
Thursday, August 14, 1980

When the trunk of the Parkers' car opened at Paya Lebar Airport, Tory bit the inside of her lip to keep from laughing. Between Chris and Sarah there was enough luggage for a year, not the five days they'd be gone. She didn't say anything, since she'd promised herself to be pleasant, if only to keep Chris off her back.

Despite her dislike of the over-priced hotels in Batu Ferringhi, she'd booked them into the one most favored by expats. It was a far cry from the guesthouse she preferred, but this trip wasn't for her. She only agreed to go because she was between assignments and it seemed to matter to Chris. Besides, if she stayed in Singapore, she'd be alone with her thoughts.

The trip would provide a diversion and get her away from Geoff. *How could I have thought I was interested in him?* After the scene at East Coast Park he stopped asking questions about her past. His questions might be below the surface, but they weren't buried deeply. If they spent time together Geoff's curiosity would get the better of him. Several times she'd watched him stop himself from saying something. It was only a matter of time before he interrogated her again.

In George Town Tory smiled indulgently when Sarah wanted to take a trishaw to their hotel. "Someone has to go by taxi with the luggage. Why don't I?" Tory volunteered.

After she registered them in the hotel, Tory scoped out the suite. There were three bedrooms and a living room. One of the bedrooms was on the opposite side of the communal living area. She claimed it before the others arrived.

Chris poked her head into Tory's room when she got to the hotel. "Are you okay?"

Tory was on her stomach, stretched out on her bed, a book in her hands. "A little tired. What do you want to do?"

Chris walked into the room and sat on the bed. "What's your favorite spot?"

"Maku Head or Rope Walk, depends on my mood."

"I don't think I've been to either. It's lunchtime. Why don't we eat the restaurant on the beach and get our bearings?"

"Sure. Let me know when you want to leave. And Chris, just so you know, I may go off by myself part of the time."

"What's bothering you?" Chris asked. "Yesterday you were manic, today you're morose. If you say it's a death one more time, I swear I'll scream."

"Yesterday I told you I didn't know. It's the truth."

After Chris left, Tory threw her book across the room. How could she explain what she didn't understand herself? For the last five nights she'd been plagued by nightmares. She'd wake up screaming, the bed drenched with sweat and looking like a war had been fought in it. When she turned the light on, she couldn't remember what had so terrified her.

At lunch she yawned frequently.

Chris laughed. "Too much night life?"

"Too much of something, that's for sure," Sarah added.

"My schedule's been a killer. Think I'll spend the afternoon napping on the beach."

"Darn. I was hoping you'd take us to see the sights," Sarah said.

"It's better to start fresh in the morning," Tory said before Chris complained that she was being antisocial. "I booked a car and driver to take us on a tour. We'll start in George Town and follow the road south. We'll visit Kuan Yin Temple, Wat Chayamangkalaram, Kek Lok Si, Nattukotai Chettiar, Ayer Itam Dam, the Botanical Gardens, have lunch at a restaurant, and spend the afternoon at a wonderful beach."

Chris laughed at the recitation. "For a second I thought you planned to spend your vacation in one place. Are we supposed to know what all the places are? I've never heard of them and I've been here several times."

Tory shrugged indifferently. "Part of Penang's beauty is the way it blends Chinese, Malay, Indian, and European cultures. Visiting the places of worship would give you an insight into the island. The similarities and differences are amazing. Sarah, if you brought your sketch pad there are some fascinating details in these places."

While Sarah went to the suite to call Barney, Chris followed Tory to the beach. "What's up with you and Geoff?"

"Nothing."

"You said you liked dancing with him. Since I doubt you meant that literally, I'm curious."

Tory shrugged. "I can't explain it better than that."

"Tory! You're a writer. How would you put it if you were describing someone else?"

Tory closed her eyes. "These two people are attracted to each other. But, for their own reasons, each of them is afraid. When things get too close for her, when he reaches for that part of her she doesn't want anyone near, she pulls back so he can't hurt her. He's no better. He does all the right things, knows just what to say. But, when she tries to tug him out of his comfort zone, he picks a fight so he can return to safety."

"Why don't you do what you always advise me to do and force the issue?"

"I planned to. Tuesday night in fact. But Geoff got caught up with Sarah. Last night he had a meeting. When we get back to Singapore, I'm off for ten days in scenic downtown Jayapura."

"If this relationship matters to you, you should spend more time in Singapore. With your travel schedules, Geoff will be transferred before you realize the music ended and it's time to stop dancing."

Tory looked at Chris as if she spoke in tongues. "I won't build my life around a man, and I won't ask him to change his schedule to accommodate me. If this thing we have matters, really matters, we'll work it out."

"Ask him? Ask him? You need a reality check. Women don't ask men. They take what the man offers and that's that. Believe me, I know."

Tory shook her head vigorously. "No! I absolutely refuse to accept that. If Geoff has a meeting and it messes up some time we might've spent together, that's too bad. Likewise if I have a job I get on a plane, even if it doesn't fit into his schedule."

"How can you be so positive? How can you be sure going to Irian Jaya won't blow things?"

"'Cause if it does, he wasn't worth my time." Tory saw the incredulous look in Chris's eyes and continued. "There's a part of me that wants to cancel this assignment, but it'd be the worst thing I could do. Geoff and I had all the togetherness we could handle last weekend. Time apart is what we need right now."

"Are you getting even with him for canceling an evening with you to stay with Sarah?"

"Life in a goldfish bowl," Tory laughed. "Is all this intrigue really necessary? Geoff and the Parkers are friends. He helped Sarah. So what? It didn't stop me from doing what I wanted." Tory paused. "How are things with Kevin? Did you have a nice weekend?"

Chris beamed. "It was wonderful."

"Then why are you here? Why'd you leave Singapore if things are good?"

"Kev says I have island fever. I think he's right."

"It's more than that. Something's bugging you."

"How can you tell?" Chris asked.

"You're pushing for happy endings. You think a vacation will heal Barney and Sarah's sham of a marriage. You're making way more of this stuff with Geoff and I than there is. When you get that caught up in making sure everyone else is happy, you're not comfortable with yourself."

"Don't project your bad mood on me. I'm not the one running away," Chris snapped.

"Yes you are. At least I know what I'm running form. Do you?"

Chris stormed off the beach and Tory rolled on her stomach so the sun could bet down on her back. If Chris wanted to hide from what was bothering her, it was her choice. Tory had enough on her mind without adding Chris and Kevin to the list. She wasn't sure why she felt so low. Why did she run when Geoff got too close? Every time her phone rang this morning she ignored it, afraid it would be Geoff. For a brief period Saturday morning she thought they were making progress. He'd enjoyed the places they visited and the things they saw. But when they stopped doing things he bombarded her with questions. She couldn't see why he was so insistent on knowing about her past. It had nothing to do with them.

She fell asleep on the beach without resolving her questions. She opened her eyes when she felt someone tugging at her arm. She shielded her eyes from the sun, squinted, and saw Sarah in a floral sundress. "Guess I fell asleep," she mumbled.

"It's nearly dinner time. We booked a table at the revolving restaurant at the top of the hotel. If you hurry you can shower, dress, and meet us for cocktails."

Tory grimaced. An over-priced restaurant was the last place she wanted to eat dinner. Remembering her promise to be accommodating, she smiled. "It's probably better if we eat here tonight. We're getting an early start in the morning."

"Hurry," Sarah urged. "Chris wanted to ring Kevin before dinner. She'll be waiting for us."

Over dinner Tory asked what Chris and Sarah had done during the afternoon.

Sarah giggled. "Nothing as lazy as you. I watched the sailboats and sketched."

"I read. Under the safety of an umbrella," Chris said.

"Don't you worry about your skin lying in the sun?" Sarah asked. "You'll be dark as a betel nut if you're not careful."

"With skin as rough as a rhinoceros," Chris added.

Tory shook her head knowingly.

"And why should you be impervious to the ravages of the sun?" Chris asked sarcastically. "Do you have a secret potion that keeps you from aging?"

"Not one you'd approve of. I visit a Chinese apothecary on Telok Ayer Street."

Chris laughed. "Why mix roots and hers with moisturizer so readily available?"

"What's wrong with that? The Chinese were the great healers before we Westerners got hung up on better living through chemistry. There's a lot to be said for some of their remedies."

"Why do you have to be so perverse?" Chris asked.

"Because I do it so well," Tory parried neatly.

Sarah smiled as she pushed her chair away from the table. "I want to ring Barney. What time are we leaving in the morning?"

"Seven," Tory announced.

The second Sarah was out of earshot Chris attacked Tory. "If you can't be civil, please go home. We came here to unwind. I'll not have you ruin our vacation because you're mad at the world."

"Really?"

Chris nodded for emphasis. "You enjoy being miserable. You don't have the right to inflict your mood on us. And that's what you're doing. Sarah has enough on her mind without having to cope with your caustic side."

"And what does pretty Sarah have to worry about? Has she broken a fingernail?"

"Sarah's suffered a great deal with Barney's arm. She needs time for herself."

"Things happen in life. And they're not always nice. You make Sarah sound as if she needs to be sheltered from life. What is she – a hothouse flower?"

"Maybe. I see her as an orchid. Too delicate to survive the harsh, cold realities you seem only too willing to push into her face."

"Such as?"

"You've been sulking all day because Geoff chose to help out an old friend and missed a gallery exhibit you were more than capable of going to on you own. This afternoon while you were off pouting, Sarah wanted to know why you hate her."

Tory sighed. "I told you before. I don't like her."

"Since you merely tolerate most people, that's hardly a news bulletin. You're using Sarah as the target of what's bothering you and it's not fair. If something's on your mind, then deal with it. Don't make the rest of us responsible for the fact that you're unhappy."

"Who died and put you in charge of the world?"

"Me. You expect us to tolerate your mood because of some vacuous complaint you refuse to explain. But when Sarah's depressed you refuse to grant her the same rights you so readily claim for yourself. It's not like you to be so mean and I won't tolerate it."

Tory put her hand out to stop Chris from leaving the table. "You're right. I've been rude. I'm sorry."

"That's it? You're sorry."

"I'm sorry. I'll keep my mood to myself in the future."

"What's bothering you?"

"I wish I knew. Think I'll go to bed and see if I can sleep it away."

Chapter 33
SARAH

Singapore
Tuesday-Wednesday, August 19-20, 1980

Sarah hummed as she painted. Penang had been delightful. For five days she hadn't thought about Barney, Trey, or Singapore. Since neither Chris nor Tory required a constant companion, she had had time to indulge her art.

She had never left the hotel grounds alone. Despite Tory's claim that it was safe to take a taxi into George Town, Sarah couldn't. If someone weren't with her, she stayed within the hotel grounds. She didn't know why Tory felt compelled to leave the hotel. There had been more than enough to see inside the hotel grounds.

Barney would be released from the hospital tomorrow. She'd visited him earlier in the day. His good mood had persisted, even while she was away. Maybe things would be all right between them. He seemed genuinely interested in the things she'd done on her holiday. He'd been amazed when she told him about snorkeling.

She was painting watercolors of the fish and coral to show him. It would be pleasant to share that part of her journey. The underwater world fascinated her. She wasn't certain she'd captured the mood properly, but she knew the aquatic life was true to form.

The phone rang, startling her. She grabbed the receiver. "Hello?"

"Hi, luv. How are you? I haven't heard from you in ages. Did you have a good time in Penang?"

"Tim, how good to hear from you. Penang was spectacular. How did you know where I was?"

"Geoff. He said you'd gone with Tory. Why would you do something like that? I've warned you she sees too much."

"Oh, Tim," Sarah giggled, "she was fine. A tad vacant at times. Nothing like the meddler you make her out to be."

"Luv, don't believe everything you see with Tory. She's a chameleon; she changes with the circumstances."

"If you say so."

"I do. You'll have to trust me on that. Tory will be trouble for the two of us if we're not careful. Now tell me about your holiday."

"It was wonderful. I enjoyed myself. I feel ready to face the world."

"Why don't you come over and tell me about it? Hubby will be home tomorrow. I'm dying to see you."

"That would be grand. Can you get out of work?"

"For you, always. When can you be there?"

"An hour."

"Fine, luv. See you then."

Sarah smiled as she changed. She hadn't seen Tim in over a month and she'd missed him. Suddenly, the change in Barney lost all importance. The mere sound of Tim's voice caused her heart to race.

Sarah rang for a taxi, and then put the finishing touches on her makeup. Although she could use Barney's car and driver, she decided against it. There was no reason for the driver to know her movements. She went in to say good-bye to Trey and tell Ah Soon that she'd be out for the afternoon.

On a whim, she carried two watercolors. Since Tim had taught her to snorkel in Phuket, he might enjoy her renderings. The fish and coral were similar to what they'd seen together.

Tim opened the door to his flat with a flourish. Sarah propped her painting on the floor against the wall and flew into his open arms. After their embrace, Tim picked up the paintings.

"These are good, very good. I never realized you were so talented, luv. Why don't you display your work in your house?"

"Barney thinks it's amateurish. He'd rather we display works of art."

Tim took the paintings and walked to the sliding glass door of the balcony, to see them in the sunlight. "But luv, these are art. If Barney won't allow the paintings in the house, may I have them?"

Sarah was touched by his question. Without meaning to, she started to cry.

Tim put his arms around her shoulder. "I'm sorry, luv. I didn't mean to make you cry. What's the matter?"

"How can you be so nice to me, especially after I've ignored you the past month?"

Tim patted her back and led her to the couch. "Sarah, luv. I know how difficult Barney's being underfoot must have been. I didn't want to be in the way. Please believe me, I missed you. Why else would I have been so anxious to see you again? You haven't changed your mind about us, have you?"

"I love you. I know that. It's just, I owe Barney so much."

Tim took an appraising look at Sarah. "What is it you think you owe him? He's a lush. All you are to him is a prize, something he won. Or something his parents bought him. Does he love you the way I do?"

Sarah shook her head. Barney might be kind and thoughtful at the moment, but she'd seen the same pattern before. And each time, Barney had started drinking again, dashing her hopes of a better marriage. It was difficult to separate what she felt from what she wanted to believe.

"Tim, I love you. If I left Barney, would you be willing to take Trey?" As soon as the words were out, Sarah felt queasy, wondering what his answer would be. It made her think of a prisoner's wait for a jury to bring in a verdict of life or death. If Tim wouldn't take Trey, what would she do? Barney was barely capable of taking care of himself, much less a child. She might have no choice but to remain with Barney.

"I must admit, luv, I'd never thought about that. I always pictured the two of us having a few years to ourselves before we started a family." He took her hand and brought it to his lips. "But I know you'd miss your son. Of course, Trey must live with us."

Sarah threw her arms around his neck. Tim's answer was perfect. Now, she could make up her mind without worrying about Trey.

Tim picked Sarah up and carried her to the bedroom. Slowly, he undressed her.

When they finished making love, Tim rested on the pillows and smiled. "A son. That could be a bit of alright. We must start making plans, luv. We can't let things keep drifting as they are. Have you any thought to when you'll tell Barney you're leaving?"

She shook her head. "I thought I should wait until he returns to work. Once he's got something to occupy his mind, I won't feel so bad leaving."

"When will that be?"

"I'm not sure. Doctor said his shoulder should be healed in another month. When that happens, his arm can go into a different plaster. I think Geoff plans for him to return to work as soon as possible."

Tim nodded. "I doubt Geoff will cover for him any longer. This project of his is too important to him."

"What's it about?"

"I'm not sure. He told me once, when we were in Auckland, but I didn't pay attention. Geoff's always been fascinated with this idea. I found it boring, so I never listened."

That night Sarah slept peacefully. It was reassuring to know that she could go to Tim if things didn't work out with Barney. Although she wanted to believe Barney's current mood would continue, she knew better. This time she wouldn't build false expectations. She'd wait and see, content in the knowledge that she and her son would be taken care of.

When she got Barney home from the hospital the following morning, she settled him in his bed and brought Trey in to see him. She left Trey on the bed showing Barney his new puzzle while she went into the kitchen to see about lunch. The next thing she heard was Trey crying. He came running into the kitchen and tugged at her hand.

"Daddy's sick. Make him better."

Sarah reached down and picked him up. "You getting heavy. Let's take you to Ah Soon and Mummy will see to Daddy." Sarah left Trey with his amah and hurried into the master bedroom.

Barney had passed out, his left hand dangling above his hip flask. Sarah winced. They'd been home for an hour, how had he gotten to the booze so quickly? The half-body cast would have prevented him from getting to the liquor cabinet. Had the bottle been stashed in his nightstand? The thought made her shiver.

Sarah picked the hip flask off the bed and took it to the bathroom to empty the contents into the sink. She then picked up the flask by her fingertips and carried it to the kitchen trash bin. Although the flask was sterling silver, Sarah carried it as if it were likely to explode. Disposing of something valuable was symbolic in her mind. It was the start of Sarah's leaving.

Her task completed, she found Trey and ate lunch with her son. There was no need to upset him because of his father. Trey was young enough to accept his mother's explanation that his father was tired and taking a nap before lunch.

Chapter 34
SARAH

Singapore
Friday, October 3, 1980

"Bye, love," Sarah called to Barney as the driver pulled the car out of the driveway. *Thank goodness he's out of here,* she thought.

Sarah's headaches got worse each day. When she went to a doctor, he told her it was stress and prescribed tranquilizers. The medication did little to alleviate the pain. *What am I supposed to do?* she asked herself over and over.

In the past month, she'd rung Geoff several times. He'd been strangely distant each time. He'd listen to her for a minute or two, then tell her he had important matters to attend to and would ring her back. He never did. She didn't understand why he refused to come to her rescue. He'd been happy to accept the role of protector when they lived in Auckland.

She needed someone to talk to, someone to protect her from her emotions. She considered ringing Chris, but what could she say? Sarah wouldn't feel comfortable pouring out her heart to another woman. Besides, Barney and Kevin worked for Trans Oil. Chris probably told Kevin everything she heard from the other wives. *Couples in good marriages do that*, Sarah thought angrily.

Sarah was shrouded in a world of fear. She jumped if she heard a loud sound, walked on eggshells when Barney was home, fearful of saying something that might send him into a rage. Most of her day was spent wandering aimlessly through the house.

When she looked at her watch, she'd see that two or three hours had passed and she had no idea where the time had gone. From time to time she'd pick up a magazine, then toss it down in disgust. She couldn't concentrate. Even cooking lost its allure. What was the sense in preparing meals no one ate?

Now that Barney was out of the house, Sarah wanted to plan her leave taking. She considered several ways of telling him. For each scenario, she tried to imagine his response. It was difficult. Even at the best of times, she had little idea how he thought. She must speak with him before he had his first drink, which meant she must do it on a night he came directly home from the office.

That night, Barney came home from work drunk and enraged. He was shouting as he walked into the house. His voice was strange. She couldn't make out his words; they were obstructed by what sounded like tears. While ranting and raving, he went into the dining room and slammed his plaster encased right arm down on her crystal collection. Methodically he destroyed each and every piece.

Confused, Sarah ran to his side, grabbed his cast, and pleaded with him to stop. She had no idea if her words registered. He gave no indication he'd heard her. When she continued to tug at his arm, he hit her in the face.

To avoid Barney's wrath, and to protect her son, she ran into Trey's bedroom. Trey was asleep. She crouched in the furthest corner of the room, between the nightstand and the wall, and cried. The sound of Barney breaking things echoed throughout the otherwise silent house. When the sounds changed, she realized he'd gone into the kitchen. He was clearly out of control. She'd have to do something before he hurt himself.

In desperation, she rang Geoff. Her voice congested with tears, she whispered into the receiver, "Geoff, you must help me."

"I was just walking out the door."

"Geoff, he's mad, absolutely mad. You must stop him. He's breaking everything. I'm afraid he'll hurt me or Trey," she cried.

"Who?"

"Barney," she whispered as loudly as she dared. "Geoff, please. Someone must stop him. When I tried, he hit me. I'm frightened."

"Ring the police."

When Geoff hung up, Sarah cried all the more. She cowered on the floor and prayed Barney wouldn't come into Trey's room. Barney was crazy. There was no other explanation for his behavior. What should she do?

Suddenly the house became quiet. The silence was more frightening than the loud rampage had been. Had Barney's furor abated or was he simply catching his breath before deciding what to attack next?

A few seconds later, she heard the car start. *He can't possibly drive with the plaster on his arm. He'll be back as soon as he tries to get the car into gear*, she reassured herself. Then she heard the screech of tires as the car turned from the driveway to the road.

She turned and stared at her son's sleeping form. Sarah was relieved that he'd slept through the ordeal. She brushed his hair off his forehead and kissed him. She waited in his room a few minutes to see if the sudden calm woke him. When he rolled on his side and put his thumb in his mouth, she left.

She walked into the living room slowly, like a sleepwalker. There didn't appear to be one piece of furniture Barney had missed. The beautiful pillows she had covered in silk fabrics were torn and strewn across the room. All the artifacts she'd so painstakingly bought were broken. Not one piece of furniture was standing upright.

Suddenly there were headlights in the driveway. She hid behind the fallen sofa for protection. Her heart pounded as she readied herself for another siege.

To her surprise, she heard Geoff call her name as he came up the walk. She ran to him and buried her head in his chest, sobbing.

Geoff whistled when he saw the hodgepodge that had once been the living room. "Where is he?"

Sarah sniffed back her tears. "I don't know. I... um... he..."

"Did Barney do this?"

"He's crazy," she cried. "I told you I needed help."

Geoff patted her back. "I got here as quickly as I could. Not to worry. I'll take care of you now. Where's Trey?"

"He's sleeping."

"What set Barney off? Did you two have a row?"

Sarah shook her head. "He got home a bit after seven. He was drunk. He walked in and started smashing things. He was screaming. I couldn't understand a word he said."

Geoff continued to rub her back in small round circular motions. "Shh, Sarah. It's over now."

"How could he do this?"

"Sarah, go make some tea while I straighten the furniture. When you come back we'll develop a plan of action."

"I can't leave," Sarah shrieked.

"Who said anything about leaving? It's time you and I had a long talk."

Sarah eyed Geoff skeptically. She was terrified at the prospect of being alone again, even if only for a minute or two.

As if sensing her dilemma, Geoff gave her a gentle shove in the direction of the kitchen. "Sarah, please. It will make you feel better to do something. When you come back, we'll talk about what went on and decide what to do next. Please go. I have a call to make."

"To Barney?" she screamed.

"Don't be ridiculous."

Sarah burst into tears when she walked into the kitchen. Barney had broken most of the dishes and glassware. As she put the kettle on the stove, she was thankful that neither she nor Trey had been hurt. When the teakettle whistled, she poured boiling water into the warmed teapot and started her tea-making ritual. Geoff had been right. It was comforting to have a familiar ceremony to perform. It made her feel in control of her world.

When she returned to the living room, Geoff had fixed the furniture to upright positions. Although it had been turned over, none of it was broken. She placed the tea tray on the coffee table and smiled shyly at Geoff.

Geoff rubbed his forehead. "Sarah, I know about you and Tim. No doubt Barney suspects as well and that's why he went on this rampage."

Sarah was furious. How dare Geoff blame her for what happened. Couldn't he see how frightened she was? Barney was the cause of their problems. Only a fool wouldn't see that. And Geoff had never been a fool. "All this time I thought you were my friend," she replied angrily.

"That's why I'm here. You have to decide, you know. You can't keep them both indefinitely. Sooner or later you must make up your mind which one of them you want. The quicker you do it, the faster things will be resolved."

"It's not an easy decision," she answered. The prospect of leaving her husband and taking up with Tim had been haunting her for the past month.

"You and Barney can't continue to rip each other apart."

Sarah nodded slowly. "Barney only attacked things that matter to me. His and Trey's things are unscathed. That proves it. Barney hates me."

Geoff eyed her skeptically. "You know better than that."

Sarah frowned. Geoff was forcing her to face reality. Slowly, she spoke. "Barney hates himself. He suspects what I feel. He can't face the thought of another failure."

"I think you're right. That should tell you something."

"Yes, it does. Someone helped him put the pieces together. Tory! She's the one. She turned Barney against me."

"Why would she do that? After Barney's accident she visited him daily. I had to go to Greece. I asked her to look in on the two of you."

"You asked her to come to my house and spy on me? How dare you."

Geoff stood and walked towards the front door. "I refuse to listen to this. You do yourself a disservice when you try to make others responsible for your life."

"You can't leave me here alone. Geoff, you can't. I couldn't bear it," she cried.

Geoff turned and stared at Sarah, a cold look in his eyes. "I'll stay and wait for Barney. But there's a price involved. One I'm not certain you'll want to pay."

Sarah thought she understood his comment. Geoff had always had a crush on her. So what if he wanted to take it past the fantasy in his mind? Nothing mattered to Sarah but her safety. She walked towards him.

Geoff pushed her away. "Don't," he ordered. "I've no desire to be included on your list of ardent suitors any longer."

"What do you want?"

"It's not healthy for Trey to live with this kind of stress."

"What do you know about children? You've never had one."

Geoff's eyes got cold, and for a moment, he looked as if he hated her. "I was one. A long time ago." Geoff sipped his tea. His tone less angry, he started to speak. "Take Trey to visit your mother. In fact, leave him in Australia while you sort through what you need to. There's no reason he should suffer because his parents are hell-bent on making each other miserable."

"Since when did you become the great protector of children? You've never evidenced the slightest interest in Trey before."

Geoff walked towards the window, turned, and gave Sarah a distant stare. "Someone must protect him from his parents. Go to bed, Sarah. I'll wait for Barney. Please consider what I've said. Because the next time I shan't cancel my plans."

Sarah stood, tears falling silently down her cheeks. "I always thought you liked me. I know you cared a great deal about me before. How can you be so hateful now? What did I do to make you change? Are you jealous of Tim?"

"It doesn't matter."

"Yes, it does. I must know. We had such lovely times. You were my friend. You liked me. Why did it have to change?"

"I didn't like you, Sarah, I worshipped you. You could do no wrong in my eyes. You were the paragon of womanhood. I compared every woman I met to you, and always found them lacking. No one measured up to the perfect Sarah. With Tory's help, I took off my rose-colored glasses, and saw you as human, not the creation I'd conjured up to fill a need I had."

"This is Tory's handiwork."

Geoff shook his head. "Not the way you think. Tory showed me what it was like to be involved with someone who wanted nothing from me other than my presence. She doesn't need anything from me."

"Everyone says she's a bitter, twisted woman."

"Considering the fact that she worried about you when the expats closed ranks, I find that a harsh assessment. Except for Chris, who else visited you and Barney?"

"You said you asked her to."

"She'd been here before she and I spoke. Go to bed, Sarah. I'll pick up as much of this mess as I can."

Sarah couldn't believe anything that had happened in the last two hours. Nothing made sense. Geoff's tone was so final. It was obvious he'd brook no further discussion.

She went into the guest bedroom and fell into the bed in tears. Until tonight, she thought the subtle changes in Geoff's demeanor were the result of his long hours at work. She presumed his travel schedule was the source of his withdrawal. Now she couldn't be certain. Something had made him change, just like something had changed Barney.

It's Tory. It must be Tory. That was the last thought Sarah had before falling asleep.

Chapter 35
TORY

Singapore
Friday-Saturday, October 3-4, 1980

"Damn it," Tory muttered as slammed the phone down. She stormed around the living room to blow out the candles. *So much for romantic moods*, she scoffed.

She and Geoff had planned a quiet dinner at her apartment. Now that he canceled, she wanted to eliminate all traces of her preparations. Hopefully his memory could be erased as readily. She cleared the place settings from the table, turned the oven off, replaced the classical music tape with a tape of the jungle, changed into shorts, leaned with her head against the sofa, and closed her eyes.

It no longer mattered how attracted she was to Geoff. The torment he caused was intolerable. While in Irian Jaya she had decided to answer his questions, if that's what would propel them into a future. For the past two days she'd steeled herself against the pain the revelations would cause. Then, at the last minute, Geoff changed his mind about dinner. How long was she expected to maintain the intestinal fortitude necessary to have this discussion?

She fell asleep and wakened to the ringing phone. "Hello?" she whispered sleepily.

"Tory, please tell me you understand."

Geoff was whispering. Tory lowered the tape player to hear him. Since she didn't understand, she chose not to answer.

"I apologize. You must believe me. This is important."

"Isn't it always?"

"Yes. How about tomorrow?"

"I'm busy."

"You said I could have a rain check. You're leaving Sunday. Tomorrow's all there is."

She heard the pleading in Geoff's whispered words. It took all Tory's strength to say, "And I said I have plans."

"Can't I join you?"

Despite her irritation, Tory smiled at the thought of her morning excursion. It would be a good place to talk. In many ways it might be easier than her apartment. "Meet me at 6 a.m."

"I can't. Not that early."

"Why don't you call me when you can fit me into your schedule? If I haven't left, we'll go together."

"Tory, please wait for me."

Something in Geoff's tone tugged at Tory's heart. She felt herself weakening, despite her intentions to the contrary. "All right," she answered, wanting to kick herself when she heard the words come out of her mouth.

"Thank you," Geoff said as he hung up.

Tory nearly threw the phone across the room. She looked at the clock. It was past midnight. Too tired to think, she went to bed.

It was nearly 10 a.m. when Geoff called. While she waited for him to get to Jurong, she carried her duffle bag and then two jerry cans of water to the street.

Geoff shook his head when he saw the paraphernalia at her feet. "You should have waited. I would have helped."

"I've told you before, I'm quite self-sufficient. I make this trip once a month. I'm used to fending for myself."

Geoff stepped back as if afraid what her next words might be. "You were cryptic on the phone. Where are we going? If I don't know, I can't drive."

Tory smiled. She'd never told him where they were going. "Jardine Steps," she answered tersely.

Geoff didn't look like he'd slept. She wondered what he'd been up to. From the expression on his face, it hadn't been pleasant. He drove in silence. Tory looked out the window without speaking. Normally she left at daybreak so she could watch the sun rise over Mount Faber. The sun was high in the sky now. Things would look different.

When they reached the ferry building, Tory and Geoff carried her packages to the wharf, where they rented a small powerboat called a bumboat. Tory started the engine.

Geoff turned his face towards the sun. "That feels good. Am I to be permitted to know where we're going?" he asked cautiously. He was doing his best to sidestep her anger.

Her tone less caustic, she said, "Pulau Sakeng," certain he'd never have heard of it. Few people had. "It's a little island about forty-five minutes from here. It's similar to where I lived with Anna. You're always so interested in my past. I thought you'd like to see what it was like."

"What's in the jerry cans?"

"Water. There's no fresh water on the island. When I visit I always carry some for my friends. It saves them a trip."

Geoff nodded. Although he didn't appear certain he understood her answer, he asked no more questions.

Since he was silent, Tory concentrated on steering the boat. When they neared the shore, she adeptly brought the boat to rest on the beach. Geoff carried the water cans and she put the duffle bag on her shoulder.

Tory loved Pulau Sakeng. It was a small Malay fishing village, reminiscent of an era that was vanishing. Sensing Geoff's curiosity, Tory pointed to the small shacks extending over the water's edge. "The houses are on stilts because of the reptiles and cobras."

"When are your friends expecting you?"

Tory shrugged. "They're not."

"You didn't ring them after I rang you? Why not?"

Geoff's question was funny. "'Cause there are only two phones on the island. If they're not home, we'll leave the things and go to the beach. We'll meet up with them sooner or later. The island's not big and they never leave."

One of the children spied Tory as they neared the house and ran to greet her. Tory stopped and chattered to the child in Bahasa. She reached into her pocket for a piece of hard candy. While the girl sucked on the butterscotch, Tory introduced her to Geoff.

"Mira, he can't speak your language. Will you speak English for him?"

Mira hid behind Tory's legs and peeked through them, her long eyelashes nearly hiding her eyes. "Hello," she whispered.

Geoff crouched down on his knees and smiled at Mira. Tory watched Geoff with fascination. He was patient and waited until Mira was comfortable before he said anything. It pleased her that he had enough sense to get down to eye level to speak to the child.

When they had had time to become acquainted, Tory handed Mira a small package from her duffle bag. "That's for you. Take it to the house. We'll be there in a minute."

While Mira skipped away, Tory turned to Geoff. "My friends are simple people. At first, they may be shy. Strangers aren't a frequent occurrence. Don't be offended if they stare at you."

"Not to worry. Did you live here?"

Tory shook her head. "I lived in Sembawang, on the north coast of Singapore. This place is a little too far off the beaten path, even for me. The Baharis were my neighbors in Sembawang. We've stayed in touch over the years. Noor, the husband, is a fisherman. If it's a good day, we'll have a wonderful dinner."

Tory watched Geoff take in the scene. He wasn't impressed. Not that she blamed him. Pulau Sakeng wasn't the tropical island seen on postcards. Rather than white, sandy beaches interspersed with bamboo cottages, there were plank houses built on stilts. Corrugated steel sheets and chicken wire surrounded anything that grew. The gardens were a mixture of cactus, coral, and seashells.

Tory leaned over and tugged Geoff's hand. "It's not as bad as it looks. Sembawang wasn't quite as Spartan, although there're a great many similarities."

"What?"

"See the gardens and vegetable patches? They're communal. Each family takes only what they need for a meal. That's why I have to carry so much when I come. Whatever I give the Baharis, they share with their neighbors."

Geoff frowned. "And you think that's nice?"

Tory nodded. "There's a safety net here that doesn't exist on the mainland. As long as you're part of the island, you're protected."

Sensing he didn't comprehend, Tory shrugged. "It's the only place I feel safe. It's also a good place to unwind. You look like you need that."

Geoff rubbed the stubble on his chin. "You might be right. Seems I forgot to shave. Why didn't you tell me?"

"No one here'll mind."

"It'll scratch your face when I kiss you."

Tory smiled and danced around Geoff. "Ah, but you can't do that here. This is Muslim territory. Open shows of affection between members of the opposite sex aren't acceptable. That's why I said to wear your bathing trunks under your clothes."

"And why you're in long sleeves and slacks?"

Tory grinned. "Come on. By now, Mira's probably got the whole family dying to meet my friend."

For two hours they sipped tea and chatted with the Baharis. Noor and his wife spoke English interspersed with Bahasa. Geoff smiled at them frequently, even when Tory was positive he had no idea what had been said. When they were offered lunch, Tory shook her head. She suggested she and Geoff go see the island by themselves.

"You feel like hiking?" she asked when they got outside.

"Not particularly."

"Just a little one? If we go this way, down the coral path through the seashells, there's a secluded spot. I packed a lunch. You can take a nap on the beach."

"Why would I want to do that? I'd prefer to talk to you. We have so little time."

"You can barely keep your eyes open. The rest will do you good."

Tory swam while Geoff slept. When she finished, Tory put her towel down next to Geoff. There was no sense in having a serious discussion with Geoff in his present state. No matter how hard he tried to hide it, he was exhausted. Even had his appearance not been a giveaway, the fact that he hadn't had a million questions about the area would have been. Fatigue was the only thing that could deter Geoff from barraging her with questions.

For the first time Tory understood the sense of loss Chris described when she complained about Kevin's working hours. It was difficult not to see someone you cared about or to see them exhausted. It was harder still to be with them while they slept and you were awake.

Geoff opened his eyes and squinted in the sun. "How long have I slept?"

Tory shrugged. Time didn't matter in Pulau Sakeng.

"When are we expected for dinner?"

"When we get there. From the position of the sun, I'd say we have half an hour. More, if you want."

"You like it here."

Since Geoff's comment hadn't sounded like a question, she merely smiled.

"Tell me about Anna and your life on the north coast."

Tory shook her head.

"Please." The jagged edge that had been evident in Geoff's tone earlier was gone. "You look so peaceful here. I watched you with your friends. You speak the language like a native. Do you miss Sembawang?"

"At times. It was idyllic then... I don't think it would be right for me now, though."

"What was it like?"

"You've seen how it is with the Baharis. Sembawang had the same feeling -- we were one extended family. There were only ten of us." Tory shrugged and struggled for the words that would communicate what Sembawang meant to her. "I felt connected when I lived there. Like I belonged. I get the same feeling when I visit here. I don't know how else to explain it."

"What about Anna?"

"You'll hear an Anna story after dinner. I always tell the children one."

"I'd like to hear one now." Geoff reached over and rubbed Tory's knee.

The feel of his hand was a shock; she hadn't expected it. Tory leaned back on her elbows. Maybe telling Geoff about Anna was a good place to begin her explanation about herself. "I'd been living in Sembawang for about a month. One morning, before dawn, I heard a funny sound and went outside to explore. Anna was swinging along the low branches of the trees. I ran inside and grabbed my camera. She was intrigued by my actions. She came over and took the camera. Apparently, she'd been watching what I did, because she mimicked my actions perfectly."

"Was there film in the camera?"

"Of course. Anna got about two complete shots of me and six of various portions of my body. It was nearly sunrise, so I walked down to the shore to watch the sun come up. Anna followed me. After that, she became a fixture in my life."

"Where did she come from?"

"I never knew. From what I've read, she must've been about five. Orangutans seldom leave their mothers before then. She was such a funny little thing. Every time she saw the camera, she'd prance in front of it. If she wanted her picture taken or wanted to take one of me, she'd go into my klang and get the camera herself."

"Isn't that a tad far-fetched? You're too intelligent to believe she understood."

"You're wrong. Anna understood more about me than anyone. She knew my moods, what made me hurt, what made me laugh. She could read me like a book."

"Why could you allow her in and not a human being?"

Tory sat up, picked up a handful of sand, and let it slip slowly through her fingers. Her tone a whisper, she answered, "'Cause I knew Anna would never hurt me."

Geoff reached for Tory's hand. "What happened to you? Who hurt you so badly? Was it Tim? Your father?"

Tory jumped up. "It's dinner time."

Geoff stood slowly. Very quietly he ordered, "Answer me."

Tory picked up their towels, shook them in the gentle breeze, folded them, and put them in her backpack. She reached down, slipped her sandals on her feet, and walked up the path.

"I'll not leave until you answer," Geoff called.

"Then you'll be standing there the rest of your life," Tory called back. Her heart was racing. She couldn't believe how close she'd come to telling Geoff the truth. *This was a lousy idea. There's no way I can explain it. Not to Geoff, not to anyone.* Why couldn't he understand?

Tory was halfway up the path when Geoff reached her. His hands were thrust into the pockets of his slacks. She could tell from his mad pace that he was raging, and she didn't care.

Chapter 36
CHRIS

Singapore
Saturday, November 1, 1980

Chris stared at Tory, her mouth open. How could she be so obtuse? Why wasn't she concerned about the change in plans? "I tell you I'm thinking of not having Thanksgiving dinner this year and your only response is fine. You sound just like Kevin."

"Chris, what is it you want from me? If you don't want to go through the ritual, that's your call. Why should you bother with a party if you're not in the mood?"

"Where will you eat if I don't do Thanksgiving dinner?"

Tory shrugged. "If I get an uncontrollable urge for turkey, I'll buy one at Cold Storage. What's bugging you? Why don't you want to have the dinner? There's more to this decision than the children's trips. You've been distant and remote since Penang and that was three months ago. Has Sarah's absence created that much of a void in your life?"

Chris shook her head. "I honestly thought things were getting better between Kev and me. He was spending more time home. Once the children got back, that changed. He's always at work."

"He's at the brink of a major coup. It's taking all his attention. You know that. We've talked about it before. What's really on your mind?"

How could Chris explain what she barely understood herself? "I'm attracted to John Horton."

Tory threw her head back and laughed. "So that's it? You can be so funny."

How could Tory be so callous and unfeeling? "What's funny about my being attracted to someone other than my husband? Don't you think another man could be interested in me?"

Tory turned serious. "Of course. It's simply I know the players too well. It doesn't fit."

"John's made me think about things. Things I'd been doing my damnedest to ignore."

Tory nodded sagely, but didn't say a word.

"You always claim Kevin doesn't cheat on me. If that's true, why am I attracted to John?"

"Why do you think? Motivation's always the key."

Chris grasped at the mosaic of fleeting ideas that filled her head. "John felt guilty when Monica died. Everyone was giving him tea and sympathy when what he felt was relief. It took him a long time to accept that he didn't have to feel guilty."

"He was ready to come out of seclusion at the same time you started questioning your life. You each needed a person of the opposite sex to talk to."

How was it that Tory always knew what went on in other people's minds? "So I'm attracted to John because he has the time to listen to me."

Tory nodded.

"I love Kevin. But something's wrong between us. I think it's more than this project. Do you have any ideas?"

Tory shook her head. "Have you tried talking to him?"

"I told him that I hated that this island was so male-dominated. He said I had island fever and should go on a trip."

"Penang. Of course. I should have put the pieces together sooner."

"Tory, you're the only woman I know who works. The rest of us are just part of the scenery. I live in a style most people can never aspire to and I'm miserable. I feel so selfish because I'm unhappy."

"Chris, you loved your life here for a long time. But people change. If you're not happy, why don't you tell Kevin? How's he supposed to know if all you do is harp on the hours he spends at work?"

"So he's told you I've become a shrew?"

Tory sighed and shook her head. "I know you and I can just picture the scene: you decide it's time to have a heart-to-heart when Kevin comes in exhausted from a fifteen-hour day. As if that's not silly enough, you probably get pissed when he won't do more than crawl into bed and roll over."

Chris couldn't believe it. How could Tory have known? "What am I supposed to do? How do I tell Kevin that I want to go home?"

"That's for you to decide, after you figure out if that's what you really want. But if you want him to listen to you, let him decompress before you jump him."

"Is that the voice of experience talking?"

"I know what it's like to be so tired that you think death is the only possible relief. When you're that exhausted you hurt all over and can't cope with more than putting one foot in front of the other. It'd be better if you waited until Kevin's not so busy before you hit him between the eyes."

"So, once again, I have to wait for Kevin to be ready. He gets to determine when we can talk?"

Tory stood up and glared at Chris who'd slumped down on the couch. "No. By all means, attack him the second he walks in the door. That way, he'll convince you once and for all that he's an insensitive brute. Damn it! If you want to go to bed with John, do it. Don't look to your husband for permission."

"That's not what I'm doing," Chris screamed. "I do not want to have an affair. I just want things to be the way they were."

"Time doesn't stand still. Chris, you're expecting Kevin to give your life meaning. No one can do that for anyone else. Do you have any idea the awesome responsibility you're placing on him? I'd rather screw up my life completely, make every wrong decision there was, than abdicate myself to someone else's desires."

"That's why you're alone."

"And you're not?"

From the look on Chris's face, Tory must have known she'd said too much, because the next time she spoke it was in a softer tone. "Chris, the toughest decisions in life are the ones you have to make for yourself I can't tell you what's right for you. No one can. You have to work it out for yourself."

Chapter 37
TORY

Singapore and London
Wednesday-Thursday, November 26-28, 1980

Tory stared excitedly out the window as the plane landed at Heathrow Airport. She could barely believe she was almost in London. She could hardly believe any of the events of the last week.

Her trip to Thailand had taken longer than anticipated. She'd returned to Singapore the same day Geoff was leaving for Greece. Since he usually left in the afternoon, she hadn't expected to see him. To her delight he was at Paya Lebar Airport waiting when she cleared Customs. He'd switched to an evening flight so they'd have time together.

Geoff drove to Keppel Harbor where they walked along the water's edge hand in hand. After a while Tory realized she had been giving a monologue. She'd just finished recounting a traffic jam that lasted for six hours and Geoff didn't laugh at the comedic scene.

"Have I done something?" she asked.

Geoff didn't answer.

Tory turned to see his face. He was lost in thought. "Will you be back by Thanksgiving? I thought I'd make dinner."

"Did you say something?"

Tory shrugged. "Why'd you stay to see me? You're a million miles away."

"Business problem. Not to worry. It'll be over soon.

"I missed you while I was gone."

"That's nice."

His answer had been so automatic, Tory was positive he had no idea what she said. They walked for several hours. Most of the time Geoff was distracted. After a while, she stopped the pretense of conversation and relished the quiet between them. It was a beautiful day and she was walking hand in hand with someone she cared about.

When she got back to her apartment she was so sleepy she dropped her suitcase and camera equipment in the foyer of her flat and went straight to bed. In the morning, she unpacked and sorted through her mail.

After the rain-filled days of Thailand that flooded the streets and brought traffic to a standstill, Singapore was a welcome relief. She took a stack of mail and went to the nearby bird sanctuary in the park. Jurong Bird Park was one of her favorite places. Most of Singapore was tall buildings inhabited by harried people. In contrast, Jurong was the site of a serene and peaceful bird park. It was here Tory came when she wanted to be alone with her thoughts.

For a while she sat and watched the birds peck at the bread crusts she threw several feet in front of her. As the birds became more comfortable with her presence, she tossed the crusts closer and closer to her feet. She knew eventually the bravest could be coaxed to put their beaks into her paper bag.

After an hour she took the mail from her camera bag and opened the first envelope. She reread the letter several times to be certain she'd not misunderstood. A publisher in London wanted her to write a book. Although she'd worked for the book publisher before, her contributions had never been more than one or two chapters on vegetation or animal life in the tropics. They wanted her to come to London to discuss the project in more detail immediately, at their expense.

She ran home and called Chris, completely forgetting their argument the last time they were together.

"Chris, you won't believe this."

"Who is this?" a cold tone demanded.

"Huh? It's Tory. Who else?"

"I don't know anyone by that name." Chris hung up.

Tory looked at the receiver in her hand. She was too excited to be annoyed at Chris or to wonder how long she planned to hold a grudge. She had to talk to someone or she'd burst. She thought of Geoff, but he wasn't due back for at least a week. He hadn't been certain of his schedule when he left. That left Tim. She called his office.

Tim was as excited as she. "It's what you've always wanted, luv. Good on you. But isn't this a bit out of your genre?"

Tory smiled. "Its a trade-off. When this book's done, I get to do one about primates. Sort of my tribute to Anna Banana. That's the book I've always wanted to write. The first book is a silly little piece of fluff. But there's big money in it."

"So the publisher agrees to your book in return for theirs? Not too shabby. How does it feel to know you were right, that if you held on long enough you'd be able to do what you wanted?"

Tim was right. She'd held on to her dream. Now it looked like her perseverance was about to pay off. As she hung up, she remembered an evening ten years before.

She and Tim were walking through Bugis Street. As usual Tim was trying to figure out ways for them to earn more money. "This is what you should write about."

Tory shook her head. "I'll leave that for the travel writers." She nodded her head at two transsexuals as they walked by. "I love this, but it's not what I want to be remembered for."

Tim leaned over, kissed her cheek, and grinned. "And what does Miss Winslow want to write? What should the world remember you for?"

"Primates."

"Bloody monkeys?" His tone had been incredulous. "All the wonders of Singapore are at your feet tonight and you want to write about Anna Banana. It'll never happen. You don't have the credentials for a scholarly tome."

Tory shrugged. "I'll do it. Mark my words. One day I'll write my book."

"And what will you do to feed yourself while you wait for your pipe dream?"

"What I've been doing."

"Then why thumb your nose at writing about what this island is like? Couldn't you make more money writing the definitive guide to S'pore?"

"Maybe. But why spoil it? The parts of Singapore that appeal to me aren't what tourists come to see. Who'd care about the hawkers in Little India or the way the sun creeps up over Mount Faber?"

Tim laughed. "When you talk like that, I couldn't agree more. But, you love this place. Surely you could write about what Singapore means to you."

Tory shook her head. "It would defile it somehow. No, I'd rather work for companies on stuff that doesn't matter, or write articles for magazines."

"So you'll keep doing more of the same. You're a fruit loop. You're passing up a golden opportunity to write about this place in a way no one else could. And all because you want to write about monkeys."

Tory nodded her head emphatically. "Primates. Tim, please call them by their proper name."

Tory remembered that day with a smile. Quickly she packed her gear and returned to her apartment. When she spoke to the publisher, he agreed that Tory should come out as soon as possible. After checking their calendars, they agreed upon Thursday. Before she could leave, she had to finish her article contrasting the Indian festival of Deepavali as it was celebrated in Singapore and Thailand, select the photographs, and pack.

The trip couldn't have come at a better time. Thursday was Thanksgiving. It wouldn't seem right to be in Singapore and not be with the Taylors. In London it would be a simple matter to forget it was Thanksgiving, since it wasn't a holiday there.

Now as her dream was about to become a reality, Tory was anxious. Her eyes roamed the huge arrivals hall to take in all she could. Heathrow Airport was a marked contrast to the small airports of Asia. Everyone rushed like they were late for a life or death appointment while Tory dawdled to allow the feel of the place soak into her pores.

She wore her old navy blue stadium jacket. It was worn and the cuffs were frayed. She felt like a waif in comparison to the polished people around her. The women at Heathrow looked so glamorous. The women in Singapore seemed drab in comparison, black and white photographs in a Technicolor world.

The line at Passport Control seemed to go on forever. She stood in the queue and craned her neck to see the end of the serpentine line. She felt a tap on her shoulder, turned, and was face to face with Geoff.

"What are you doing here?" she asked. The second the words were out of her mouth, she knew they'd come out wrong. "I thought you were in Greece," she added quickly.

He nodded. "I was called to London for a meeting. Isn't this a tad out of your jurisdiction? I almost didn't recognize you. Then I saw the camera bag and knew my eyes weren't playing a trick on me."

"Want to wait with me?"

He shook his head. "This isn't my queue. Why don't we meet after Immigration? Where are you staying?"

"The Dorchester."

"You must have spoken to someone at Trans Oil. We can share a taxi."

During the ride into London, Tory marveled at the passing sights. She tugged at Geoff's sleeve constantly to point out something that caught her attention. By the time they arrived at the Dorchester, she was talked out. She peered at Geoff through her eyelashes, embarrassed. "That was some performance, wasn't it?" she asked sheepishly. "I'm sorry."

He smiled indulgently. "I take it you've never been here. It's a glorious city. I'm sure you'll enjoy your stay."

When Geoff handed his bags to the porter, she looked at him questioningly.

"I'm booked here as well," he offered.

Tory wondered who would make the next move. She was uncomfortable about the way she'd rambled on in the taxi and was certain Geoff thought her an imbecile. She was pleased when he took her hand in his.

"I've some calls to make. If you've no plans for dinner, we must eat together. I'll book a table for 7:30 and meet you here at 7."

Tory unpacked swiftly and went out to see the city. She was anxious about tomorrows meeting and bumping into Geoff only added to her agitation. Geoff was part of her Singapore world; he didn't belong in London. But then again, neither did she.

To calm herself, Tory decided to go on a walking tour. She carried a map from the concierge and wandered through the narrow lanes, planning to see the sights. Instead, she mentally reviewed her book proposal and followed the crowds.

Before she knew it, she was in front of Harrods. While she'd walked, she realized she'd need more to wear than her thin silk dresses. She'd be chilled to the bone if she didn't buy warmer clothes. Tory hated being cold more than anything. She selected two dresses and was surprised at how easy it was to spend more than anticipated. She also needed a coat, hat and gloves.

That evening, she wore a new dress. It was cranberry cashmere with a cowl neck and a soft tie belt of the same fabric. She liked the feel of the dress against her skin and knew it would go perfectly with a silk scarf she had with her.

"How long will you be here?" Geoff asked over dinner.

"I'm not sure. I have a meeting tomorrow. I'll know more then. Why?"

"I thought that, if you could fit it in your schedule, we might stay for the weekend. I've meetings tomorrow and Friday. I'd relish a brief holiday before going home."

Tory nodded eagerly. It was a dream come true. She was afraid that any minute, she'd wake and be in a tent in the middle of a jungle.

"Did I mention I like your dress?"

"At least ten times. Do I look that different from home?"

Geoff nodded. "You look lovely. You always look lovely. Tonight though, there's something different about you. Or is it me?"

Tory shrugged. "The last time we saw each other, you barely knew I was there."

Geoff paused, then looked embarrassed. "The day I left. I was preoccupied. I trust you didn't take it personally."

Tory shook her head. There was so much that she wanted to say. But this wasn't the right time. A great deal was riding on tomorrow's meeting. She couldn't allow anyone to come between her and her dream. Not when it was this close.

Geoff also had things on his mind that he didn't choose to discuss. They ate the balance of their meal in silence. Neither ordered dessert. They each sat with an untouched glass of cognac in front of them. It was as if they each understood that when the snifters were empty, they'd return to whatever captivated their attention. Tory stared uncomfortably into Geoff's face.

Geoff broke the silence. "I'm surprised you've never been to London before. I expected you'd been everywhere."

She shook her head. "I pretty much confine myself to Asia."

"Why?"

Tory paused. The lie she so often gave to that question didn't seem appropriate tonight. It was time for the truth. She saw Geoff reach for his wallet, and put her hand out to stop him. "I'm not going to change the subject. I've woven a tale about my past for so long that it's hard to remember what's real and what's fantasy. Bear with me. Please."

"Not to worry. I've waited long enough for this. A few more minutes one way or the other won't matter." He took her hand in his and squeezed it gently. "I'm interested. With your reputation, you could live and work anywhere you wanted."

"It's warm... I like the people... I don't know... Actually, I can't imagine living anywhere else. There's something magical about Asia. If you don't try to live like an expat, it's relatively inexpensive."

"You're doing it again. What is it that you detest about us expats?"

"It's not all of you. Just the ones who come to Asia and live in big houses and complain bitterly about how everything's not up to some mythical standard they have in their head. They're leeches. They don't understand the people or how they think. They make no attempt to get to know the country that's their home."

"What was it like starting out in a strange country? You didn't have all the perks we expats get."

"The first few years were a struggle. Some months, there was barely enough money to pay the rent, but I survived. That's when I resented the expats most. I was twenty-four, and kids my age were living in palatial houses with cars, drivers, and hot and cold running servants. Did they appreciate their lifestyle? No. All they could do was whine about what brand of butter was available at Cold Storage. I lived in a barter economy, and these spoiled brats, who had it all, valued nothing. They acted as if it were their due, that they had some divine right to the wonders that were at their feet."

"What do you think now?"

"Expats are people, some good, some bad. I can't imagine being one, though. It's like being trapped in a mammoth jar of peanut butter. Bland, textureless ooze."

Geoff smiled. "Does Asia remind you of home?"

Tory laughed. "Heavens, no. I grew up on a farm in North Dakota. Crops, animals, pretty countryside, the whole nine yards. It was a bucolic area. But it was always cold. When the wind blew, you'd swear there wasn't a tree between you and the North Pole. At night, the wind'd blow through the cracks in the walls and I'd shiver until I thought I would die." Troy shuddered visibly at the memory. "Asia's different."

"Asia's not cold, at least not the parts you stay in. What appeals to you besides the weather?"

Tory shrugged. "There were all these cultures that live together in harmony. I couldn't believe that people could be so tolerant of differences, but they were.

"After the Peace Corps, when I got back to the States, I didn't feel like I belonged. I taught for a year and hated it. I tried to get a job in journalism, but I didn't have the proper qualifications. A degree in education doesn't prepare you to work for a publishing house or a magazine. I couldn't face the prospect of teaching for the rest of my life. It would have taken years before I could save enough to go back to college for a degree in journalism.

"One day, I got an idea. I wrote to the Peace Corps and suggested that, if they'd pay my expenses, I'd write about the good they were doing in Asia. To my surprise, they took me up on my offer.

"After that I got pretty good at figuring out where a company was missing a golden opportunity. When I saw what their weak point was, I'd send them a proposal. I visited the preserves and took photos of what they were doing, you know, training animals to live in the wild, rehabilitating animals that'd been injured. After I got home I'd send them the photos with a business card. The next time they were looking for a photographer, they called." Troy shrugged.

"How often do you go home?"

"Last year was the first time."

"Doesn't your family miss you?"

Tory shifted uncomfortably in her chair. "There's no one left who'd care if I went back."

"I can't believe that. Surely you have friends who'd like to see you."

"Not really. I told you, I left home when I was sixteen. No one in my family's spoken to me since the day my father threw me out." Tory clutched herself for strength. Her next words were almost whispered. "The only person who even tried to see things from my perspective was my school teacher. She died last year. That's why I went back."

"And you didn't look up your family? Why not?"

Tory bit her lower lip. How could she explain her behavior without giving away too much? "It's been twenty years. I've made a life for myself. When I needed them, no one was willing to stand up to Papa. Why should I give them the chance to hurt me again?"

"And you think they would have?"

Tory nodded. A tear trickled down her cheek. Before she could open her purse for a tissue, Geoff dabbed at the tear with his handkerchief.

Geoff leaned over, kissed her cheek, and took her hand in his. "Why'd you choose tonight to open up? You've hidden behind your wall for so long. Why now?"

Tory wanted to explain, but was terrified she'd burst into tears if she spoke. She reached for Geoff's handkerchief, which was on the table.

"Tell me, please," he asked softly as he stroked her hand.

"I'd planned to do it months ago. We've not had much luck connecting recently, in case you haven't noticed... I knew if I didn't tell you tonight, I'd never do it."

Geoff nodded. "I realize my schedule's been erratic lately. I apologize for that. I was also immensely tired of your ostrich game. It didn't matter how attracted I was to you, or you to me. I couldn't penetrate your wall. I was starting to question if you were worth the effort."

Tory was confused. "Earlier you mentioned staying for the weekend. Which one of us is playing games now?"

"I know. I almost rang you to cancel dinner. I couldn't face another evening that ended in our usual argument. I've important negotiations over the next two days. I thought an encounter with you might ruin my concentration."

"You've been avoiding me?" she asked. She pulled her hands away and reached for her purse.

"Don't leave, Tory. Please. I've never canceled dinner for anything other than business." He stopped. "No, that's not quite right. I canceled once for a friend. For Barney. It was a crisis. Before he and Sarah returned to Sydney.

"When I saw you at Heathrow, I couldn't believe my luck. I thought we might have a chance to be together, away from phones and work and all the things that interrupt us in Singapore. Tonight I realized how tired I am. This project's taken its toll on me. You sap my strength as well. I can't tolerate two forces pulling me in opposite directions. This project is important to me. If I'd been forced to make a choice, it would have been the winner."

"So? What's changed? I'm still me. If that's too stressful for you, why should it be different now?"

"It's serendipity our being in London at the same time. We must make the most of it."

"What's your project all about? You and Kevin have been working ridiculous hours. Trans Oil isn't usually that type of company."

"I can't discuss the matter now," Geoff answered firmly.

"Can't or ...?" Tory stopped before she finished her question. Since she didn't want to tell Geoff about the book until she spoke to the publisher in the morning, she understood his hesitation. "I understand. Well, what do you want to do from here?"

"What I want and what we are about to do are not the same at all. We've both meetings in the morning. I have no way of forecasting how long I'll be involved. I expect my work will be done sometime on Friday. I'll ring when I'm free. If you're available, we'll take it from there. If you've left for Singapore, I'll understand."

"What if I'm not back from my appointment?" she asked, suddenly afraid he might leave for Singapore if he finished before she did.

Geoff laughed at her unspoken words. "Your insecurity amazes me. If you haven't checked out, I'll keep ringing until you return. Does that meet with your approval?"

Tory didn't trust her voice, so she offered what she hoped was a seductive smile.

The meeting with her publisher went well. Tory was excited about their proposal. When the topic was initially raised, she'd thought a book on a wife's guide to surviving her husband's assignment to Singapore, was little more than a humorous look at what could go wrong. She was surprised to realize the book could be made fascinating if approached properly. It wasn't quite the no-brainer she first described to Tim. If nothing else, it would stretch her in a new direction. For two days, all thoughts of Geoff disappeared, while she worked on an outline and chapter summaries.

The phone was ringing when she walked into her hotel room Friday evening. She practically jumped on it. "Hello?"

"I thought you'd never return. How are you?"

"I feel like celebrating," she laughed.

"That makes two of us. I'll meet you in the lobby in an hour. I booked a table at Beotty, it's my favorite London restaurant."

They had champagne with dinner. Tory was tipsy. Knowing champagne had that affect on her, she wondered why she'd asked Geoff to order a bottle.

Geoff refused to discuss his meetings. "Trans Oil will make an announcement next month. I'm not at liberty to say more than that. What has you so fired up?"

She giggled, afraid the book would sound silly, or worse, simplistic. "I'm going to write a book about living in Asia. For expat wives. What they should expect, how to buy things, that sort of stuff. There's nothing written from their perspective. Travel books don't fit the bill. The few books that have come out are written by self-proclaimed experts who've spent, at most, a week in the area."

"Why should you write a book for wives? It's the same for men."

She shook her head. "It's not. Not at all. I've watched it for years. The men go to work all day, just like they would at home. Their world stays the same. The only thing that changes is the venue. The wives have to wind their way through the maze of Asia, where things are never quite what they seem. Their husbands think that because they have servants, they should be happy. They don't give any credence to how difficult it can be to get things accomplished. Actually, they understand damned little that goes on in the wives' world."

"That remark sounds like you're about to discuss Singapore and the people we know." He offered the waiter his credit card. "Tonight we must forget Asia and concentrate on ourselves."

Geoff's lips brushed the nape of her neck when he helped her on with her coat, sending shivers down her spine. She forgot everything but her desire. They rode the taxi in silence, each hesitant to ruin the mood. At the Dorchester, Geoff asked for his key only.

Tory fought to catch her breath when Geoff touched her. The sensation of his fingers sent shock waves through her body. It felt like a million butterflies were fluttering across her. Geoff pulled her face towards his and kissed her. Tory returned his kiss, hungrily. How could he be so calm? Tory wanted to tear off their clothes this second. Geoff continued his teasing caresses. She reached for the buttons to his shirt.

Geoff put out his hand to stop her. "There's plenty of time for that."

Was there? Every inch of her body ached for Geoff. It took all her restraint to keep from ripping his shirt, to get closer to him. Tory gasped when Geoff's right hand moved up her thigh. When she looked at his face, Geoff was grinning. "You're enjoying this, aren't you?" she asked.

He nodded. He moved his hand from her quivering body. "Shall I stop? If you're not enjoying this, I must stop."

"No. Please. Don't stop," she managed to croak.

Silently, he took her hand and led her to the bed.

Chapter 38
CHRIS

Singapore
Friday, December 12, 1980

"Damn Kevin. Damn the holidays. Damn Singapore," Chris ranted to the air, as she attacked her roses. She'd been pruning the bushes when Kevin called. Afterwards she was so angry, she took her frustration out on the bushes. Instead of cutting back two inches, only stumps remained. When she saw what she'd done, she cried.

Angry with herself now, she stormed into the house lest she wreak more havoc. She found no solace indoors. She was lonely in the house she once loved. The children were each with friends for the weekend. They never wanted to be home anymore. Not that Chris blamed them. She could barely tolerate being there herself.

Kevin was at work from early morning until late in the evening. When he managed a cameo appearance in their lives, he spent most of his time on the phone. At first she'd thought his whispered conversations were to a woman. Then she heard him say Geoff. Geoff represented the world of work, the only world that mattered to Kevin. When Chris asked what was so important, he ignored her, the same way he avoided everything else in their lives. It had been months since they'd sat down to a meal as a family, and at least nine months since she and Kevin had gone out together. Usually when Chris returned from a party, Kevin was asleep. Nothing in her world was as it should be.

The Parkers were still in Australia. Chris didn't know if, or when, Sarah would be back. Tory was off someplace. Chris had no idea where she was. For weeks she'd regretted hanging up on Tory. She'd called several times to apologize. Tory was never home. It wasn't like Tory to be away this long without a word. Chris considered calling Geoff, but was mortified she'd sound like a child who'd had a spat with her best friend. Chris didn't want to admit to being so needy.

Over the summer, Alison had matured. Club meetings and new friends filled her afternoons. Marc had developed a passion for the science club. Coupled with swimming and soccer practice, his afternoons were as full as his sister's. For years Chris had listened to wives talk of the freedom they experienced when their children were older. Why did she find their independence a loss?

There was little to be fascinated by in afternoons of bridge and coffee. Although the faces might change, the conversations seldom varied. The topics were the same. The women were content to remain in the expatriate compounds or the shops on Orchard Road. Chris longed for the days when she and Tory explored Singapore and the surrounding countries.

When Chris suggested to Janet Adams that the coffee service she was looking for could be bought at Arab Street for a quarter of the sum being asked at the Emporium on Orchard Road, Janet scoffed, "Why waste our time digging through all that junk?"

"You never know what treasures you'll find."

"Who cares? Whatever I spend here is less than I would've at home."

Chris nodded. "I know. But think of the fun we could have."

"What's fun about poking through dusty stores? Phil won't mind what I spend. It's a gift for his mother."

It seemed to Chris that her life was getting smaller, while her family's got larger. Although she made the pretense of working at Mount Elizabeth, it was fraudulent. She was a glorified gofer. She'd had more responsibility as a candy-striper. She was furious at her family for leaving her behind. Chris needed something. The fact that she couldn't decide what she wanted made it all the worse.

Her only comfort came from John Horton. He was the consummate gentleman. He escorted her to dinner, the symphony, or lunch. No matter what she wanted, John was happy to oblige. It was pleasant to have someone listen to her, someone in whom she could confide, someone who was cognizant of her existence.

She paced the solarium's marble floor. Finally she poured herself a glass of wine to calm her nerves. On a whim she tried Tory, even though she didn't expect to reach her. To her surprise, Tory was home.

"Where have you been?" she asked the second she heard Tory's voice.

"Here, there, everywhere."

"Look, I'm sorry about ..."

"Don't give it a thought. I'm fine. How're you?"

"Miserable. Why don't you come over and we can have a long chat? I need a shoulder to cry on. The Murphys are having a party tonight. If you want, we could go together." *Please don't let me down,* Chris thought silently.

"I'd like to, I really would. It's just..."

"You're angry at me," Chris muttered sadly.

"No. I'm on a tight deadline. I have to finish an article this weekend."

"And you can't spare me a few hours? Well, thanks for nothing," Chris answered sarcastically. Her eyes filled with tears. Tory had been her last hope. Even she didn't have time.

"Don't hang up, Chris. Give me an hour or two. I can't go to the Murphy's party, but I can always make time for you."

Chris heard the hesitation in Tory's voice and wasn't convinced. Tory sounded distracted. Chris pictured Tory engrossed in her darkroom, unwilling to leave. "Look, if you're busy, it's okay."

"It's no big deal. You may be able to help me with my next project. I've been dying to talk to you about it."

"Great. I'll send the car so you don't have to wait for the bus."

When Tory arrived, Chris recounted what had happened in her world over the last few weeks. When she ran out of stories, she could think of nothing to say. "You've just heard all that's new in my life. What've you been up to? You're becoming a recluse. No one's seen you in ages." She looked up, saw Tory's Mona Lisa grin, and wondered what it signified. When she could take the silence no longer, she asked again, "What's up?"

"Two things. I'm trying to decide which to tell first," Tory giggled.

Chris watched a hint of pink grow from the base of Tory's throat until it covered her face. "It is Geoff, isn't it?" she asked tentatively.

Tory nodded. "Who else? We bumped into each other in London. The music didn't play there, so we stopped dancing."

"London? What were you doing there?"

"That's the other news. How would you like to collaborate with me on a book?"

"A book? I don't know the first thing about writing. I don't even write my mother, I call her. Haven't you heard Kevin complain about our phone bill often enough to know that?"

As Tory explained about the book, Chris forgot her initial skepticism. This was something she knew only too well. Her mind wandered back to when she'd arrived in Singapore. Suddenly, she recalled all the difficulties as if it had been last week. Simple tasks seemed Herculean efforts until you understood the Asian mentality.

The concept of time was so radically different. People call it "rubber time." When you first arrived, it was infuriating. Appointments didn't symbolize what they did at home. If a repairman agreed to fix something on Tuesday, he meant some time in the future, when the spirit moved him.

Whereas Westerners often raise their voice to emphasize a point, the more important the subject matter, the quieter the Asian voice would get. It could be difficult to understand their whispered tones.

The Asians tendency to laugh out of context was confusing. Asian laughter didn't indicate humor. Rather, they laughed when they felt shy, nervous, or embarrassed. Tory claimed the laughter was meant to mask what they saw as a "loss-of-face."

It had taken Chris a year to be comfortable with the differences. Had it not been for Tory's advice, she might not have made it through the first months. After all the years, she still had difficulty with the contrasts.

Chris would enjoy letting others know what they were getting into before they arrived. Most companies gave wives a road map and travel guide, expecting they'd learn the rest on their own.

Chris was so excited, she talked for two hours about things that had happened to her and the stories she'd heard from other women. When she finally stopped for a breath, Tory was grinning. "What's so funny?" Chris asked.

"I haven't seen you this excited in eons. It's great. But there's more to writing a book than little anecdotes about what can go wrong."

"What?"

"Research, research, research. We'll have to look at it all from the eyes of someone coming here for the first time. Take schools. We have to list each school, the curriculum, the fees, and the admission standards, do the kids wear uniforms, and is there transportation, all that and more. I have an outline of what's to be included."

Chris laughed. "If you're trying to tell me that there's hard work involved, so what? I need something to sink my teeth into. When do we start?"

Tory put up her hands. "Hey, not so fast. I've got other assignments to finish before I can start. I thought after the holidays, if you really wanted in, we'd go over the outline and you could do some research. It'll probably take me 'til mid-March to clear my calendar. I'll be in and out of town until then."

For the first time in recent memory, Chris was enthusiastic about something. The project was just what she needed. If she had something to do, maybe she wouldn't resent Kevin's enthusiasm for his job. "I want in. Now. There's no reason for me to wait." She got up, pulled Tory to her feet, and hugged her. "Tory, this is fantastic. Do you realize you've just given me a new lease on life?"

Tory shook her head. "I've offered you drudge work for minimal pay. I'm doing the book for royalties, and have to support myself while I write it."

"I don't care about the money. I want to do something."

"I take it nothing much's changed with Kevin."

Chris nodded. Silently, she struggled for the right words. "Well, how do you feel about the command performance next Sunday?"

"Huh?"

"This morning Kevin called and informed me we had to be at the Managing Director's house for brunch next Sunday. If the children or I had plans, they were to be canceled. Immediately. Geoff has told you, hasn't he?"

Tory shifted in the chair. "Sort of ... He asked if I'd be in town. And, um... well... he said he'd appreciate it if I tried to make it."

"See, you get asked, I get told. Not only that, I have to force the children to cancel their outings. I don't even like this MD."

"Neither do I. He looks like a ferret." Tory scrunched her face to mimic the man. "Aren't you dying to know what's taken up Kevin's time this year?"

"What makes you think the brunch has anything to do with Kevin's behavior?"

"In London Geoff said there'd be an announcement this month."

"Well you know more than I do. If I ask Kevin anything, he turns a deaf ear. And before you give me a lecture, I have tried waiting for a quiet time when he's relaxed and the children aren't around."

"Then get dressed up in your Sunday best next week and find out. I wouldn't miss this show for anything. I switched an assignment so I could be here."

"You really think it'll be that good? Why? You must have a clue or you wouldn't be so agreeable."

"Too much stuff's happened in the last year that doesn't make sense unless Trans Oil plans a major coup. Think about it rationally for a second." Tory motioned for Chris to sit down.

"Forget all the stuff between you and Kevin and focus on the facts. If you're going to help with the book, you'll have to learn to separate fact from emotion."

Chris tried, but couldn't come up with a logical explanation. "I give up."

Tory explained. "Kevin used to be busy at the start of the year. Busy to him was a ten-hour day once or twice a week. Suddenly he's working insane hours. Even weekends. He's probably got a phone surgically attached to his ear when he's home."

Chris laughed nervously. Why was it that Tory always sounded like a fly on the wall of her life? "How'd you know?"

"Any time Geoff and I go out, he gets calls. Sometimes he puts me in a cab and leaves. Since Tim's been on leave, we've been using their apartment. Geoff spends more time on the phone than he does with me."

"And that doesn't bother you?"

"No. I enjoy the time we have. Now I bring an article with me and edit. When Geoff gets a call, he stretches the phone cord as far as he can, until he's in a room with a door. I know there's an extension in his bedroom. He never uses it. He probably figures I'll hear something I shouldn't if he asked me to hang up the other phone. I think it's comical."

"What else?"

"Geoff goes to Greece an awful lot. Last I heard Trans Oil didn't have an office there. Something's up."

"Maybe not," Chris countered. "Did it ever occur to you that Kevin and Geoff are obsessed with work and Trans Oil figured out it had a good thing going and kept dumping more on them? Kevin obviously doesn't want to be home. Geoff's a bachelor. They always work more. You always claim bachelors use Singapore as the springboard to the rest of their career."

Tory shook her head. "It doesn't ring true. Kev's in a fog. I bumped into him, literally, on Orchard Road about a month ago. He didn't recognize me. I stooped down to help him pick up his papers. He shoved them back in his portfolio and scurried off without a word. That's not like Kevin. Usually he's so polite.

He'd've been more concerned about hurting a stranger than his papers."

That comment made Chris think. It was a perfect description. Kevin had been in a fog for a year. Even when he pretended to listen to her or the children, he didn't hear them. "Now that you mention it, he's put a lock on his desk. I never gave it much thought. I guess we'll have to wait and see. Tell me what I can start researching, so I can get started. I've nothing to look forward to but Christmas parties. And I don't like going alone."

After Tory left, Chris considered their conversation and realized it didn't matter. Nothing at Trans Oil could be so important that it was worth deserting your family. And there was no other way to describe Kevin's actions. It was time for Chris to make a stand of her own. Research might not be the answer, but it was a good place to start. After the debacle earlier in the day, it was clear she should stay out of the garden. She poured herself another glass of wine and tried to remember what she felt when she first arrived in Singapore.

They'd been put in a suite in the Shangri-La Hotel, in the center of the city. The children loved room service, the pool, and the weather. Even with a babysitter for Marc and Alison, she'd been hesitant to leave the children at the hotel while she looked for a house.

The traffic was horrendous. There was no subway and the buses weren't air-conditioned. She never left the hotel unless she took the car and driver. The city looked like one huge skyscraper. She was terrified if she left the hotel alone, she'd never find her way back.

It had taken several weeks to find this house. At first she didn't believe that Trans Oil would pay for what looked like a mansion. There was so much space that it overwhelmed the children. For weeks they followed her wherever she went. Marc actually cried if she were out of his sight.

Everything was so alien. There was a cloying, sweet smell permeating the air. It was a mixture of orchids and sandalwood. It made her nauseous at first. As she thought, she made notes. It was important to remember the little things, like the smell you later failed to notice.

Lifestyles changed in Singapore. With their allowances, expats were upper class. With the increased money came increased socializing. Entertaining was done on a larger scale. At home their friends had been a combination of family, college chums, and people from the hospital. In Singapore, their social world was other expats. Suddenly what a woman did was seen as a reflection of her husband. Chris quickly lost her identity as anything other than "Kevin's wife."

As if the loss of self-esteem weren't enough for a woman to cope with, there was the added stress of the husband's travel schedule. Singapore was the gateway to most Asian cities. Most men traveled on a regular basis. Whereas they might have left town four times a year at home, in Singapore they were out of town several times a month. The wife was left to cope with all the responsibilities of the house and the children. It was easy to feel like a single parent.

The luxury of household help was a double-edged sword. With increased leisure time, the wife gained a new sense of freedom and a sense of uselessness. Boredom became part of her routine. How do you fill up a day when you pay others to run your house?

Chapter 39
SARAH

Sydney, Australia
Saturday, December 13, 1980

Sarah wondered how much longer she could tolerate the masquerade. Barney's parents acted as if their son had been injured in a battle rather than a drunken rage. Why had she agreed to return to Australia with him? It would have been much better if she and Trey had returned alone.

They would be going back to Singapore in less than a week. Sarah didn't think she could bear the prospect. She needed to talk to someone about her trepidation. Maybe her mother would understand this time. Chloe had been horrified at the tale of Barney's destructive fit.

They sat in the living room of the small, terrace house. Chloe was embroidering and Sarah sketching. Sensing that the time was right, Sarah put down her pad and looked at her mother. "I want to leave Barney," she said quietly and firmly.

"Sarah, be serious. So he got drunk one night and made a fool of himself. That's hardly a reason to leave your husband."

"Mother, it's more than that and you know it. Barney's a drunk. Why can't anyone but me see it?"

Chloe shook her head vigorously. "I don't care. He's a good provider. In the long run, that's the most you can expect of marriage."

Irritated that her mother wouldn't take her seriously, Sarah slashed a pastel chalk across her sketch. "I've met a man. I'm in love."

Chloe put down her embroidery, her face suddenly pale. "What?"

"I've met someone who cares about me. Mum, it's so wonderful with Tim. You've no idea how he makes me feel."

"You're daft, Sarah. I'm sure what you felt was a momentary thing. No doubt by the time you return the young man will be seeing another woman."

Sarah shook her head. "You're wrong. Tim would never do that. He loves me. He tells me so all the time. He's different from Barney. He doesn't come from money. What he's done, he did for himself His father didn't buy it for him."

"Child, be reasonable. A little fling now and then appears to be the current vogue in marriage. Please see this dalliance for what it is. You were angry with Barney and lashed out by becoming infatuated with another man. Now that it's out of your system, things can continue as they should between the two of you."

"I'm miserable with Barney," Sarah screamed. "Doesn't that matter to you? Surely you don't want me to be unhappy for the rest of my life. Shall I tell you what life in Singapore is like in the Parker household? Barney drinks every day, sometimes an entire bottle of gin. On weekends drinking is the only thing that matters to him. Trey and I don't exist in his world."

"Then give him a reason to stop. If you were doing your share, you wouldn't be in this predicament."

"Mother, I have tried. More than you can imagine. It's no use. Barney's not about to change. And I won't spend the rest of my life shackled to a man who views me as a trophy his parents bought and paid for."

"Sarah, if it weren't for your father-in-law, I could never afford this little cottage. The Parkers are very generous people. You can't ruin this for me. I dearly love this place and I don't want to move."

"What about me?" Sarah pleaded through her tears. "Don't I matter? Don't you care that I'm unhappy or that I have a chance to get out of a horrible situation?"

"Sarah, it's time you grew up. Life is not a fairy tale. People don't live happily ever after. Do you think I was in love with your father every day of our marriage? I wasn't. But we were mature enough to work through the hard times. You should do the same."

When Sarah started to say more, Chloe put her hands over her ears. Sarah soon stopped her arguments. Her mother was on Barney's side just as Geoff had been. *Why couldn't anyone see things from her perspective? Why did everyone side with Barney? Were they all blind to what he did to her*, she wondered.

The night before they were scheduled to leave for Singapore, Barney Senior took Sarah aside. "I understand that you two have been facing some rough times. Not to worry. It happens to us all from time to time. Barney feels terrible about breaking your crystal. Mother and I ordered replacement pieces. They've already been shipped to Singapore. They should be there when you return."

Sarah stared at the floor. Broken crystal was not her problem. Part of her wanted to tell Barney Senior what she felt. Instead she said nothing, posing as the demure little doll of a wife she was expected to be.

Apparently satisfied that Sarah was not about to challenge him, Barney Senior continued. "It might be wise to leave Trey in Australia. For a while, at least, until you sort through your differences. Just think, Sarah. Without Trey, you and Barney can have a second honeymoon in a tropical paradise. I know that's what you wanted to do in Bangkok. Barney told me how disappointed you were when he had meetings and couldn't go with you.

"Promise me if things get rough you'll ring me. I'd be more than happy to send you a little pin money to go on a holiday with one of the wives. Now be a good little girl and make my son happy."

Sarah hadn't expected more from Barney Senior, yet she was livid. He saw money as a balm that could heal all wounds. Money wasn't the problem with her marriage. All she wanted was time alone with Tim. These months without speaking to him had been torture. There'd been no way for her to ring him without explaining the overseas call to her mother. It would have been impossible for Tim to contact her; No one in Singapore knew that they'd gone to Cairns.

Chapter 40
SARAH

Singapore
Wednesday, January 7, 1981

It's lovely to be back in Singapore, Sarah thought as she went through her morning exercises. The past few months in Australia had been fraught with people pushing and pulling her in different directions. She felt like a rag doll-limp and lifeless, and tossed forgotten in a heap in the corner.

Barney was at work. Without Trey and Ah Soon, the house was empty. There was nothing for Sarah to do. When she rang Tim's office, his secretary said he was on holiday. When Sarah rang Chris, she babbled about a project for Tory and tried to interest Sarah in it. Sarah now regretted her hasty rejection. Much as she disliked Tory, it would be nice to have something to do. She had rung Chris several times to say she'd changed her mind, but Chris was never home.

Today was Wednesday and there wasn't a movie to look forward to. Barney claimed to be tied up at work. She was uncomfortable ringing Geoff. She still hadn't decided. In Australia, Sarah had been certain she wanted Tim. Now that he wasn't here, she wondered. Logically her mother was right, she should stay with Barney. But how? He had no interest in her as anything more than a trophy or a bed partner. It wasn't enough. Her mind and body screamed for more.

She couldn't believe Tim had left while she was on leave. He must have known how desolate she'd be if he was gone when she returned. The fact that she'd left and never rung to say when she'd return didn't enter into it. Tim should have been in Singapore when she got here.

Her thoughts were a blur as she exercised. The angrier she got, the more fast-paced her workout became. When the phone rang she jumped up so fast, the room spun.

"Hullo."

"You're back, luv. I'm so glad. It was intolerable having you away."

"Tim! When did you get back?"

"Last night. I'm not due in the office until Monday. I thought maybe you missed me as much as I missed you."

The second she heard his voice Sarah knew what she wanted. Try as she might, there was no way to ignore the butterflies in her stomach at the sound of Tim's voice. "It's been agony, darling. Absolute agony."

"Where's hubby?"

"The office. Why?"

"Geoff's at work as well. This place is all mine for hours. Why don't you come 'round and we can say hello properly?"

The invitation was what Sarah needed. Every nerve in her body twitched at the expectation of seeing Tim. "I could be there in an hour."

"Why so long?"

"I've been exercising. I'll have to shower first."

"You'll only have to do it again later. Sarah, luv, I've missed you. Come as soon as humanly possible. I'm not sure how much longer I can live with only the memory of your touch."

Sarah hung up in a daze. As was his wont, Tim had pushed the right buttons. Despite his request that she hurry, Sarah showered, and fixed her hair and makeup. There was no way she'd look less than perfect for their reunion. It would never do.

Tim met her at the door in an electric blue silk robe which he flashed open to reveal he wore nothing underneath. The second she was inside, Tim's arms encircled her. He pressed her back against the closed door. Sarah's clothes came off, piece by piece, as they hurried into Tim's bedroom. There was no need to worry about the trail of clothes through the living room. Geoff wouldn't return for hours.

In the privacy of his room, they made love. Quickly at first and then slowly as they accepted the reality of the other's presence. Try as they might, they couldn't make up for the drought of the last few months in one afternoon. By four o'clock, they were exhausted and hungry.

Sarah went into the kitchen. The refrigerator was barren, and she doubted the pantry was stocked any better. After moving some beer, she found an overripe pineapple and a wedge of Brie. Since she couldn't find a cutting board, she put them on plates, and proudly carried her feast to the bedroom.

While she was gone, Tim had picked up her clothes and folded them neatly on top of his bureau. The two of them sat in bed and ate. In between feeding each other slices of fruit and cheese, they touched constantly, gentle, reassuring strokes that proved today wasn't a dream.

"Sarah, we can't continue like this. I want more than stolen seconds of your time."

"Tim, it's been a lovely day. Please don't ruin it."

He kissed her nose and placed a sliver of pineapple on her tongue. "While I was away. I thought about us. I want to go back to Adelaide. I had a job offer when I was home. If we went together, we could start a new life. Just you, Trey, and me. Wouldn't that be lovely as well?"

Sarah frowned. "I need more time." She saw the sadness on Tim's face and reached over to soothe his furrowed brow. "I'm not saying no, love. I'm only saying I can't do it now. Can't we wait until after the holidays?"

"And what will be different then? Sarah, don't you see? It's what we both want. We're meant for each other. Can you honestly tell me you're in love with Barney?"

She shook her head no.

"Well then, what's the problem? The sooner you tell him it's over, the quicker we can start our life together."

Tears welled in Sarah's eyes. This was not what she expected. Tim had never pressured her before. Why must he do so now? Why did everyone think they knew what Sarah should do? She wanted Tim. At the same time, she wasn't positive she could give up the lifestyle Barney provided. It saddened her to realize how spoiled and pampered she had become. And how much she liked the expatriate life. Could she survive in Australia without the money and position Barney provided? Tim made a good living, but Sarah had no delusions that it would compare to what she was accustomed to.

Tim brushed the tears from her cheek. "Don't cry, pretty Sarah. I didn't mean to hurt you. I've missed you so. I can hardly think when I don't see you every day. I'm so afraid if we don't run off together, you'll disappear. All the time I was home, I was frightened that I'd get back and find you'd left Singapore forever. I was terrified I'd never see you again."

"I missed you. All the time. Oh, Tim, you've no idea how hard all this has been. Barney's family will fight to keep Trey. His father as much as said so. I think my mother would help them."

Tim paused. "I hadn't given any thought to Barney's parents wanting their grandson. I'm sorry. It was selfish of me, I know. The only excuse I can offer is that you've bewitched me. I can think of nothing but you and our being together. It's all that matters."

"I feel the same. Barney's parents insisted Trey remain in Australia while Barney and I work things out. I'm worried I'll never see my son if I leave Barney now."

Tim brushed the tears from her eyes. "Pretty Sarah. Don't worry. We'll work it out. We must figure a way around Barney's parents. How is hubby, anyway? Is he still perfecting a way to pickle himself inside the gin bottle?"

Sarah shook her head. "He's not drinking."

"Not to worry, luv. He can't ignore the lure of the bottle forever."

"I know."

"Then we'll have to wait. Once he starts to drink again, he'll clear the path for us."

They fell asleep in each other's arms. They woke to noise coming from the living room. Tim put his finger to Sarah's lips, went to the door, put his ear against it, and listened. Frowning, he motioned Sarah to his walk-in closet at the far side of the room. In whispered tones, he blurted, "Geoff's here. With Barney, no less. There's someone else with them, I'm not sure who. Barney's drunk. Geoff just ordered the other person to make coffee. We'll have to be quiet until they leave."

Sarah paled visibly. "Barney? What if he comes in here? Tim, what are we going to do?"

"I've turned the lock on my door. No one can come in unless I unlock the door. Sarah, please pull yourself together. This is no time for hysteria. We best get dressed. With clothes on, we're less suspect."

Sarah was shaken. This was too close for comfort. How on earth had Barney ended up here of all places? It wasn't like him to be drunk at the office. But where else would he see Geoff? Surely Geoff hasn't been out drinking all afternoon. Not staid, proper Geoff.

Sarah nearly jumped out of her skin when the phone rang. Tim stared at the phone, waiting for Geoff to pick up the extension. Shortly, they heard the front door open. Tim went back to his listening post at the door. He stayed there several minutes. When he turned, he was grinning. "Geoff left in a huff. Whoever else is here has been ordered to take Barney upstairs to the deck, and keep him walking until he's coherent enough to take home. They've already gone upstairs. I could hear two pairs of feet."

"What now?"

"If there's no noise in ten minutes, you slip out, hail a taxi, and go home. I'll slam the front door when you leave and pretend I just came in. I'll make sure Barney stays here for at least an hour. That should give you enough time to shower and change your clothes. When I get the lay of the land, I'll ring and tell you what's happening."

Sarah's heart pounded and her pulse raced. When Tim gave the signal, she snuck out of his flat. She had the doorman ring for a taxi, rather than go to the street, where she might be seen. The wait seemed interminable. Sarah was convinced Geoff would return any minute and find her.

Chapter 41
TORY

Singapore
Wednesday, January 7, 1981

Tory did not want to get out of bed. She was desperate for just ten minutes more sleep. Ever since London she had felt like a whirling dervish, engaged in constant spirals of motion that led nowhere. In order to schedule time for the book, she readjusted her calendar. She postponed some assignments; those that couldn't be pushed back, she accelerated. Unfortunately, there were more of the latter than her schedule could accommodate.

Daily she commuted to the neighboring Asian countries. It seemed she was on a plane each morning. Evenings were spent developing film and writing. No matter where she was, she had a pencil and pad in her hands. The article she planned to edit today had been started on a plane from Bangkok and completed on one to Kuala Lumpur.

She was too busy to see anything when she traveled. Since she didn't have time for research, she relied on her memory to provide background filler. There was only enough time to get the information or photos she needed before it was time to get on yet another plane.

Her apartment was the worse for wear from her rapid comings and goings. She'd allowed things to pile up. Clothes were strewn all over. What little food was in the refrigerator had long since grown into a different life form. There was no way she could work in this chaos, so she called a Singaporean neighbor who ran a cleaning service. It would be worth the investment to come back to a more settled atmosphere. As she got out of bed, she flexed her muscles to get the kinks out of them. Her neck and upper back were in knots.

The phone rang. Tory groaned, certain it would be Chris with another wonderful idea for the book. Although she was pleased Chris was excited about the project, at the moment Chris's enthusiasm was another pressure. In Tory's mind, the book was placed in a separate compartment she dared not open until ready to give it her full attention.

"Hello. Grand Central Station."

"You sound in good humor. Can you spare me an hour tonight?"

Despite her exhaustion Tory, laughed at Geoff's question. "That's what we've come to? An hour. Somehow, I expected the thrill to last longer."

"Not nice," Geoff countered. "Tim's back. There's no longer a quiet haven on Grange Road."

"You could come here."

"No, Jurong's too far. If you meet me at the Hyatt at seven, we could share a cup of coffee."

"I'm not that cheap a date. I'm holding out for my very own cup. And I want tea."

"Greedy little wench," Geoff laughed as he hung up.

By now Tory was accustomed to the curt starts and ends to Geoff's phone calls. They no longer worried her. What did was their inability to meet for more than an hour. Geoff was completely involved in what was going on at Trans Oil, and she was always dashing to or from a plane. The Hyatt was their second home. A place to rendezvous for an hour. She wanted more, and it disturbed her. Geoff was taking on too much importance in her life.

Time was what she wanted, time for the two of them. Not fragmented hours sandwiched into their too-full schedules, but real time, when one of them didn't have an eye constantly fixed on their watch.

She showered quickly and reviewed her diary while she sipped chamomile tea. As usual, the brew had a calming effect.

The canister was nearly empty; she made a note to pick up more. She looked at her watch and grabbed her camera bag. There was barely enough time to catch the 9 a.m. shuttle to KL. On the plane, she reviewed the questions for her interview with a prominent zoologist.

The interview took twenty minutes longer than she'd allocated. The afternoon rains started before he finished talking. That meant she had to wait to get the photos she needed. Instead of being on the 2 o'clock shuttle, she barely made the 4:30 plane.

When she landed in Singapore, Tory realized there was not enough time to return to Jurong and get back to the Hyatt by seven, so she went to Chinatown. Tory adored Chinatown. The small buildings, the hustle of the people. The smells that filled the air, this was her Singapore-not the modern skyscrapers, but the ramshackle buildings with tin roofs and brightly colored facades, where paint peeled off the shops like decaying bark on a tree in the jungle. Families lived above their small shops. You could see laundry hung from poles out their windows.

The streets were crowded at the end of the workday and the area pulsated with people. She felt herself get pushed from passersby as she walked towards Chun Chun, her favorite herb shop. Tory savored the feeling of life that was so evident in the area. She paused at Sago Street and smiled at the colorful paper dragons being made to ward off the evil spirits that might otherwise posses the dead. The funeral parades of Chinatown were sights to behold. She made a mental note to bring Geoff here one Saturday morning.

In the midst of bargaining over the price of the tea, she thought she heard someone call her name. She ignored the sound; positive she'd been mistaken.

"What's the matter, Tory? Don't you remember me?"

She turned slowly. Her jaw dropped when she came face to face with Barney Parker. His shirt was coming loose from his trousers, his tie was askew, his face had smudges of dirt on it, and he wore only one shoe. He was drunk. This was the last thing Tory needed. "Hi, Barney. How goes it?"

"It goes. You know how it is. Let's have a drink. Okay?"

Barney hung on Tory's arm. She smelled gin on his breath. The last thing he needed was another drink.

"I'm in a rush. How about a rain check?"

"Be a sport. We had so much fun with that racetrack game. I've got it in my pocket. Play with me again. Please." Barney reached into his slacks and caught his hand in the lining of his pocket.

Tory knew that she had to get Barney out of there. If nothing else, he'd lose his wallet in the crowd. She led him to the nearest bar so she could think. The minute she got him into a chair, he passed out. When she tried to lift him, she knew she could never move his dead weight. To placate the owner, she ordered two shandies. It was a little after six. If she hurried, she might be able to reach Geoff at his office. She looked in her diary and realized she didn't have his phone number.

With the change from the shandies, she went to the pay phone and dialed Trans Oil's main number. When the line was answered, she was thrilled to hear an operator she knew.

"Hi Grace. It's Tory Winslow. Could you connect me to Mr. Melbourne, please?"

"Hi, Miss Winslow. Mr. Melbourne's not here anymore. He works at the Shaw Building now. You know, on the corner of Orchard and Scotts Roads."

What's Grace talking about? Trans Oil doesn't have an office in the Shaw Building. Orchard Road sounded familiar, though. Then she had it. That was where she'd bumped into Kevin. And she always met Geoff at the Hyatt. But why were they there? "Of course. How silly of me. Could you give me that number then?"

"I'm not supposed to give that number to anyone."

"I know, Grace, and normally I wouldn't ask you to betray a confidence. But it's urgent I reach Mr. Melbourne. He's expecting me and I'm held up." *Please don't offer to give him a message*, she implored the air. "How are your children? Would you like more photos of the baby?"

"If you want to take them. Mr. Taylor had a meeting with us before he and Mr. Melbourne moved. He said we weren't to ask you to take pictures unless we could afford your fee. He said if we accepted free pictures of our children, we put Trans Oil in a compromising position. Something about conflict."

"Conflict of interest," Tory said. "I like taking pictures for my friends. Grace, I really have to talk to Mr. Melbourne. I promise you he won't be angry if you give me the number. I don't have my appointment book, otherwise I wouldn't have to bother you."

"Okay," she agreed reluctantly.

Tory wrote the number on the back of her hand and put more coins into the phone. She stood with her fingers crossed and pleaded with the air. "Please, please answer, Geoff."

"Trans Oil."

"Hi, Kev, it's Tory. I need to talk to Geoff. Is he there?"

"How on earth did you get this number?" he demanded.

"That doesn't matter right now. Please get Geoff."

"Tory, I demand you..."

"Fine, Kevin. Demand all you want. Either put Geoff on the phone or come to Chinatown yourself."

"Chinatown?"

"Barney's out cold. We're at One-Eyed Sams. Tell Geoff or come yourself." With that, she slammed down the receiver, and ran back to Barney. Two men pretended to be asking about his health. She cursed at them in Mandarin. When she checked Barney's pockets, she found that the bulge the men had probably assumed was his wallet was only the computer game.

She drummed her fingers on the small table. The wait was agony. Each time she looked at her watch, only a minute had passed. If Kevin gave her message to Geoff, it would take him at least half an hour to get to Chinatown. She had no idea how long it would take him to find One-Eyed Sams. She hoped that the owner's name would be enough information.

What if Kevin didn't give Geoff my message? If' Geoff's not here by 7:15, I'll page him at the Hyatt, she promised herself. She hoped Kevin wouldn't ignore her pleas. She sipped her shandy in a daze. It was the only way she could drink beer at all, mixed with lemonade. Shandy was a drink that grew on you. It was cheap. She'd acquired a taste for it over the years.

After what seemed like hours, the door to the bar opened, cautiously. She was ecstatic to see Geoff. "The cavalry to the rescue," she joked.

He was not amused. "Where's your head? Why would you take a drunk to a bar?"

Tory was irritated at Geoff's attitude. He sounded as if it had been her idea. This was not the time to argue. All that mattered was they get Barney out of there. That seemed to be Geoff's intention as well. He looked at Barney and picked him up from his seat roughly. "Grab him under his left shoulder," he ordered.

"Careful. You might hurt him."

"Be quiet. Please. Can you walk with him and carry your ubiquitous camera?" he asked sarcastically.

Tory was stunned into silence. Geoff acted like she'd done something wrong. *Who does he think he is*, she raged silently. She struggled to keep pace with Geoff's rapid movements. They dragged Barney's limp form between them through the thick crowds. The car was parked blocks away. When they reached it, they poured Barney into the passenger seat of Geoff's sports car. Tory climbed into the space behind the front seats.

During the ride, Tory bit her tongue several times. Geoff would only talk when he was ready, and she had no intention of making a bad situation worse.

"I tried Sarah before I left. She's not home. When we get Barney to my flat, will you stay with him until he sobers up?"

Now her allotted hour with Geoff was to be used in getting Barney to safety. For a moment, Tory wished she'd left Barney in the bar and gone to the Hyatt. *No, I'm annoyed because Geoff's reverted to his arrogant old self. I honesty thought that he'd changed. Was I ever wrong.* "What's your problem?" she asked belligerently.

"Shall I enumerate? First, you have Kevin apoplectic. He's positive you'll give that number to Chris, and no doubt wonders what else I've told you. Second, you've spent the afternoon drinking with a man we all know should be kept away from booze at all costs. Third, when you determine the situation's out of control, you ring me to bail you out. Next time you find yourself in a situation such as this, don't expect me to rescue you."

"Are you through?" she screamed. "I bumped into Barney in Chinatown. He was drunk then. That bar was the first place I could find. I knew I had to get him off the street or he'd've been found mugged and dead in the morning. I couldn't let that happen to anyone I know. Pardon me for having a conscience. Next time I go out, I'll leave it in the pantry."

He lifted his eyebrow. "I take it I'm not about to win a popularity contest. You must admit, what I assumed made sense."

"Can't you apologize? I feel like I need a code book to understand you."

When they stopped at a traffic light, Geoff reached behind his seat for Tory's hand. "I am sorry. I'm annoyed that what little time we have is spent picking up after the Parkers. It was wrong of me to take out my frustration on you."

"Damn straight," she said. "You can be so ... oh ... I give up."

"Careful, you nearly smiled. I apologize, Tory, I do. There's nothing more I can say at the moment. Someday we'll talk about today and laugh."

She was not convinced. At the moment, she wasn't certain she wanted to see Geoff again. Tory thought about the day's events. It was obvious that Geoff didn't like raised voices. This was new information. She tried to synthesize it with other facts she knew about him.

When they got to Geoff's apartment building, Tory followed Geoff and the doorman into the elevator. The two men carried Barney between them. She could see Geoff was uncomfortable with the spectacle they made.

At the door to the apartment, Barney started to wake up. He looked confused. Geoff ignored him and sent Tory to make coffee. She thought she heard a lock turn and realized her imagination was working overtime. In the kitchen, she caught an aroma that was vaguely familiar. As she started the percolator, she tried to place the scent.

Geoff poured the hot, steamy liquid down Barney's throat so fast Tory was sure he'd be scalded. Geoff was so intent he didn't hear the phone start to ring.

"Shall I get it?" Tory asked.

Geoff handed her the coffee and put the phone to his ear. His conversation consisted of grunts and the words "I know." When he hung up, he looked ready to kill.

"I must go back to the office. Immediately. See if you can get him upstairs. The fresh air may help. Whatever you do, don't let him near the pool. Ring Sarah every ten minutes until she's back. Have her come 'round and fetch him."

Tory saluted Geoff's departing back. She heard a noise from Tim's bedroom and the penny dropped: Sarah's perfume, the lock turning. Part of her wanted to knock on Tim's door and ask Sarah to tend to her husband, but she wasn't up to that scene. The important person was Barney.

She walked Barney back and forth across the patio until she could stand it no more. As she collapsed in a chair, she heard the front door slam and readied herself for the farce that was about to be played with Tim.

Chapter 42
CHRIS

Singapore
Monday, February 2, 1981

It had been two months since Trans Oil announced its entry into the oil trading and shipping segment of the business. At the start of the year, when Kevin and Geoff had been given adequate staff to run their operation, Kevin had returned to a more normal work routine. Now that he was ready to be a husband and a father, he acted as if his family had been in suspended animation, waiting for him to bring them to life. Kevin and Chris argued about his point of view constantly.

She'd expected things to be strained between them at first. She also thought that after a period of adjustment they'd find equilibrium. Things weren't working out that way. No matter how she tried to ignore it, Chris always came back to the same thought: Kevin hadn't trusted her. Although he insisted Geoff had demanded absolute secrecy, she couldn't believe Geoff had meant her. When Kevin tried to absolve himself by reminding her that Geoff hadn't said anything to Tory, she couldn't believe his audacity. Geoff and Tory weren't married. The rules for a married couple were different.

Their battle had been raging for weeks. It was worsened by the work Chris did for Tory. Chris felt invigorated by the time spent with new people. Now she came home tired and wasn't interested in listening to the petty annoyances that Kevin faced during the day. After all she was out in the world herself.

She no longer expected Kevin to give her life meaning. She was doing that for herself. Their relationship had always been dictated by Kevin's schedule and needs. Their future would have to take both of them into consideration. Chris wouldn't settle for being an afterthought in Kevin's life.

Chris threw herself into her volunteer work and research. The world of bridge and lunches had lost their allure. She and Kevin went to parties together. Once again they were seen as the perfect couple. They play-acted well in public. At home the facade fell apart.

Chris wasn't due at the hospital today. All she had to look forward to was organizing the data she'd so diligently collected. So far she'd filled three notebooks with information that would have to be sifted and organized. While she enjoyed gathering the data, she had no idea what to do with what she found. It was the same way she'd felt in school when it was time to write a term paper. Her mind had always drawn a complete blank and she ended up in tears. In school she'd had Kevin to turn to. Now she was afraid to ask for his help. And she dreaded facing Tory with so little to show.

She'd been staring at a blank piece of paper for hours when John called. He'd been in Kentucky on leave. When he suggested lunch at his house, she agreed. John had been so gentle and patient with her. For months he held her hand and listened to her complaints about life. He'd been there when Kevin was too involved to notice she was alive. She and John had developed a closeness she no longer shared with her husband.

She went to the closet in the master bedroom to find the appropriate dress. Her eyes searched the rainbow of dresses in the closet, looking for the perfect outfit. Then she saw the buttercup yellow silk dress Sarah had convinced her to buy. She'd never worn it. As she held it against her body, she smiled at her image in the mirror. Sarah had been right after all.

All her life Chris had avoided wearing yellow. As a child, her auburn hair had been carrot-colored and she'd been told that yellow didn't look good on redheads. Sarah had insisted that, with her alabaster skin and auburn hair she had nothing to worry about, the color would be lovely.

The dress had a boat neck and was fitted at the waist with a gently pleated skirt. Instead of a belt, she tied a multi-colored, albeit mostly green, scarf around her waist. The swirling colors brought out the green in her eyes. She hesitated for a second when she touched the pearl choker in her jewelry box. The necklace was from Kevin. Was it right to wear it for an assignation with another man? She started to discard the pearls, stopped herself, picked up the pearls, put them around her neck, set the safety catch, and grinned. After all, Kevin had bought them to salve a guilty conscience.

Her hands shook as she used the knocker to John's front door. She felt as nervous as a teenager on her first date.

John opened the door and bowed gracefully. "You look lovely, my dear. Just like the daffodil you remind me of."

"Daffodil?" Chris asked, taken aback by the imagery.

"I think of all women as flowers," John explained as he led her to the sunroom where he poured them a glass of champagne. "You have such a lovely garden. Surely you recognize people in the flowers. In their own way, each flower is beautiful, but they vary so."

"Why a daffodil?" she asked. "It's just a run-of-the-mill flower. I'd rather think of myself as an orchid."

John kissed her cheek. "No, my dear. You could never be an orchid. The daffodil's a beautiful flower. It's long and sleek yet sturdy enough to survive strong winds. A perennial, it comes back each spring, eager to face the world again. So like you. You have this marvelous ability to bounce back from life's little punches and return stronger than before. That's a rare gift, you know."

Chris felt her face flush. John was so gallant. Kevin hardly noticed her garden. Even though he knew she spent hours working there, he was oblivious to her efforts. He smiled indulgently when someone commented on the effect Chris had achieved; yet he had no idea what was involved.

"Why not an orchid?" she asked. "I think they're the prettiest flower."

"An orchid's beautiful. But it's such a fragile flower -- too fragile, really. It only flourishes in the proper environment, preferably a hothouse. Even here in Singapore where the orchid grows abundantly it must be cared for and treated tenderly. If not, it withers and dies too soon. You, my dear, are beautiful, but there's nothing tragic about you."

Chris smiled at John's description. How many times had she seen her friends in flowers? She'd never seen orchids as tragic before and yet she knew exactly what he meant. "I know who's an orchid -- Sarah Parker."

John nodded sadly. "Yes, Sarah's a delicate creature. She's far too fragile for the life here. That brute of a husband of hers has no idea how to give her the tenderness she needs."

Chris raised her glass. "Barney's not the only man I know like that."

"Speaking of Kevin, that was some coup he pulled off for Trans Oil. Is he pleased to have gotten the brass ring?"

Chris looked surprised. Kevin insisted it was Geoff's idea. "The brass ring? Doesn't that go to Geoff?"

"To both of them. It would never have worked without Kevin. Geoff may have had the idea. He could negotiate the contracts and work out the myriad of details, yes. But he needed someone with Kevin's intimate knowledge of Singapore to pull it off."

John placed his fluted glass on the small table between them and stood. "If you'll excuse me, I'll just check on the status of our luncheon."

While John was gone, Chris found herself comparing him to Kevin. John's hair was graying at the temples and he had more laugh lines than she remembered. So different from Kevin, whose hair was the same brown of his youth. Kevin only had wrinkles when he frowned, although that was a common occurrence these days. Despite the slowness in John's step, there was lightheartedness in his voice. He was pleased about something that much was certain.

The words brass ring made Chris think of Coney Island. She closed her eyes and could almost smell the surf and hear the call of the gulls, while she and Kevin walked hand in hand on the boardwalk after eating Nathan's hot dogs. It was the week before they moved to Singapore. Kevin had been so excited about the adventure before them.

"I want my chance for the brass ring, Chris. I know Singapore's the place. Promise me you'll stand by me. We're a team. I'll never be able to do it alone. Together we can do anything."

Chris was so lost in her memories that she swore she smelled the hot dogs' spicy mustard. She didn't hear John come back into the room until he spoke.

"What were you thinking of just then? You looked happy."

Chris opened her eyes with a start. "Kevin," she offered weakly.

"Don't be embarrassed. I wanted to have lunch today to tell you I'm leaving. I put in my retirement papers this morning. I'll be returning to Kentucky in three weeks."

Her jaw dropped. "John, why?"

"I've never cared for Singapore, you know that. It's time I went back to what I miss: the smell of new mown grass, the changing seasons."

Tears filled her eyes at the prospect of losing the man who'd become her closest friend.

John handed her his handkerchief "Don't shed a tear for me, my dear. It's what I want. I shall miss you, though. You've been an important part of my life. It's better that I leave while we're friends. If I remained, one night when we were both a bit too lonely, we'd do something we wouldn't easily forget. I'd never have been able to forgive myself if that happened."

Chris blushed. "You've been reading my mind. I planned that today would be the day."

"Had we met at another time and another place it might have been different. But not now. And most definitely not here."

"I'm not sure I understand."

"Chris, you're a treasure. I've been through too much with Monica's affairs to be party to a liaison myself. You and I became friends because we both were starved for attention from the opposite sex."

"Tory and I decided the same thing, months ago."

"Tory's a very wise woman, except when it comes to herself. I worry about her solitude."

"Tory and I are friends."

"I know. After Monica died, Tory and I were very close. I don't know how I'd have survived those first few months without her gentle ministrations."

"Tory?" Chris was in shock. John and Tory? It couldn't be. The thought of Tory and John together was incomprehensible.

John brought Chris's hand to his lips and kissed it gently. "Not in the way you think. Tory helped me see things clearly at a time when the world looked like I was seeing it through a kaleidoscope. With her help, I learned to focus. She has the ability to help others find themselves while still lost herself. I hope that someday she finds peace."

John stood and offered his arm. "Lunch is served. I thought we might be more comfortable in the garden."

While they ate, John steered their conversation to pleasanter topics. "I've told you what I miss about Kentucky. What do you miss about New York?"

Chris smiled. "My family, especially my brother. He and Kevin were best friends from junior high. Even after we married, Mike was a big part of our lives. Until we moved to Singapore, Alison and Marc were like brother and sister to their cousins. It was nice to be connected with people we shared a history with."

"You lack that here. Everyone comes and goes. There's no permanence."

Chris nodded. "We've been in Singapore nearly eight years. Each year my Christmas card list gets longer as friends move on. The only constant besides my family is Tory. I don't think she'll ever leave."

"Probably not. She's found a hiding spot. Is there anything you've enjoyed about life on this island?"

Chris nodded. "I've seen so many places I'd only read about. The children are getting a marvelous education. We wouldn't have dreamt of sending them to private school in the States. Then there are the servants. At home a cleaning woman every two weeks was considered the height of luxury. I can't remember the last time I've had to do more than plan a menu. The lifestyle here can be fantastic."

"Yes, it can. Does the allure of so much free time appeal to you?"

"For a long time I relished it. Then it became a sort of bondage."

"And now?"

Chris smiled. "I'm enjoying it again. I'm doing research for Tory's book. Without the house to worry about, I can devote my entire day to investigation if I want."

Chris paused. "Seems like I've been seeing only the negatives for a long time. Singapore's not the root of my problems with Kevin. They would've surfaced anywhere he excluded me."

At the end of the meal, she and John savored a glass of Remy Martin. As the last drop of the amber liquid was finished, John took a box from his pocket. "This is for you. It's my way of saying thank you for all you've given me."

Chris held the box unsure whether she should open it. At John's prodding, she did. Inside was a gold daffodil on a thin gold chain. With trembling hands, she unhooked her pearls and replaced them with the pendant.

"I don't have anything for you. I should do something to repay your kindness."

John smiled. "A mutual friend of ours has a saying, if you get a kindness from someone, pass it on."

He leaned over and kissed Chris on the cheek. "You've been very important to me. I shall never forget you. I do hope you and Kevin work out your differences, Chris. You deserve happiness, and it appears to be a scarce commodity among our friends."

"I'll miss you, too. You've helped me in so many ways. I wish things could have been different."

"They can never be anything but what they are. You know that. Now give me one last hug before I change my mind. And, Chris, watch out for Sarah. I suspect of all the flowers, she's the one most in need of kindness."

"What about Tory?"

"Tory's war is with herself."

"Can't I can help her?"

"No. If you're truly her friend, all you need do is be there. If she ever decides to face what frightens her, I think she'll need all the support she can find."

There were tears in Chris's eyes when Suradmin started the car to take her home. On the way, she thought better of going home and asked him to take her to Scotts Road. Her heart raced as she took the elevator to the fifteenth floor of the Shaw Building to see Kevin. If she wanted to make a change in her life, what better place to start than with Kevin. She wondered what Kevin would think of her impulsive behavior. She wanted to see where he spent his day. It was the most important thing she could think of doing with the rest of her afternoon.

To her delight, Kevin was pleased to see her. When she walked in, he was standing over a computer screen looking at something Geoff pointed to. They both looked pleased with what they saw.

"Chris, so good to see you again," Geoff said. He stood, bowed, and started for the door. "If you'll excuse me, I've a matter of some importance to attend to."

"What brings you here?" Kevin asked.

"I thought it was time I saw what's captured your attention for so long. The wife's always curious about the other woman, you know that."

The smile faded from Kevin's face and was replaced by a frown. "Chris, we've been through this before. I did what I had to. It was my shot at..."

"The brass ring," she offered. "I know. I wanted to see what it's all about. Is this your office?" She turned to see get a better look at the room. The decor surprised her. The furniture was Scandinavian with straight lines and no frills, just the opposite from the furniture they had at home. The two walls without windows had huge photos of the jungle, their stark reality the antithesis of the Impressionist paintings Kevin claimed to like.

"It's Geoff's. Good grief, can you picture me comfortable in a place like this? It reminds me of a waiting room." He pointed at the pictures on the wall. "The photos are from Tory. A Christmas gift, I think. She's such a good photographer, I half expect a tiger to jump at me from the bushes."

"But Geoff got up... I thought... I mean..."

"Geoff's the consummate gentleman. Don't worry. As long as he's found a phone, he'll be content. Why don't I give you the guided tour of the place? While you're here, you might have some suggestions for what I can do with my office."

Kevin's office was as large, but on the opposite side of the building. It had a panoramic view of Orchard Road and the comings and goings of the city. If possible, his office was more barren. The only decorations were photographs of Chris, Alison and Marc on his desk, in the silver frame she'd given him several years before. She recognized the pictures. They were from Sentosa. "It doesn't look much different than Geoff's."

"No, but you could change that." He leaned over, kissed her, and tugged at the chain on her neck. "Is that new? I like it. It suits you. What is it?"

"A daffodil."

"I'm happy you stopped by, Chris. I really am."

"So am I."

Chris waited eagerly for Kevin to get home. She practically flew into his arms when he walked into the solarium. "I've missed you."

Kevin returned her embrace. "It's been all of three hours since we saw each other," he kidded.

"Can't I miss you?"

Kevin pulled away and looked at her lovingly. "It's been a long time since you cared when I came home. If I knew all it'd take was your coming to my office, I'd have invited you."

"Why didn't you? Didn't you think I'd want to see where you spent your time?"

Kevin led Chris to the rattan sofa. He nodded in the direction of the bar. "Care for a martini?" When she agreed, he went to liquor cabinet, made a pitcher of martinis, and carried them to the table. Kevin took Chris's hand. "Actually, I have no idea what you want. Lately you seem hell-bent on punishing me for keeping Geoff's idea a secret."

Chris nodded. "I know it must seem like that. I was angry at you, because I missed you. Geoff found time for Tory. You didn't have any time for me."

"Chrissy, I was so exhausted, it was all I could do to drag myself to bed. Geoff gave Tory stolen minutes. She was happy with a cup of coffee at the Hyatt. Would you have settled for so little?"

Chris shook her head. Kevin knew her better than that. "Tory's so terrified of commitment, all she wants are fragments. She was upset for months after she and Geoff were together for a long weekend last August."

"Oh, I don't know. Geoff claims they're together a lot these days."

"Right. In between her flights to hither, thither and yon. Kevin, be serious. Tory's always on the move."

"So are you. What's capturing your attention?"

"I told you before, I'm doing research for a book. Tory asked for my help."

Kevin laughed. "That's rich. You never liked doing research when we were in school. When did that change?"

Chris shifted uncomfortably in her seat. This wasn't progressing as she'd hoped. Kevin wasn't taking her seriously. "I know it sounds strange, especially from me. But, there's something about what I'm doing that makes me see things differently."

"What?"

"Take a look at our house. What do you see?"

Kevin's eyes scanned the room. "A big room and the garden."

Chris got up, tugged Kevin to a standing position, and walked quickly into the living room. "See the tiled floors? They can't have been part of the original structure. They must have been additions. They were probably installed when the air conditioners were put in."

Kevin looked around the room, as if he would find the answer written on the shutters. "How can you be so positive the tile floors weren't here all the time?"

"I've read about the original construction during the time the English were here. The floors in the formal parts of the house were solid marble. Tile wasn't used until after World War II. At least not tiles like these."

"What's your point?"

"Things aren't always what they seem. I wanted to describe the housing in Singapore. There are so many differences in the old colonial mansions that I went to the National Library to read up on what the construction had been like. That's when I discovered that marble tiles weren't made until the 1950s."

"And that's symbolic of something?"

"No. It's interesting."

Kevin shook his head. "If you say so. What are we doing this weekend?"

Chris glared at her husband. "Can't you pretend to be interested in what I tell you?"

"Chris, I'm glad you found a hobby. Don't expect me to make more of it than that."

"So my research is only a hobby? Do you think what Tory does is a hobby?"

"Of course not. Tory does more than study arcane facts. She takes photos, strings words together, and comes up with articles that get published in books and magazines. You can't honestly compare what you're doing to what she does."

"Why not?"

Kevin tugged Chris's hand and returned to the solarium. He reached for his glass and swallowed his martini in one gulp. "For one thing, Tory supports herself."

"So if I got paid, you'd take what I'm doing seriously?"

Kevin shook his head. "Geoff told me Tory was paying you. I'm sure you like having money of your own."

"It's more than making money. I feel alive. For the first time in ages, I feel like I'm contributing to the world. I'm not a parasite."

"Doesn't making a home for me and the children count for something? That should be more than enough to keep you fulfilled. Running a house this large can't be easy."

"It's not. But I need more. The book's made me see how bored I am. Now I have a purpose when I get out of bed in the morning."

"Has Tory seen what you're working on? I doubt she'll be fascinated about when marble tiles came into style. Tory writes about serious matters, not frivolity."

"Kevin, this is not trivial information. It explains what's happened to housing. It might help some woman decide what type of house she wants before she arrives."

"I'm sure her husband will be thrilled to know that decision's reached before they set foot on the plane. He'll sleep better knowing that housing won't be a problem. No one cares when their house was modernized."

Chris wanted to slap the smirk off Kevin's face. "Why not? At home, people spend tons of money restoring old brownstones."

"I hadn't thought of that. So what are our plans this weekend?"

Chris closed her eyes and sighed. "We were invited to a party Friday evening at the Burkes." She looked over and saw the blank look on Kevin's face. "They're new. He's with a bank. Their son's in science club with Marc, although he's in Alison's grade. Since I'll be at Sarah's garden party that afternoon, I turned Penny down."

Kevin nodded absently. "Some shipping guys will be in town Thursday. I'll probably be out late with them. A night off will be a relief. It's amazing how much those guys can drink."

"Am I supposed to find that interesting?" she asked sarcastically.

Kevin looked puzzled. "You always wanted to know stuff like that before."

What's the use, Chris thought. Kevin didn't care what she did during the day, why should she care about his? "It's been so long since you shared things with me, I forgot."

"Do we have plans Saturday night?"

Chris nodded. "The entire day's programmed. Marc has a soccer match. I promised we'd go. The team is coming over for a barbecue. Several of the parents will be here, too. Geoff and Tory are coming, the Adams, the Murphys. Most of the usual crowd."

"That's nice. It's been ages since we've had a party. I was afraid that you'd lost interest in everything but the book. Glad nothing's changed."

Chapter 43
SARAH

Singapore
Friday, February 6, 1981

The lovely weather matched Sarah's mood. Although it seldom happened at this time of year, she'd been afraid the day would be overcast, or worse, that it would rain. Today she was hosting a lunch for twenty women. She'd not left one detail to chance. The house was perfect. She followed the servants around, and readjusted each accent pillow to guarantee they weren't a fraction of an inch out of place.

The menu had been chosen with the utmost care. The food would be low calorie and artfully displayed. For a week she'd tried various combinations until she found just what she wanted. The colors and presentation were exquisite. No matter which foods a woman chose from the buffet, her plate would be a work of art.

The pool was sparkling. The water was so pristine you could see the design on the bottom. Five small rattan tables were set on the flagstone patio surrounding the pool. Each had a pastel umbrella to ward off the sun. The umbrella colors had been chosen because they looked like sherbet: cotton candy pink, pale aqua, robin's egg blue, pistachio green, and buttercup yellow. The pale colors would accent, rather than overshadow, the women's dresses.

When Sarah decided to throw this party, she'd been afraid no one would accept her invitation. After the afternoon she and

Tim had nearly been caught in his flat, they decided Sarah should adopt the pose of the perfect corporate wife.

What should have been a slow process was made easier by the influx of new families in January. Although the new wives might have heard stories about Barney's drunken accident, they'd never know the truth. Sarah held her head high and acted like all was perfect in her marriage. It was impossible to differentiate the falsehoods from the truth in the gossip mill. If she put on a good front, no one would believe the stories. After all she was married to Barney Parker.

In the past month she'd accepted every invitation, regardless of how insignificant. She played bridge two afternoons a week, shopped, went out to lunch or coffee every day. When she and Barney went out as a couple, she stayed at her husband's side. Although her eyes might search for Tim, she acted the dutiful wife.

Barney had been transferred to Trans Oil's new venture and, for the moment, was happy at work. Although Sarah had seen him start new jobs with enthusiasm that dwindled rapidly, she tried not to let the past color her thinking.

She and Tim agreed that four months of self-imposed isolation should be all the time they needed. Once Barney's drinking increased, no one would fault Sarah for leaving him. Now that the Parkers were in the social whirl, Barney's drinking wouldn't remain a secret. It would be easier for Sarah to get custody of Trey if Sarah were seen as the wronged party in her divorce.

After the first of the year their movie night had started again. It was torture for Sarah. There was no way to dissuade Barney from the idea without arousing his suspicion. She'd hoped Geoff would refuse and put an end to the matter. Surprisingly, he'd been all for the plan. Apparently Tory didn't share Geoff's enthusiasm for movies. Rather than ask her to do something she didn't care for, Geoff preferred to go with friends who shared his passion.

Each week she prepared a suitable meal and went to whatever horror movie Geoff and Barney suggested. Even when a lovely film was in town, one that she and Tim would enjoy, the four of them went to Barney's choice. It was easier that way. Sarah didn't trust herself. She could only speculate on what might happen if she were alone with Tim. She trembled with anticipation all day each Wednesday, knowing she'd see him that evening.

This would be the first time she'd entertained in her house since her in-laws' visit. Sarah had purposely decided upon a women's afternoon. It would be easier without Barney. She could ensure the day went as planned. To her amazement, everyone she invited accepted, even Tory. Now that there was only fifteen minutes until her guests arrived, Sarah was apprehensive.

Lately everyone seemed different. Tory was changed; her caustic wit had been replaced by a withdrawn silence. Much as she'd disliked Tory's acid tongue, Sarah found her reticence more difficult to comprehend. Even when she was at a party with Geoff, Tory appeared off in her own world.

Chris, too, was standoffish. She'd lost her interest in parties and socializing. Sarah had been amazed when Chris did nothing to introduce the new wives to each other. Chris was always racing off to look into something for Tory's book.

Not to worry, she chided herself. *They're only two of the guests. Anyway, they're always thick as thieves when they're together.* They could ignore the rest of the guests, for all Sarah cared. As long as they were there, it was a good omen. It would indicate the most prominent women in the expat world accepted Sarah.

Sarah took the last few seconds before her guests arrived to make certain she looked as good as the house. She wore an off-white silk dress. It had flowing sleeves and a tulip bottom to the skirt. Her hair was pulled off her face with combs that had small orchids attached to them. The color of the dress matched the orchids in her hair.

It was a lovely afternoon. Everything worked as planned. The ladies raved about the food, said it was so pretty that it was a shame to eat it. At last Sarah's talents were being appreciated. She was surprised when Tory complimented her on her eye for color and placement. Everyone had commented on the decor, but from Tory it meant more because she understood design details.

When the other women left, Chris and Tory stayed behind. Sarah was flabbergasted when Chris launched into a tirade about men. It was so unlike her. She sounded at odds with the entire male population. Sarah wondered if she and Kevin were having problems. It wasn't a topic discussed in a large group. The jungle drum was not above using an inadvertent comment against the husband of the wife who made it. A wagging tongue at the bridge table could destroy careers. Knowing that and how protective Chris was of Kevin, Sarah couldn't believe she was complaining so openly.

The three women sat by the pool with a carafe of wine. Sarah watched Chris with interest. Her eyes were moist. Her voice sounded as though it was strained by unsheds tears.

Chris said something that hit a nerve with Tory because Tory's dark eyes clouded and her body turned rigid. Sarah wondered why. Chris had been complaining that Kevin treated her like a possession. A comment like that had nothing to do with Tory. Geoff didn't do that. Over dinner on their movie night, Geoff often spoke about what Tory was working on. He didn't trivialize her work. From what he said, Tory breezed in and out of his life at will, a situation he accepted.

Chris seemed so emphatic when she spoke. "Doesn't it ever bother you, Sarah? Wives are nothing more than decorations in Lotus Land."

Before Sarah could say anything. Tory jumped into the conversation. "Come on, Chris. Nothing's changed here except you. Don't globalize your feelings. Own them."

"What would you know about it? Kevin calls all the shots. What I want doesn't matter to him. I thought things would get better with him not working so much. The only change is he's home more. You have no idea how lucky you are. No one's ever told you what to do."

Tory closed her eyes, opened them again, and gulped down her wine.

Her motions were so rapid that Chris stopped in mid-sentence. "Don't you dare tell me I should say all this to Kevin. I have and he doesn't hear me."

"I'm sure you have."

"What's that supposed to mean?"

Tory sighed. "Exactly what it sounds like. Kevin only hears what he wants. It's a male characteristic, I think. It probably has something to do with the Y chromosome."

Sarah was stunned. Tory, who had an answer for everything, had said someone else was right. More than that, she'd admitted she didn't know the motivation behind every action. From the look on Chris's face, Sarah could tell she was just as surprised.

Sarah looked at the two other women. "There are times when I think I'm something Barney's father bought him to keep him out of trouble," she offered weakly.

Chris laughed. "Don't say things like that around Tory. She thinks if you tell someone what you want, it happens, like magic. I've told Kevin I want to go home, and he ignores me. When I tell him about the research I'm doing for Tory's book, he calls it my little hobby, and asks what's for dinner. I'm sick and tired of not being taken seriously."

Sarah was in shock. All this time, she thought Barney's lack of interest in what she did was an indication of their problems. She'd never considered it universal. But if it happened to the golden couple, it must be. "Does he ever ask you what you've done all day, and then laugh if you describe a day spent marketing and planning menus?"

Chris laughed. "I gave that up last year. Now I say outlandish things like I had a mad passionate affair with the pool boy. Kev just smiles and says that's nice."

Sarah turned to Tory. "You don't know how lucky you are. You've never been in a position where a man owned you."

Tory paused. When she spoke again, she appeared to weigh her words carefully. "I think it happens to all of us. We simply experience it in different ways. It happens nonetheless."

"Right," Chris answered snidely. "Like Geoff would ever question your work. No one tells you what to do or how or when. You come and go as you please, without ever having to consider anyone but yourself. Do you realize how lucky you are?"

"Freedom's not what it's cracked up to be. There are times I... oh, forget it."

Sarah couldn't. Tory had more to say, she was positive. Sarah was curious. Was it possible that self-sufficient Tory was no happier than the rest of them? "Geoff isn't condescending about what you do. He often talks about articles you've written."

"The fact that he knows what you're working on is more than we get from our husbands. Tory, you have no idea what it's like. You don't. You have it all. Now that Geoff's in the picture, I'm jealous. I wish I had a career I could lose myself in."

Sarah nodded her head in agreement. *Tory does something she loves and has a man to love. What more is there?*

Tory smiled a little grin, the sides of her lips ever so slightly upturned. "No one has it all. No one. If you think it's a career you want, Chris, then go for it. But be careful. Sometimes you get what you dream about, and then you wake up and realize it's a nightmare masquerading as a dream. And you'll be forced to live in terror for the rest of your life."

"Do tell," Chris said.

Tory shook her head. "You'll have to trust me on that score."

Chris was indignant. "I tell you everything. Why do you always clam up? Geoff adores you. Any idiot can see that. Why can't you accept a simple fact without turning it into a melodrama?"

Tory's eyes lit up and she smiled in earnest. "Geoff's wonderful, I admit it. If it were possible for me to love anyone, he'd be on the top of the list. But I learned a long time ago that I'd always be alone. When his work permit expires, he'll leave. Like the rest of you will. I'll be left in Singapore. Alone."

Chris frowned at Tory's remarks.

Sarah said, "If the two of you married, you could go with Geoff. You could work anywhere. It doesn't have to be here."

Tory shook her head sadly. "There's a price to pay for decisions you make in life. Marriage isn't in the cards for me. My independence appeals to certain men, especially ones like Geoff. He's afraid of commitment, and I don't ask for promises. I know there won't be a tomorrow. I accept that today's all there is. If I tried to make more of it than that, Geoff would be on the next plane out of here."

Chris looked at Tory as if she'd lost her mind. "Have you and Geoff had a fight? Is that what this is all about? I can't believe the garbage you're spouting. Geoff would do anything you want, and you damn well know it. From what I've seen, you're the one who pulls back, not him."

She turned to Sarah. "What do you think, Sarah? Is Tory over-dramatizing?"

Sarah nodded. "Definitely. Tory gets all the freedom she wants. And she gets Geoff at the same time. It's an ideal arrangement."

Tory seemed to withdraw physically, even though she never left her seat. Sarah was about to say something and Chris shook her head. Much as she wanted to pursue the subject, Sarah followed Chris's lead. Apparently Chris knew when it was wise to stop asking questions.

Sarah wondered about appearances. Chris was angry with Kevin, angry enough to broadcast it publicly. She'd chosen a safe refuge. Tory never repeated anything. And Sarah was too concerned about her own marriage to tell tales about anyone else. Tory, who gave the impression of being satisfied in her world, was anything but. What the problem was, Sarah couldn't tell. Tory talked in riddles. It was impossible to understand her. For the first time, Sarah saw Tory as human and vulnerable like, the rest of them.

If no one's happy what's the sense in it all, she thought. No matter how hard she tried, she couldn't find happiness with Barney. Her thoughts wandered to Tim all the time, especially in bed. If she closed her eyes and pretended Tim were her husband, it made it easier for Sarah to sleep.

The year before Sarah had envied the Taylor's marriage. But Chris was unhappy. If that could happen, anything was feasible. She wondered if it would be different if she were with Tim. She'd always assumed that their similar interests would provide a strong basis for their future. Yet Geoff and Tory also seemed well-suited. They each had a career the other respected, they shared a cynical view of the world, and each admitted to caring for the other. If that was all it took, they should have been happy. Tory wasn't.

Sarah looked at Tory. "Have you ever made a decision that was really hard? One that could affect the rest of your life?"

Tory turned her head slightly and nodded, her eyes fixed on a point in the pool.

"How did you do it? Did you make a fist of pros and cons, or toss a coin? How did you know what was right?"

Tory was so silent Sarah thought that she'd not heard the question. Just as she was about to repeat it a bit more loudly, Tory answered.

"I did what I had to do."

"But how did you know it was what you had to do?" Chris asked.

"I just knew. It was the only path out. As I did it, I knew I'd have to live with the ramifications of my actions for the rest of my life."

"Do you ever regret the decision?" Sarah asked. She wanted to know what Tory had decided, but knew that she'd never get an answer to that question.

"Regret's a waste of time. You can never know how things would've been if you made a different choice. Once you pick a path, you're committed. There are no second chances in life."

Sarah looked at Chris and shook her head. The old Tory was back.

After Chris and Tory left, Sarah sat by the pool and thought. The afternoon had been an eye-opening experience. She'd never realized that other women shared her frustrations. *Have I been too hard on Barney?*

When he came home drunk and fell in the pool, she was no longer sure of anything.

Chapter 44
CHRIS

Singapore
Saturday-Monday, February 7-9, 1981

After Sarah's garden party, Chris was relieved to find Kevin asleep when she got home. She was irritated that Kevin had belittled the research she was doing for Tory's book. She'd planned to discuss her anger with Sarah and Tory. Instead of the sympathy Chris expected, Tory lit into her.

She walked into the kitchen for a glass of juice and saw a note from Alison. "Mom: Dad said I could spend the night at Debbie's. See you at the soccer match. Love, Alison."

She went upstairs and stuck her head into Marc's room. "Ready for the game?" she asked.

Marc grinned. "Yep. Dad says he'll be there. Will you?"

"Of course. I promised, didn't I?"

"I know. It's just ... Dad said you might have things to do with the barbecue and I shouldn't pressure you."

Chris moved to sit next to Marc on his bed. Absently, she brushed a lock of hair off his forehead. "Sometimes your father worries too much. I promised I'd go to your game. I'm sure I can manage a barbecue and a soccer match in the same day."

"I'm glad. Aunt Tory's coming. Dad said he saw her this morning and she said she's gonna take photos of the game."

"Going to, not gonna."

"Going to take photos of the game. Isn't that neat?"

"Yes, it is. Marc, don't be upset if Aunt Tory doesn't make it. She and I were together this afternoon. I don't think she feels well."

"Now who worries too much? If Aunt Tory told Dad she'd be there, she will."

Chris nodded. There was no reason to disturb Marc. She was probably overreacting. Between Tory's travel schedule, and the time Chris spent researching, they'd barely seen each other.

"Well, Marc, you better get some rest or you won't make the game yourself." She leaned over and kissed his cheek.

She went downstairs and poured herself another glass of juice. The way Chris calculated, in less than a month, Tory would be ready to think about her book in earnest. What would she say when she saw the notebooks full of information in no order?

Damn Tory's mood, she thought angrily. She'd hoped that when they lagged behind at Sarah's, Tory could suggest the best way to structure her data. Instead of providing the support Chris expected, Tory had jumped over Chris before she could explain where her conversation was leading. After Tory's outburst, there was no way Chris felt comfortable raising the subject. Something was on Tory's mind, something serious.

She wondered what to make of Tory. She'd seemed about to explode. The only time she'd seen Tory so rattled before had been after a death. Then, too, Tory hadn't explained why she was perturbed. Why was it that Tory knew what was right for everyone but herself? *She's trapped in her thorny bush,* Chris thought. Absently, she flipped through her notebooks until she found a page with "psychologist" printed in red capital letters. When she looked at the page, she laughed. Who was she kidding? Tory was the last person who'd seek help for what bothered her.

Although she'd convinced herself that Tory would be at the soccer match, Chris was relieved to see her walk into the stadium with Geoff. Geoff waved and joined Chris and Kevin in the grandstand. Even though the game wouldn't start for half an hour, Tory stayed on the sidelines with the team. Chris looked at Geoff with a puzzled frown. "Isn't she going to sit with us?"

Geoff shrugged. "She must have a headache. She scarcely said a word in the car."

Kevin smiled. "Tory quiet. Now that's a day I've longed for. Let's hope she doesn't find her tiger balm."

Chris laughed at Kevin's attempted joke. Tory's allegiance to Chinese herbal remedies was well-known. She doubted that Tory's head hurt. Whatever was wrong was more deep-seated than a headache.

"How's your research coming, Chris?" Geoff asked.

Chris smiled. "It's a lot harder than I anticipated."

"Most things are," he agreed. "Kevin and I find that out daily."

"So he says. It is going well though, isn't it?"

Geoff nodded. "With no small thanks to your husband. We'd not have gotten where we are without him."

Kevin scoffed at the compliment. "Anyone could've done what I did."

"Not so. Do you realize how impressive your husband can be? He had the ship owners eating out of his hand Thursday night."

Chris smiled, leaned over, and kissed Kevin on the cheek. "I never question Kevin's brilliance."

"Or my taste in women."

Alison came into the grandstand, a sad look on her face. "Sweetie, why aren't you with the cheerleaders?" Chris asked.

"I thought I'd come up and say hi. Is something wrong with Aunt Tory? I said hello and she didn't hear me."

"Mr. Melbourne thinks she has a headache." Chris hoped she sounded convincing.

"I knew something was wrong. When I walked by, I would've sworn she was crying."

Kevin kissed his daughter and pushed her towards the steps. "Don't worry about the grown-ups. The sun was probably in her eyes."

When Alison left, Chris looked at the men. "Who's going to be the brave soul who goes down to see what's wrong with Tory? I vote for Geoff."

Geoff shook his head. "If I know one thing with absolute certainty, it's that the wisest course of action is to leave Tory alone. When she puts up her wall of silence, no one can find the door. Not to worry. She never remains this way for long. By the time the game's over, she'll be fine."

Chris wondered if Geoff knew what he was talking about. At the same time, she didn't want to be on the receiving end of Tory's scathing tongue. By the time the game started, Tory was talking to the coach and taking photos of the action. She seemed engrossed in what was happening on the field. During the break, she took individual photos of the team and the cheerleaders.

Given that Tory had seemed to return to normality, Chris was surprised when Geoff arrived at the barbecue late and alone. There were so many people at the house; it took her an hour to catch up with Geoff. "Where's Tory?" she asked.

"Jurong. She said this was the only time she'd have to develop the film from today's game. I'm to stop by later this evening, pick up the photos, and give them to Kevin at work on Monday."

"Is she all right?"

Geoff nodded. "She leaves for Jakarta in the morning. I think she's worn out from her schedule. She's not spent an entire day here since December. Three months on the road is too much, even for Tory."

"Are you certain that's all it is?"

"Yes. She said she was sorry to miss your party, but was certain you'd understand how important the photos are to Marc and his friends."

"She's right," Chris agreed. Geoff wandered off to speak to some of the men from Trans Oil and Chris quickly forgot about Tory.

Monday morning, how she should organize the data came to Chris as she worked in her garden. To keep John's memory alive, she had planted daffodil bulbs and had been tending them, when suddenly the idea was in front of her. She didn't need Kevin or Tory. The answer had been inside her all the time.

Chris went into town and bought large index cards, a pair of scissors, and several rolls of sello tape. It took her over a week to go through her notebooks, cut up the pages, and put them on the cards. When she finished, she had far too much data for the book. She'd amassed a wealth of material on doctors: their education, medical specialty, philosophy of treatment, as well as personal details. When she looked at the cards she realized that at her fingertips she had all the information needed to refer people to the correct doctor for any problem.

All the time she spent gathering the data, she wondered what had led her to start with doctors and not schools or stores. She smiled at the stack of cards on the table. It made sense when she thought about it. She was trained as a nurse, and she was obviously still called to the field.

Now that she had all the information, she wondered what to do with it. There was no doubt in her mind that Tory would pare it back for the book. The fact disturbed her. The data should be used for more, and she had a good idea what. Before she could call Tory to discuss her idea, she got a frantic call from Sarah.

She had a headache and couldn't stand the pain any longer. As Sarah explained her symptoms and what the doctor she'd seen previously had said, Chris sifted through her cards. She was positive Sarah had described a migraine, not a stress headache. When she found the card for a doctor who specialized in migraine treatment, she called him, made an appointment, and volunteered to accompany Sarah.

The second she saw Sarah, Chris knew she'd been right. Sarah wore dark glasses and gripped her stomach as if nauseous.

While Chris waited for the doctor to examine Sarah, she wondered why a doctor would have given her tranquilizers. On the trip back to Sarah's house, they stopped at a chemist to fill Sarah's new prescription. Chris stayed at Sarah's while she took the pills and rested in a darkened room. While Sarah slept, Chris took a notebook from her purse and started to make notes about how to put her idea into action.

A referral service would be a boon to expat families. The question was how to do it. Getting a doctor in Singapore was a process of asking a friend for a reference. There were not many private practitioners who expats felt comfortable using. While the locals might be content with clinics, the expats wanted a physician who gave them an appointment and offered Western medications.

When they'd first arrived, Chris had taken the children to Tory's doctor. He treated their maladies with roots and herbs. Although his regimen cured the children of their afflictions, Chris hadn't liked his methods. Boiling roots and herbs into tea was not her idea of medical care. It took so much time to find what she needed at Cold Storage. Then she had to grate the root, put it in boiling water, and make a compress. She had continued to search for a pediatrician. In the end, the children went to the doctor at the American School. It hadn't been an ideal solution, but it was the only one available.

When Sarah woke without her headache, Chris was pleased. She had proof of how beneficial a referral service could be. She could hardly wait to tell Kevin. This was much more interesting than research. There was no doubt in her mind Kevin would share her enthusiasm.

While they sipped a martini after dinner, she explained what she wanted to do. Kevin listened in rapt silence, and she assumed he was as excited as she. Since she knew she had his undivided attention, she continued to talk. Her ideas poured from her mouth like rain in the monsoon season. When she finished, she grinned at him. "Isn't this a great idea?" she asked.

"Who'll do it?"

"Me."

"You don't need a job," he answered. While Chris sat dumbfounded, Kevin continued, saying, "Taking care of me and the children is your job."

"Kevin, be serious. This is important to me."

"Last week, doing research was important. This week, it's a referral service. What will you be interested in next week, Chris?"

"The referral service. Can't you see? This is something I can do. Think about the years I spent studying. I'll get a chance to use my nursing again."

"I thought that's what you did at Mount Elizabeth."

Chris shook her head. Why couldn't Kevin understand? "You don't need a nursing degree to fluff pillows. Ask your daughter. She goes to Glen Eagles Hospital one afternoon a week. Alison doesn't want to be a nurse. She's working on a science project."

"Chrissy, I admit your idea has merit. But it will take a lot of time. Have you given any thought to that? It isn't something you can start and stop to suit your whim. It would have to be open every day. You don't have that kind of time. Or the attention span."

The more Kevin spoke, the angrier Chris became. It was as if he'd heard nothing she'd told him in the last few months. She'd expected him to be happy she'd found something that interested her. The children were at school all day and had after school activities. They barely got home in time for dinner. There was no need for Chris to sit in the house all day to wait for them. The servants took care of the house. They'd been doing it for so many years they didn't need her guidance. In fact, she was in their way when she was home.

For every argument Chris could think of, Kevin had a rebuttal. "It'll take too much of your time. And for what?"

"For me. You have a job. Why can't I?"

"You have a job. Taking care of your family is your job."

"I need more than that. I've told you a million times, I can't spend the rest of my life playing bridge."

"Why not? It sounds great to me."

"I feel like a parasite, a freeloader. You got your chance for the brass ring. Why can't I?"

Kevin picked up the newspaper. Chris grabbed the paper from his hands and threw it on the floor. "Damn you, Kevin. Listen to me."

"When you say something that doesn't have Tory written all over it, I'll listen. Chrissy, this isn't like you. Your family needs you. The children and I depend on you to be here for us. If you want to do something, why not decorate my office?"

Chris ran up the stairs to the bedroom and slammed the door behind her. She knew what she felt. Why couldn't Kevin understand? He might listen to her, but he didn't hear what she said.

They'd been in Singapore too long. Her natural fast pace had slowed within the first two weeks of moving. The oppressive heat made it impossible to function at breakneck speed. If the climate weren't enough to make you sluggish, the pace of the island was slow. In the beginning there had been so much to keep her busy. Now time hung on her hands like humidity. Chris was no longer satisfied to putter in the garden, do volunteer work, play tennis, and go to lunch. It had been a wonderful existence for a few years, but the time had come for her to do more.

She smashed her fist into the pillows on the bed. *Who died and put Kevin in charge anyway? If he won't support this venture, I'll do it anyway. I don't need his permission.*

Chris started her referral service on an informal basis. Within a week, when word got out that she could find the right doctor for any complaint, friends started calling her with their symptoms. Soon she had calls from people she'd never met that'd been given her name from someone they knew.

She never told Kevin. There was no reason to fight with him. She had no intention of stopping. He'd insist she abandon her dream if he found out. Since most of the calls came during the day, she was able to keep her venture a secret from Kevin. As long as dinner was on the table and his world didn't change, Kevin wasn't suspicious.

They continued to go to parties together and she was the perfect wife. She said the right things to people and told Kevin any snippets of gossip she thought he'd find interesting.

Chapter 45
TORY

Singapore
Saturday, February 7, 1981

Tory met Geoff on the corner near her apartment. "Thanks for coming for the photos. I hope the kids like them."

"I'm sure they will. How long have you been waiting here?"

Tory shrugged. "I don't know. I finished making the enlargements about 8:30. What time is it?"

Geoff looked at his watch. "About a quarter to nine. How nice for you that I left the Taylors when I did."

"Mother Luck smiled on me," she joked. She didn't want to get into another argument with Geoff.

"Have you time for coffee? I'd like to talk."

Tory smiled slowly. "I'd love to, Geoff, but I'm tired. May I have a rain check?"

"No. I've had about all I care to take of your moods. If you can't take an hour out of your schedule for me, there's no sense in continuing this charade."

Tory stared at Geoff in disbelief. "This from the man who spent over a year working on a project practically twenty-four hours a day."

"That's not quite true. I made time for you whenever you were in town. Admittedly it wasn't much time, but I made certain there was always time for you."

"And you'll walk away because I can't find time for you one day? That sounds pretty harsh to me."

Geoff reached for Tory's hand. "There's a world of difference between making time and finding time. I'm surprised you missed such a salient point. You must be more tired than you realize."

Tory eyed Geoff skeptically. She detected a hint of sarcasm in his words, yet he was smiling. It didn't make sense. "I'm tired."

"So am I. Tired of your games. Chris was disappointed you didn't come to her party. There was no need to develop the film tonight. You used the photos as an escape. What are you hiding from?"

"It doesn't matter."

"It does. You know that."

Tory tried to wrest her hand from Geoff. He stood firm, refusing to release her. "Geoff, please leave me alone."

"Tory, if I do, I leave permanently."

"Damn you! I want one night to myself and you insist on making a crime out of it. Can't you understand? I'm tired and need time to think."

"How can you think when you're exhausted? You spent the better part of last night curled up on your couch."

"How do you know? You were asleep when I slipped out of bed."

"I'm a light sleeper. I woke when you got out of bed. You do that whenever I spend the night. Is it having me in bed that disturbs your sleep? If so, I'd go home."

Tory shook her head. "It's not you, it's me. I'm having nightmares. It's gotten so I'm afraid to sleep."

Geoff let her hand slip from his and put his arms around her shoulders. "Tory, what's bothering you? Please don't say nothing. Something's on your mind. It was so obvious even Alison was concerned about you today."

"Geoff, I wish I could explain."

"I think you know what's bothering you and why it disturbs you."

Tory thought silently. *Why can't Geoff leave well enough alone? Why does he have to push for the truth?*

"I'm certain this has to do what happened when you left home. What was your argument with your father about? If you talked about it, you'd see it wasn't so bad after all."

Tory shook her head. She knew what she felt. How could she make Geoff understand the sense of abandonment she'd felt when her family turned their backs on her?

"Tory, please. I want to help you. I hate to see you in so much pain."

"I know. And I appreciate it more than you'll ever know. I can't explain it to you. I'm sorry, Geoff. You have no idea how much I wish I could tell you everything."

"So do I. Tory, there's nothing you could tell me that would stop my loving you. You must know that. Take my hand. We'll go for a ride if that will make it easier for you."

Tory shook her head. "Geoff, you really are a sweet man. I'll never forget what you've meant to me." Tears streamed down her cheek. "I wish I could tell you the whole story, but I can't. Not today, not ever. I wish things were different. You deserve so much more than I'm able to give."

"Isn't it a tad presumptuous of you to decide what I need?"

"Geoff, please don't make this harder than it has to be. You've already said you want answers. I can't give them to you. I've tried, I really have. But I can't go any further."

"You're willing to close the door on me? I thought it odd that you met me on the street. I didn't realize it was the harbinger of our farewell. There's poetic justice in ending things on this corner."

Tory tried to smile. "I know. It's where we met."

"Do you always end things where you think they started? Is that how you and Tim separated?"

"Geoff, please leave."

"After I escort you to your door."

"Always the gentleman. How can you be so gallant? I'll not change my mind as we walk up the stairs."

Geoff nodded. "I realize that. I want to make certain you make it up four flights. At the moment, you don't look too steady on your feet." He put out his arm for Tory. "I promise I'll not ask any more questions. We each must do what we see as being in our best interest."

Geoff kissed her good-bye at her front door. When she heard his footsteps on the stairs, Tory fell onto the couch in tears. *Why wouldn't the past stay buried where it belonged?* For years, she'd forgotten Prairie View. Recently the past was an ever-present companion. Even if she filled her days so there was no time to think, her dreams kept the memories alive. Since Sarah's garden party, she hadn't been able to shake the urge to return home.

Maybe it wasn't such a bad idea. Geoff could be right. Things might not look so bleak if she went back. She'd only been sixteen. She was no longer a frightened child. Tory smiled at the course of her life. She was a respected, self-supporting photographer and writer, she had friends, she was falling in love. All in all, she had a good life. If only she could get past the nightmares.

Geoff's good-bye had sounded so final. Tory knew it was up to her. Was she willing to let one childhood mistake ruin the rest of her life? No. She reached for the phone to schedule a flight to North Dakota.

Tory decided against letting anyone know that she was leaving town. Her recent schedule had been so erratic that no one would think twice about her absence. In a week, when she came back, she could tell them.

Chapter 46
TORY

Prairie View, North Dakota
Wednesday, February 11, 1981

Tory was in such a fog that she nearly drove past Prairie View and back to Bismarck without stopping. It took two tries before she could park her rental car in front of Jack Talbott's office.

Jack smiled when Tory walked into his office. "What brings you here? I thought you said you'd never return."

"I'm not really sure. It goes back to Dora's letter. Jack, I want to face the past again. I need your help."

"Anything. Let's have a cup of coffee while we talk."

Distractedly, Tory sipped at the coffee, not noticing the bitter taste, since it matched the bile in her throat. "I want information on my family. I've written down the names of my parents, brothers, and sisters. I want to know everything, where they live, if they're married, the ages and sexes of their children, who drinks too much, who beats his wife, anything you can find."

"Tory, I'm not a private detective. That's what you need."

Tory shook her head. "Prairie View's small and I doubt any of them left. It's probably just a matter of asking questions of the right people."

Jack put his coffee cup down and peered across his desk. "You're sure this is what you want? From what Dora told me, it won't be pretty."

Tory nodded. "I have to know."

"Why?"

"Dora said I should open up my heart. I can't. Every time I try, the past hits me in the face. If I'm going to get beyond this point, I have to face some things. The problem is, I don't know where to start. I was hoping, if I approached it like I was writing an article, I'd figure out who to see. There's always a weak link. If I know more about my family as they are today, I'll know where to start."

Jack nodded. "I see. Well, it may take some time. Will you stay with me while you're here?"

"I thought I'd stay at a motel between here and Bismarck."

"From what Dora said you've spent more than enough time alone. There's plenty of space in the house. You'll have privacy. I'd welcome the company. I need to talk about Dora and no one here besides you cared for her."

To pass the time, she drove around town to get the feel of it. In her mind it was a journalistic endeavor. She explored the town as if in search of background material for an article. It was easier to view the sights if she divorced herself from them.

It was amazing how much had changed. How had she missed it all last year? The feed store, the pharmacy, and the general store were still there, but they were more modem than she remembered. The rest of the storefronts were for new businesses. Turner's Restaurant was now a bank.

On a whim, Tory walked into the pharmacy. The dry air made her throat ache. She wanted rock candy. She scanned the shelves and couldn't find any. The man standing behind the counter looked vaguely familiar. He couldn't be old man Tyler. Bob Tyler had been one of her father's poker buddies. He'd also been older than her father. Tory did some quick addition. If he were still alive, her father would be in his seventies.

"Hi there. Bobby Tyler at your service. Can I help you find something, ma'am?"

Tory smiled. *Bobby, of course. It's the son.* "I was looking for rock candy."

The man laughed. "We don't get much call for that. Not with the newfangled throat sprays the drug companies have come out with. Why don't you tell me how your throat feels and I'll suggest an alternative?"

Tory frowned. "Do you think the general store would carry it?"

"Couldn't say. We Tylers don't have anything to do with the Masons."

"Thanks, anyway." Tory turned to leave, spied a small bottle of aspirin on the display counter, and picked it up. "I'll take these." There was no reason not to buy something. He had given her information.

Despite the changes in the stores, the people were the same. The feud between the Tylers and Masons was still going on. This must be the third generation who didn't speak. She wondered if they knew what the initial argument had been about? It didn't matter, although it reminded her that the people in Prairie View had long memories.

In many ways Prairie View was still a whistle stop town, so small it didn't even have a traffic light. Tory wasn't certain what disturbed her more, that so little had changed or that her mind had accurately recorded what was there. Although she prided herself on her ability to recall minute details, she'd wanted to believe that the cosmetic overhaul indicated a tolerance that hadn't been there before.

Despite her initial misgivings, Tory was happy that she was staying with Jack. She hadn't realized how hard the trip would be. She no longer felt like the person she was in Singapore. Memories of the past came back with every step she took. With Jack home in the evening, when the pain was at its worse, she had a friendly face to turn to. Jack listened to Tory without passing judgment on what she said.

When Jack completed his research, Tory sat in his office and read the dossiers. She was surprised at the wealth of material he'd amassed in a week. He'd set up a separate file for each family member. Her mother was dead-one beating too many from her drunken husband. Tory scanned the folders. Most of her brothers were similar to their father: they drank too much, beat their wives and children, and barely scraped together enough money to keep a roof over their heads. Her sisters hadn't fared much better. "Am I related to these people? It hardly seems possible."

"I've checked all the records. They're your kin all right."

Tory frowned. She was painfully aware that the folders contained but a fraction of the truth.

It took her two days to decide how to make the next step. Even then, she was barely able to sleep the night before. At 10:30 a.m., she drove to the address of her youngest brother Matt. He lived in a development of houses that had gone up since she left.

Tory sat in the rental car for over an hour and stared at the house. It was bitterly cold. No one was outside. She sat undetected while she summoned the courage to knock on the door.

Finally she got out of the car and rang the bell to the house. A small boy who eyed her cautiously answered it almost immediately. While he looked her up and down, he put his middle finger in his mouth. Tory's heart raced. It was the same finger she'd sucked as a child.

"Is your mommy home?" she asked softly.

When he nodded his head, and made no move to call her, Tory was at a loss what to do. Before she could decide, a woman who asked if she could help her opened the door.

For a second, Tory lost her voice. When she regained her composure, she smiled weakly and asked when Matt would be home. The woman looked at her oddly. Tory was uncomfortable under her penetrating gaze. Maybe the information she had was wrong and Matt didn't live there after all. But it must be true. The little boy looked like Matt.

Before she could say anything, the woman told her, "We ain't buying nothing."

Tory tried to reassure her she wasn't selling anything. Strangers were rare in Prairie View. No wonder the woman eyed her suspiciously. The words she'd rehearsed the night before were gone.

"Are you Jane Winslow?" she asked in desperation. The woman nodded and Tory continued, saying, "You're married to my brother Matt. I know he's at work and I don't want to disturb him there. I'd like you to do me a favor. If I give you a number, would you please ask him to call me there this evening? Tell him Tory ... I mean Eliza ... wants to talk to him. If he doesn't want to call, tell him it's okay, and I understand."

The woman's face lit up in recognition. "Eliza? After all these years. I knew there was something familiar about you. Don't you remember me? Janie Simmons. Tommy, this here's your Aunt Eliza." The door opened and Tory went inside.

Jane filled her in on what had happened to the Winslow clan since she left. "Your Papa ain't going to want to see you. Not sure much else of your family will either. Matt and me, we don't see much of them ourselves. We've worked real hard to make a good life for our family. Why'd you come back? You fall on hard times?"

The question was so funny, Tory laughed. The hard times had been so many years before. Tory and Janie spent the day sipping coffee and discussing what their lives were like. Tory regretted not having brought photos of Singapore to show. When she'd left, the thought of sharing her life with her family had been the furthest thing from her mind.

When Matt came home, he echoed his wife's sentiments. "Papa crossed your name out of the Bible the day you left. You knew that. I heard Mama tell you, the one time you called. If it's money you need, we could scrape some together."

Tory laughed nervously. "I came to see Papa."

"You're dead to him. Don't you understand?"

"But he's not dead to me. Matt, please, I'm afraid to go out there alone. And I need to see him again so I can put the past to rest for good. I wouldn't be here if it weren't important."

Matt shook his head. "Eliza, you don't know what you're asking. If anything, Papa's gotten worse with age. Why don't you stay for supper, meet the girls, and go back where you come from tomorrow? Sounds like you got a nice life now. Be thankful you got out of here."

Tory shook her head stubbornly. "I can't run away again. This time I've got to face Papa and tell him the truth. I wouldn't be here if there were any other way."

"Okay. We'll go Saturday afternoon. I work mornings. Janie, you and the kids stay here. There's no sense in upsetting everyone 'cause Eliza and me are going to see Papa."

Saturday morning Tory couldn't eat. She paced Jack's living room until she was certain she'd worn a new path in the old carpet. Just before she left to meet Matt at the bank, she fixed a cup of chamomile tea.

During the ride, Matt tried to dissuade Tory.

She was as adamant as he. "Matt, I know you mean well. But this is something I have to do. Stop reminding me how stubborn Papa is."

"Okay, after you explain why you're dragging me along. You've been gone over twenty years. What's so important you gotta go back?"

"I'm falling in love with a man."

"That's wonderful. I never believed what Papa said about you. What's love got to do with coming home?"

"Geoff insists on knowing about me. He wants to know why I'm afraid to let him get close."

"I've seen some of your articles in magazines. You write well. Make up something. He'd never know the difference."

Tory shook her head. "I can't. Over the years, I've developed this public persona who doesn't need or want anyone. Geoff doesn't buy my act; he sees it for the facade it is. Besides, deceit isn't a good starting point for a relationship."

"No, it's not. As long as there's a purpose in all this, I'll do what I can. I don't expect Papa'll be keen seeing me. He and I fell out years ago. Janie got pregnant and we got married when we were sixteen. I worked days in her father's feed store and studied nights to take the high school equivalency test."

"Papa must've thought you were putting on airs."

"Papa never put much store in school learning. We lived in town with Janie's parents. They had a christening party when Tara was born. Janie's dad took the party as the time to announce that I'd passed my high school tests. As a gift, he planned to send Janie, Tara and me to Bismarck, so I could go to college. Papa was drunk. He slammed me on the back so hard I stumbled into the wall. He was laughing the whole time. Said I'd never amount to anything. He called Janie's dad a fool for wasting his money."

Tory reached out to touch Matt's arm. "I'm sorry. Papa was wrong."

"I know. That day, seeing our family with the Simmons and all, I realized there was no way I'd be like Papa. Mr. Simmons offered me a way out. You can't believe how good I felt. He had faith in me. Considering I'd knocked up his daughter, he had every right to hate me. Instead, he was willing to help me make a better life for my wife and daughter."

"Are Janie's parents still alive?"

Matt nodded. "We see them every week for Sunday dinner. You're invited tomorrow. They want to see you. Doug, that's Janie's dad, and I have coffee Saturday morning when I get out of the bank. He remembers you as a skinny, tall kid, with her nose in a book. He never put you together with the articles he reads."

"Most people wouldn't." Tory paused. Something didn't add up. "You said you'd seen my work. How'd you know it was me?"

"I didn't at first. One day, Miss Martin came into the bank. While she waited for me to finish with a customer, she was reading a letter. The envelope had foreign stamps on it. Since Tara collects stamps, I asked if I could have the envelope for her. I put the envelope in my briefcase and forgot about it. That night when I was looking for some papers, I saw the envelope. The name Winslow was on the return address, as was Singapore. I picked up a magazine and looked at what it said about the author of the article on orangutans. It seemed too coincidental that someone named Winslow had written the article, lived in Singapore, and kept in touch with Dora Martin. I didn't think there'd be too many Winslows living in Singapore. You'd always been close to Miss Martin. I thought of asking Miss Martin about it."

"Why didn't you?"

Matt shrugged. "I wanted to believe you were happy, and you'd found your own route out of this place. Since I try not to look back, I figured you lived pretty much the same way."

It took nearly two weeks for Tory to see everyone in her family. Matt hadn't been far off the mark when he predicted none of them would be happy to see her. She considered calling Geoff several times, and always stopped herself. Now that she was ready to tell him everything, it would wait until she returned. This was not a conversation to have over the telephone.

Chapter 47
TORY

Singapore
Saturday, March 7, 1981

Now that she was back in Singapore, Tory wondered if Geoff would understand why she hadn't told him before she left. When she had called him at his office on Friday, his voice had been icy. He had called later in the evening and barked orders. Even during his second call, Geoff sounded as if he were barely able to control his rage. She wondered if he'd be any calmer this morning.

His demeanor when he stopped the car did little to alleviate her fears. Geoff frowned as he tossed her canvas tote into the trunk of the car. She started to say hello and stopped. She'd never seen him so angry. He drove in silence; his jaw was clenched, and his hands gripped the steering wheel so hard his knuckles where white. His continued silence only added to the knots in her stomach. She was surprised to see Keppel Harbor. She'd been so intent on watching Geoff that she hadn't paid attention to their journey.

Geoff asked if she knew anything about sailing. When she shook her head, he said, "Wonderful. Then, for once in your life, do exactly what you're told, and stay out of the way." Those were the first and last words he uttered until the boat was in the middle of the harbor.

Tory followed his instructions and stayed at the opposite end of the boat. While Geoff sailed, she looked around. The harbor was full of small boats floating among the oil tankers and freighters. The contrast was amazing. The oil tankers and freighters were huge, overshadowing the sailboats and motorboats of the weekend day-trippers. She wished she had her camera, but Geoff had specifically barred it from the day. There was an interesting juxtaposition of boats ahead. It would make a fantastic photograph.

The sun danced off the water and nearly blinded her. She went towards the front of the boat for her sunglasses.

Geoff saw her approach and blocked her movements. His arms were folded and he was prepared for battle. "Is it too much to ask for an explanation?"

"I went home. Please try to understand."

"When you say something that makes sense. Everyone goes home sooner or later. The rest of us tell our friends before we leave. It's a social convention. I know you're not partial to such niceties yourself, but I did think you must have read about them. You're always so in tune with social customs."

Tory ignored his sarcasm. "I'm not like you, and Singapore is my home. That's what you don't understand."

She stopped. This wasn't the time for that argument. "You told me once that I run from things I don't like. You were right. It was time to stop. The only way to do that was to go back to where it started."

Geoff reached for her trembling hand. "Tory, it doesn't take a month to see that what hurt you as a child looks different through the eyes of an adult."

Tory shook her head. "The demons are still there, and they hurt just as much."

"You're shivering. Do you want a sweater?" he asked as he reached for her canvas bag.

"Hold me, please." Geoff sat down and leaned against the side of the boat. When his arms enveloped her, Tory leaned her head against his chest. She sat with her back to him, so she wouldn't see his face while she spoke.

"I told you I grew up on a farm. It wasn't quite the bucolic paradise I described. The only things that grew there were dirt and despair. My two older sisters married before they were sixteen, just to get out of the house. It didn't change anything for them. They married guys just like Papa, angry men who drank too much on Saturday night and beat their wife 'cause she was there."

"Why didn't someone put a stop to it?"

"Who? We grew up watching Papa do it to Mama. My sisters took it from their husbands as their due. It was what we expected. Papa liked their husbands. He'd never've believed my sisters didn't deserve what they got. If they'd come home crying, he'd only have dragged them back. It's different where I come from. Girls don't count for much." She felt Geoff stiffen at her description. "You didn't cross Papa, not if you wanted to live to tell the story. When I was seven, I tried to stop him from hitting Mama. He twisted my arm until he broke it. After that I closed my eyes and ears and waited 'til I was old enough to get out."

"Tory, I'm sorry. I never realized what haunted you was so physical. Can I get you anything?" he asked solicitously.

She shook her head. "I've got to finish this before I lose my courage. I used to read all the time. Guess I hid even then. School wasn't a big deal in my family. But as long as I got my chores done, no one much cared what I did, so I went.

"I had this great teacher, Dora Martin. She told me life didn't have to be what I grew up with, that I could control my destiny. She paid the money so I could apply to college. The day I got accepted, I ran home to tell my parents. I was so excited. No one in my family had ever finished high school, and I'd just gotten into college. Papa ripped up the envelope I was holding and told me I was going to marry one of his drinking buddies. The guy was nearly forty and I was sixteen. Papa said I had to do it, that this was my way to pay him back for all the years he'd supported me."

Tory pulled Geoff's arms closer around her. "It was a Thursday. The wedding was scheduled for Saturday. I tried to go to school on Friday morning. Papa dragged me back into the house by my hair. He pulled it out in clumps. That night, he beat me as a warning. He swore he'd kill me if I tried anything at the church. I believed him. He had my oldest brother sleep in the room with my little sister and me so I couldn't run away. When my brother fell asleep, I crept down the stairs. Papa was there, like he'd been expecting me. The next day I got dressed in the wedding dress Mama and my sisters had worn and went to the church. I was crying, my face was black and blue, and everyone acted like it was the most normal thing in the world."

"You're married?" Geoff asked.

Tory put her hand over his mouth. "Let me finish. Please. When the ceremony started, something inside me snapped. I couldn't go through with it. It didn't matter what Papa thought I owed him. Nothing mattered except getting out of there. I couldn't run. One of my brothers would've stopped me before I got out the door. I was desperate. I did the only thing I could think of. When the preacher asked if anyone knew a reason why we shouldn't be married, I said I did. I said I was a lesbian."

"What?"

"It was the most horrible thing I could imagine saying. It worked. My would-be husband left the church in a flash once the preacher told him what the word meant. There was no way I could go home after that escapade. I'd just embarrassed Papa in front of his friends."

"What did you do?"

"I went to Dora's. She was the only one I thought would take my side. She did, but she couldn't buck the town -- they paid her salary. She called a friend, and then drove me to Bismarck. The friend was a woman she'd gone to college with. She taught at the university. She agreed I could stay with her. I finished high school in Bismarck. I worked in the library to help pay for my keep, and in the fall I went to college.

"As the years went by, Prairie View was nothing more than a place that crept into my nightmares from time to time. Then things changed, and I started to think about it more and more. I had to go back and see it again, to see how much of what I remembered was real, and how much was my imagination."

"What did you find?"

"As far as most of my family's concerned, I'm dead and have been for years. That's okay with me now. I've faced it and it can't hurt me anymore. All this time, I thought it was my fault. I was sure there was something wrong with me. I blamed myself for wanting more than the life I would've had if I'd done what Papa wanted. When I saw it again, I realized I'd done the only thing that was right for me."

"Tory, you did the only sane thing. What could possibly have changed enough to make you go back to a place like that?"

Tory ignored his question and continued with her story. "I've been virtually on my own since I was sixteen. I learned to protect myself from anyone who could hurt me. It made sense. Dora was self-sufficient and she seemed so much happier than Mama or my sisters.

"Dora died last year. I went home for her funeral. She left me a letter. When I read it, all my illusions were shattered. What I'd seen as Dora's greatest strength, her ability to five on her own, was a reaction to a love affair that hadn't worked out. It was really only in the last few years, after she'd been reunited with her lover, that she was happy. The letter made me consider my own life. I'd paid a high price for my independence.

"While I was puzzling through it all, Anna died. In a matter of a few weeks, I was alone. The cornerstones of my life were gone. There was no one who understood or cared about me. Then, as if things weren't insane enough, you came into the equation. No matter what barriers I put up, you were always there. But you wanted more than I could give, you demanded answers. No one had ever challenged me before.

"At times I'd feel myself letting down my guard and giving you a glimpse of the real me. I was so terrified when that happened that I'd run, so the feelings would go away and I could breathe again. Finally I got tired of hiding, but I didn't know how to stop. I was so frightened of ending up like Mama and my sisters, but I didn't want to be alone like Dora. There didn't seem to be a happy medium anywhere."

"Tory, no one's happy all the time."

"I know that. Try to understand what was going on in my head. As long as Dora and Anna were alive, I was never really alone. Without them I had no center. On top of that, I had to face the fact that so much of what Dora taught me was based on a lie. I was bewildered. What was true and what wasn't? I had no idea what I should do, and there was no one I could talk to about it.

"When I stopped thinking about myself so much, I started to really look at the lives of the people I thought had it all. Chris was hurting and Kevin was oblivious to it. He was too involved in work to notice. Much as I defended Kevin, I knew Chris was right. But I was too self-absorbed to offer my best friend the comfort she needed. Then I looked at the Parkers. I always thought Sarah was a bitch, 'cause she cheated on her husband. Then I saw that Barney was like Papa, only with money and better manners."

"Tory, why didn't you tell me where you were going? I was worried. I thought something had happened to you. For weeks I've vacillated between wanting to find you and hoping I never laid eyes on you again."

"I wanted to see what would happen between us if I got over my fears. I thought if I told anyone what I was doing, they'd stop me. I wasn't thinking clearly when I left."

"What did you just say?"

"I wasn't thinking..."

"Before that," he said as he tickled the back of her neck.

She turned and smiled. "You heard me."

"Loud and clear. Now, if you'll follow me below, I'll show you the marvelous things that this boat has to offer."

"Whose boat is it?"

"For the weekend, it's ours."

"The weekend?"

Geoff nodded. "Things between us can't continue as they've been. I thought, if I got you out here, we'd end it for good or work it out."

Tory sat silently. Geoff was right. His methods might be extreme, but he was definitely correct. "What if I'd gotten seasick? Would we have stayed here then?"

"You'd have gotten over it."

"What if I wanted to leave?"

"Tory, what do you want?"

She sat cross-legged, with her arms folded on her chest. "I want to go back to Jurong." She saw the stricken look on his face and stood to kiss him. "I'm nauseous. It's nerves, not the boat."

"Fine, then you can get over it here. Can I do anything to help?"

"Don't leave. Please."

Chapter 48
CHRIS

Singapore
Thursday-Friday, March 19-20, 1981

Chris wiped the sweat from her forehead. She was not up to a tough tennis game. By the time the game was over, she could barely catch her breath. "Do you have time for iced tea? I need to pick your brain about something."

"I'm on the two o'clock flight to Bangkok."

"Geoff and Tim's party is Saturday night. Don't tell me you won't be there."

Tory shook her head. "I promised Geoff I'd make it."

"What's so important in Bangkok that can't wait 'til next week?"

"I had something made to wear to the party. It doesn't fit right. I need to go to Jim Thompson and have them do the alterations."

"You had something made for Geoff's party? That doesn't sound like you. What's gotten into you?"

"I want to look good. What was it you wanted to talk about? How's your business coming? I hear about it all the time."

"It's not a business."

Tory grimaced. "Don't you dare call it your little hobby or I'll scream. Don't belittle what you've done. You've got a business, whether you see it that way or not. It really is a fantastic idea. Just what this island needs."

Chris beamed. "A business? You think so?"

"Yes. But if you're going pull it off, you have to start believing in yourself. If you don't take yourself seriously, why should anyone else?"

"You know it means I won't have time to help you."

Tory shrugged. "I never expected you to."

"What?"

"I hoped the book would give you the chance to find what you wanted, and it has. Don't look at me like that. Writing's what I do. It's not your thing. Likewise, I wouldn't know the first thing about setting up a medical referral service. You're you, and I'm me."

Chris was confused until she remembered John's words. He'd been right. Tory had helped Chris to find herself. "The referral service is my problem. I can't keep it going by myself. I figure in a month I could be ready to make it into a full-time service. Already, several women have volunteered to work either one morning or one afternoon a week."

"That's great. What's the problem?"

"Beside the fact that I haven't mentioned it to Kevin after our last argument?"

Tory nodded.

Chris pulled out the pad where she kept the work schedule. She smiled triumphantly as she looked at the list of days of the week and hours of the day. "I can keep the phone lines open during business hours of the workweek. What I don't have are enough phone lines."

"Are you planning on running the service out of your house?"

Chris nodded. "Why not? The only additional cost would be another phone line. I can squeeze the money for that from the grocery budget without Kevin noticing."

"Chris, he's going to find out. You should be up front with him."

Chris shook her head. "He's opposed to the idea. He claims I'll lose interest in a week."

"Will you?"

"No," Chris shouted.

Tory smiled. "I didn't think so. Okay, so what we have to do is package your concept like a business plan. That way Kevin will know you're serious."

"Will you help me?"

Tory nodded. "Get some paper and pens. I better call SIA and cancel my flight."

"What about your new outfit?" It was so unusual for Tory to be interested in clothes. Chris didn't want her to change her plans.

"I can go to Bangkok tomorrow and be back Saturday afternoon." Tory shrugged. "Heck I can get the alterations done here if I have to."

Chris wasn't convinced. There were dressmakers galore in Singapore, yet Tory had gone to Jim Thompson. Thai silk was heavier than Chinese silk. Singaporeans often found the weight of the fabric difficult to work with. "I'm sure Geoff would like to see you looking your best at his party."

"Probably. But he knows me. When something captures my attention, I forget everything else." Tory put her hand out to touch Chris's arm. "Don't worry. I'll look smashing Saturday night. That's two days away. At the moment we need to concentrate on drawing up a business plan."

"Where do we start?"

"Let's see, you've got at least two people working each shift. That means four phone lines."

"Four? How'd you come up with that? Two should be more than enough."

Tory shook her head. “Two people, one phone line each. Then, you'll need an extra line, to cover any overflow. That's three. A fourth might be useful if you ever have to call out while the lines are busy, or so you can leave a phone line open for calls from your families. It'd be a shame to have a phone line taken up with Alison telling you about the cute guy in her algebra class."

"She's told you? I never see you. When did you see her?"

"At the American School. Now that I'm going to be in town on a regular basis, I thought I'd see about teaching photography again."

"Four phone lines. What will that cost?"

"Read the inside of the phone book. The rates are listed there. While you've got the book out, get the number for Chang Realty. You'll need a place for this operation. Madame Chang will know just where to find it."

Chris stared at Tory. She couldn't be serious. "I don't have the money to rent office space."

"Well, you can't run it from your house."

"Why not? You work out of your apartment. You say it's fine since no one has to visit you. The referral service will be the same."

Tory shook her head. "I live alone, you don't. It wouldn't be fair to the kids to have you here and not available to them."

"You sound like Kevin," Chris snapped.

"I'm sorry. I didn't mean to sound negative. I think it would be better if you set up the referral service in an office somewhere else. You'd be surprised how hard it can be to separate yourself from what you do if it's always staring you in the face."

"Does that happen to you?"

Tory nodded. "I never noticed it when I traveled. Now that I'm in one place, every time I look at my typewriter I feel guilty."

Chris nibbled on the top of her pen. "Where do I get the money for an office? You don't think Kevin'll be willing to subsidize my venture, do you?"

"Probably not. Why not charge the doctors a fee to be included? They pay for their ads in the phone book. Being listed by your referral service is another form of advertising."

"How much could I charge?"

"Check what the phone book charges and discount their rate by a third."

Chris grabbed the phone book and flipped through the front until she found what she wanted. Quickly, she jotted figures on a pad of paper. "Even considering the cost of the phone lines, it might work. Why would a doctor pay to have his name included in a referral service?"

"Now who's being negative? Chris, you told me you've gotten calls from doctors who want to be sure they're included in your listing. If that's the case, I doubt they'd have a problem paying for the privilege. Call one and see."

Chris called a doctor she knew from Mount Elizabeth and was stunned at his positive reaction. The doctor would be willing to pay after he reviewed the information to be sure it was correct. Chris thought about her index cards.

Chris looked over at Tory. She was busy writing on her pad. "I've come up with a flaw in charging the doctors. Doctor Brown wants to see what I'm listing about him."

"Sounds sensible. You get to review your ad in the phone book before it's published."

Chris went to the bottom drawer of the china cabinet in the solarium and took out a section of her index cards. She handed several cards to Tory. "This is how I store my data. How impressed do you think Doctor Brown would be with this?"

"That was going to be my next question. Now that you know it's feasible to get doctors to pay for their inclusion, you need a good retrieval system. If you get the information typed, copied, and laminated, it should be fine. At least, until you can afford a computer system."

Chris scoffed at Tory's latest suggestion. "You live in a dream world. Even forgetting your idiotic idea about a computer, it'll take money to get done what you suggest. There's no way I can find that much money in my grocery budget."

"Probably not. I inherited some money last year, when my friend died. I could finance the start-up costs."

Chris stared at Tory in disbelief. Was she that certain the referral service could be self-supporting? "Why would you do that for me?"

Tory shrugged. "A lot of reasons. I believe in your idea. You're my best friend. Heck you've fed me so much over the years, I probably owe you more than this will cost."

Tory stopped, stood up and starting pacing. "Look, I've been pretty much a bitch for a year. Except for Geoff, you're the only person who's hung around waiting for me to work through what was bothering me. I owe you. I don't think I've ever told you how important your friendship is to me. For someone who makes their living with words, I'm not good at speaking to people about what matters. You've made me part of your family. It gave me a chance to see what a normal family was like."

Tears streamed from Chris's eyes. Tory's offer of financial help would get her idea off the ground. Chris knew her tears had more to do with Tory's disclosure. Tory had admitted she cared about someone.

"Tears won't get your business plan written."

Chris tossed a pen at Tory. Slowly, she sniffed back her tears. "Right. Let's take a break and get some lunch. I'm starving. Aren't you hungry?"

Tory nodded. "Emotional outbursts always give me an appetite."

They worked on the business plan until the children came home from school. Alison walked into the house from cheerleading practice as they were rereading the last page of the proposal.

"You're both still dressed from tennis. I wish I could be so lazy. I had a rough day."

Chris looked at Tory and shrugged her shoulders. When Alison went upstairs to change, she held up her crossed fingers. "Wish me luck talking to Kevin tonight."

"Good luck. I'm sure he'll see the sense in it. Make sure to let him read the plan completely before you start talking."

"I know, I know. You've told me that at least a dozen times. Are you sure you don't want to stay for dinner?"

Tory shook her head. "You don't need me to hold your hand. The way your eyes light up when you talk, he'd be an idiot not to be supportive."

"Okay. You'll go with me in the morning to see the office spaces Madame Chang finds?"

"Tomorrow we go to see office space and typing services. Then I go to Bangkok and get my outfit altered. See you at 9 a.m. sharp."

While Chris showered and changed, she mentally reviewed the business plan. It made so much sense when it was put down on paper. So much of what they ended up with was her own ideas. She'd expected Tory to want to change everything. Instead, she'd made suggestions where they were necessary and left most of the details of the service up to Chris.

After dinner, when the children had gone upstairs to do their homework, Chris walked into Kevin's study. He looked up from his newspaper and smiled. "Kev, I've got something I'd like your opinion on. Do you have time to read it?"

"What is it?"

"A business plan for my referral service. I'd appreciate your professional advice about the plan." She extended the typed pages. "Why don't I leave this with you? I've some things to sort through in the solarium. When you've got some spare time, maybe you can read it and give me some suggestions on how to polish it."

Before Kevin could argue, Chris left the room. Her heart was pounding when she got to the solarium. *So far, so good,* she thought. Although she wanted to review her notes for tomorrow's meetings, she was too anxious to sit still. She went upstairs to see if the children were doing their homework. Alison had a phone extension in her room. She was only supposed to spend an hour on the phone each night, but Chris was positive she stretched the time limit. To her surprise Alison was sitting at her desk working.

"How's it going, sweetie?"

"May I take photography next year? Aunt Tory's going to teach again. If I use a free period, I could take her class and still take the courses Dad and you think are so important."

"Is that next year's schedule you're working on?"

Alison nodded. "See, I can fit in all the college prep courses and photography." Alison smiled triumphantly and handed her schedule to her mother.

Chris was looking over the paper when Marc burst into the room. "Did you ask her, Alison? Can you take Aunt Tory's class? Which one do you want? I don't want to be in your class."

Alison glared at her brother. "Mom hasn't said yes yet."

"No bickering, please. Marc, where's your class schedule?"

Marc pulled a piece of paper from the back pocket of his jeans.

Chris compared the children's schedules. Marc planned to take photography on Monday and Wednesday, whereas Alison had listed it as Tuesday and Thursday. How many classes was Tory teaching? "When are these due at the school? Don't your father or I have to agree?"

Alison became the spokesperson. "I was going to talk to you about it when I got home from school, but Aunt Tory was here. The two of you looked busy, so I decided to wait until after dinner. I was about to go downstairs when you came upstairs."

Chris smiled. "Why don't I take these downstairs so your father and I can look at them together? I'd also like the course listing for next year."

In the solarium, Chris opened the course listing and turned to the section on electives. Tory was teaching four classes. She was shaking her head, when Kevin walked into the room.

He pulled out a chair, sat down, and put the business plan on the table in front of them. "This is incredible, Chris. I thought your idea was farfetched. Reading it in this format, I can see how it might work."

Chris nodded. "I know it'll work."

"Are you planning on working at the referral service?"

"I'm going to run it. It's my brainchild."

"That's what I thought. Your plan says you have the financing. Where'd you come up with that?"

Chris took a deep breath. She wanted Kevin to see this as a serious business venture and was concerned that if he knew about Tory's part, he'd dismiss the idea. "Tory offered me the money. Before you say a word, I told her all I'd accept was a loan. I signed a promissory note. Tomorrow, after I go to see the typing services, I'll know how long it will take to get the materials into shape. We should be ready to open two months after that."

"Why'd you go to Tory for help? Why didn't you come to me?"

Chris almost laughed at the absurdity of Kevin's question. "When I told you about my idea, you laughed. Tory didn't. She believes in me. She thinks this is an idea that's long overdue."

"So the master of I-can-do-it-for -myself is helping someone else get started. Doesn't sound like the Tory I know. Then again,

I've stopped being amazed at your friend. How much of your time will this venture take?"

"In the beginning, all my time. Once it's operational, I'll work nine to five, Monday to Friday. It won't change our lives. You and the children will be at work or school while I'm working." Chris looked expectantly at Kevin. His face was impassive. She had no idea what he was thinking.

"You need to be prepared for the unexpected in a new venture. That's something I learned from Geoff. You haven't left enough room in your scheduling or financing to cover contingencies." Kevin turned the business plan to a particular page. "Here, let me show you what I mean."

Chris smiled. Kevin wasn't arguing. She listened to her husband's suggestions. They made sense. But if he were right, she'd need more money than she'd told Tory.

Kevin paused and looked at the frown on Chris's face. "Looks like I hit a nerve. What's the problem?"

"If any of the things you enumerate happen, I'd be out of capital before I could get the venture up and running."

"I could see where that might be a problem."

Chris saw the silly grin on her husband's face. "Are you doing this to frighten me?"

"Not really. I'm warning you what could happen. The money you got from Tory will cover you, if everything goes according to plan. Life seldom works that way. I think you'll need more seed money than either of you counted on."

Not to be deterred, Chris shrugged. "Guess I'll have to find it then. How much more do you think I'll need?"

"Where will you get the money?"

"That's my problem."

"We discuss things in this family. If you need more money, I might be willing to invest in your business."

Chris picked up her business plan and put it on her lap. "Don't patronize me, Kevin. I'm deadly serious about opening a referral service."

Kevin reached for Chris's hands, which still clutched her plan. "I know you are. As I said when we started to talk, it's a workable idea. My concern is under-capitalization. Look, Chrissy, I know I hurt your feelings when I didn't take you seriously before. I'm sorry. I know you can do anything you set your mind to. Guess I've been so busy chasing after my dreams, I failed to see you were doing the same."

"Kevin, I don't want money from you."

"Why? Isn't my money as good as Tory's?"

Chris brushed a tear from her cheek. "I wanted you to believe in me. If you do, that's all that matters. The referral service will work with the money it has."

Kevin looked quizzical. "How can you be so certain?"

"'Cause that's all the money there is. Now if you'd consider putting..." she moved the business plan back on the table and looked for the page where Kevin had made pencil notations, "five thousand Singapore dollars into a special interest-bearing account in the name of Physicians Referral Service, I wouldn't object."

"Oh you wouldn't, would you? And what collateral do I have against my loan? Will you sign a promissory note like you did with Tory?"

Chris shook her head. "I have a better idea. This business will need someone with a business background to look over things from time to time. I'll let you have the honor. After all, you know more about business than I do."

Kevin laughed. "Why do I get the suspicion that you knew you needed more money? I feel like I've been conned."

Chris laughed. "Why? Because I beat you at your game?"

Kevin leaned over and kissed Chris. "You're a shrewd businesswoman. There's no way this idea will fail, not with you at the helm."

"Do you mean that, Kev?"

"Yes. Let's go upstairs. I've never slept with a business tycoon before. Chrissy, I love you."

"I love you, too."

Chapter 49
CHRIS

Singapore
Saturday, March 21, 1981

Chris was so tired she considered not going to Geoff's party. Friday, she and Tory had visited five offices and seven typing services. By the time Tory left for the airport, Chris's feet hurt. She was still reviewing the notes she'd made when Kevin came home.

To her surprise, Kevin was interested in hearing about what she'd done during the day. He volunteered to go see the office spaces with her Saturday morning. Since the children were both leaving to spend the night with friends, they made a day of it. After looking at each of the offices, they went to Raffles for lunch. While they ate, they discussed the pros and cons of the various places they'd seen.

"I'm leaning towards the Jurong building."

"Chris, don't make the decision on price alone. Jurong's a long haul. Will your volunteers want to spend an hour traveling in each direction? Instead of the three hours they've agreed to work, it'll take them five."

Chris paused. There was merit to Kevin's argument. At the same time, the rent was two hundred dollars less a month than the next cheaper space. "I hadn't thought of that. Even I'd have trouble getting out there every day."

"You can have Suradmin and the car. Now that I'm working in town, I can get most places by taxi."

Chris reached for Kevin's hand and squeezed it. "That's a nice offer, and I might take you up on it when I have to visit doctors. You're right. Jurong is too far off the beaten path for an office. I don't know how Tory lives out there."

"She may be moving soon."

"What do you know?" When Kevin folded his arms in front of his chest, she laughed. When he adopted that pose, he was begging to tell her a confidence. "C'mon. Tell me what you know."

"Geoff said he should have one party in his apartment before he moves out. He's talking about getting a house."

"Are you suggesting that he and Tory might move in together? I can't imagine her giving up her independence." Chris paused. Was Kevin guessing, or did he know more? "Did Geoff say they were going to live together?"

"He said Tory and he planned to look at houses together next month. I can't see Geoff moving out of the apartment unless the two of them were up to something. He can walk to work from his apartment. Has Tory mentioned anything about moving to you?"

"No, but I've hardly seen her recently. Yesterday and Thursday, we were too busy working to talk about what she's up to. She does seem happier."

"That's good. Now what about the office space? We've crossed Jurong off the list. That leaves four alternatives."

Chris nodded. "They're equally easy to get to, in the city center, the buildings are about the same age, and the only differences are the amount of space available and the cost. With your concern about contingencies, do you think I'd be better off going with more space?"

Kevin shook his head. "You can always move. Now that you've gotten Jurong off your brain, cost can be the determining factor."

"How'd you know Jurong would be my first choice?"

"Geoff and I were discussing the referral service at lunch yesterday. He suggested you might be too easily swayed by rental costs."

"How would he know that? Geoff hardly knows me."

"He knows Tory though. Apparently she told him she was underwriting things. He said he hoped her frugality didn't rub off on you."

"That's ridiculous. Tory's one of the most generous people I know. She'd give a stranger the shirt off her back if she thought they needed it more than she did."

Kevin nodded. "I know. But she doesn't spend money on herself unless it's a necessity. Don't give me that look. I never thought about it until Geoff said something."

"Do the two of you always spend lunch discussing the women in your lives?"

"If we did, we'd never get any work done. Chris, we've been together more than half our lives, and I don't think I'll ever understand what goes on in your head."

At that moment, a doctor Chris knew by sight stopped by their table. "I'm sorry to disturb your lunch, Mrs. Taylor, but Dave Brown said you'd called him about paying a subscription for your referral service. Since I hadn't heard from you, I was wondering if there was a reason you were excluding me from your listing. I know my office staff spoke to you several months ago."

Chris smiled. "We've put sales calls on hold until the material is back from the printer. I expect someone will be contacting you in April. May at the latest. We thought it advisable to have the information we'd be using ready for perusal at the time we discussed the cost of the advertisement."

The man smiled in relief. "I look forward to hearing from you in due course. Terribly sorry to have interrupted your lunch. I didn't want to think I'd been forgotten."

Chris shook her head. "No. Production time is longer than we anticipated. You know how those things go, I'm sure."

When the doctor left their table, Kevin took Chris's hand and brought it to his lips. "You handled him perfectly. Where did you learn language like that?"

"From listening to you talk about work all these years." Chris laughed. "Actually, I surprised myself. I heard myself talking and wondered who I was. What was really a hoot was the good doctor believed every word."

"Why wouldn't he? You were very professional and quite convincing. Guess I'm going to have to learn what it's like to live with a superstar."

Chris smiled at the compliment.

After lunch, they stopped at the Long Bar for a Singapore Sling. By the time they got home, Chris realized how tired she was.

Despite her desire to skip the party, Chris was pleased she'd come. All night, people came up to her to thank her for their referral. They were pleased with their new doctor. It was reassuring to know that her venture was such a success, especially since she was working from her solarium with index cards.

The party was wonderful. Half the top floor of the apartment was a patio and a pool. There was a spectacular view of the city from the thirtieth floor. Chris felt as if she were on the top of the world as she surveyed the lights below.

After two hours, she realized she hadn't seen Tory. She met Geoff by the stairs to the first floor of the apartment, and asked, "Where's Tory?"

"I'm here," Tory called as she came up the stairs.

Chris was struck by how different Tory looked. She wore electric blue, form-fitting silk slacks and a long-sleeved blouse of the same color. Her hair was pulled back in a braided ponytail, which looked wet. There was more to her changed appearance than her clothes and hairstyle. There was a radiant look in her eyes. Chris wondered what it meant.

Geoff took Tory's hand, smiled, and kissed her cheek. "I'm happy you made it. I heard traffic in Bangkok is at a complete standstill."

Tory giggled. "It is. But if you really want to get someplace, you can always find a way."

Geoff bowed to Chris. "If you'll excuse us a minute, Tory and I must talk about something. I promise to bring her back in a few minutes."

When Tory came back, Chris looked at her quizzically. "What was that about?"

"Geoff wanted to say hello. And to thank me for showing up. He didn't think I'd get here."

Chris grinned as Tory blushed.

"Well, enough about me. How did things work out with Kev? Is he friend or foe tonight?"

"Friend. You can't believe how supportive he's been about the whole thing. He even went with me to look at the office space this morning."

"That's great. I told you he'd come around. Once the service was packaged in terms he understood, his business sense would take over. Your husband's always been a sucker for a good business plan."

"How did you know that?"

"Who do you think taught me?"

Chris was dumbfounded. Kevin had taught Tory to write business proposals? "You've got to be kidding. Why didn't you tell me sooner?"

Tory shrugged. "It was a long time ago. I was working on a marketing campaign for Trans Oil. Kev was one of the junior flunkies on the project. One night, after a few beers, we started talking about how I got my jobs. Kevin, of course, told me I was writing my proposals all wrong. He drew an outline I should follow. On a cocktail napkin, of all things. I thought he was nuts, but I tried out some of his ideas. They weren't half bad."

"You never cease to amaze me. No wonder Kev liked the idea -- it's his format."

"Bull. Your husband liked the idea because it's good."

"It was a good idea when I first suggested it. He didn't think much of it then."

Tory shook her head. "You're looking at the situation emotionally. Review the facts."

Chris groaned. Tory and her blasted logic. "All right. Fact: I proposed my idea to Kevin. Fact: Kevin reacted like it was a harebrained scheme. Fact: You showed me how to dress my idea up in more business-like terms. Fact: Kevin understood the idea because it was in a format he's accustomed to seeing business data in."

"Kevin needed to have your idea look like a business proposal before he could think about it that way. What did he think about the office space? Have you decided on one yet?"

"I think so. I called Madame Chang this afternoon, but she was gone for the day."

Tory put out her hands. "Well? Are you going to tell me which one?"

Chris laughed. "I forgot, you weren't with me when I made up my mind. The next to the last place we saw, the one off Scotts Road."

"Good choice. It's easy to get to. It's also close to two hospitals. That'll make it easier to visit doctors." Tory lifted the pendant from Chris's throat. "That's nice. Is it from John?"

"How is it you always know things?"

"Luck, I guess." Tory laughed. "You said you planted daffodils because they reminded you of John. Are you sad he's gone?"

"Yes, but I'm happy for him. How's the book?"

"Slow. I've started to take an assignment or two to get out of the apartment. You have no idea how nuts I get staying in one place. Now that you're so busy, there's no one I can just hang out with and relax. If it weren't for Sarah and the odd assignment, I'd go nuts."

"Sarah?"

"She's doing some work on the book."

"I'll say it again. Sarah? I can't see her doing research."

"She's not. She's got a wonderful eye. She sets up displays of indigenous fruits and vegetables so I can photograph them."

"I thought you didn't like her."

"So did I. Can we leave it with I decided Sarah is more a victim of circumstance than I thought? I know you don't like half-answers, but that's all I want to say on the topic."

"Chris, I'd quit while I was ahead," Geoff said, as he walked over and handed Tory a rose. Tory took the flower, kissed Geoff, and he left.

Chris stared. "What was that about?"

Tory shrugged. "Geoff likes to give me roses."

Chris wondered if Geoff understood the symbolism of that particular flower. She looked at Tory again and saw the light in her eyes. She seemed so happy. "Why were you late? I thought you were coming back this afternoon."

"I've already had all the lectures I plan to hear about being late tonight. I had one from Tim. Sarah, and Kevin, before I got upstairs. Sometimes things don't work out as planned, you know that."

"Only too well. How are things going with Geoff, or is that topic off limits?"

Tory sniffed the rose in her hand and smiled. "Fine."

"Tory! Will you talk to me?"

"Geoff and I see each other a great deal, and so far at least, it's working out okay. I know you'd like to know more, but I'm superstitious."

"What?"

Tory nodded. "I'm afraid if I talk about how good things are, I'll jinx them. I told you once, if it were possible for me to love anyone, Geoff would be at the top of the list. Can we leave it at that, that I'm fumbling with how to make what I want become a reality?"

Later, when Chris saw Tory dance with Geoff, she smiled. Tory was at peace. That was what was so different about her. What had been bothering her at Sarah's garden party was a distant memory. She no longer fought Geoff's advances. She seemed comfortable with him and their relationship. It was reassuring to think that one of the flowers was at peace.

The thought made her see that she too was at peace. There was no sense battling life in Singapore. It was what it was, a male-dominated world if you were an expat wife. No one would change that unless you did it for yourself. Tory had told her that for years and she'd never understood. Now that she did, she couldn't figure out why she hadn't seen it earlier.

By the time she and Kevin left the party, she'd forgotten how tired she'd been. She thought the buzz she felt was the result of too much wine. Then she realized she was happy.

As they changed for bed, Kevin took her hand. "I heard a great deal tonight about your referral service. You've made quite a hit with the wives. And their husbands, I might add."

"Are you angry?"

Kevin pulled her down on the bed and smiled. "Yes. At myself mostly. I wanted to protect you from the world. Don't you see that?"

Chris laughed. "I'm not a hothouse flower. You can't possibly protect me from everything. Don't you see that?"

"It's my prerogative to try. Why didn't tell me what you were doing?"

"I followed the example you set with your project, she answered calmly.

"That was different."

Chris's smile vanished instantly. "Why? Because you get paid and I don't?"

Kevin shook his head. "You always tell the kids that they don't have to do idiotic things just because their friends do them. You want them to think things through for themselves."

"So?"

He leaned over and pinned her beneath him. "I don't expect my wife to be a jerk because her husband is."

Chapter 50
SARAH

Singapore
Wednesday, May 6, 1981

The four months of separation Sarah and Tim had given themselves was finally over. Instead of waking relieved, Sarah was overwhelmed with a sense of foreboding. She rolled on her side, looked at her carriage clock, and groaned. It was past 10:30 a.m. Usually she was up before the alarm rang at six. The bed was empty. Barney's side hadn't been slept in.

She stood, felt the room spin, and put her hand against the wall for support. Her silk kimono was on the chaise lounge. She slipped it over her shoulders and walked into the living room. When she saw a lamp shattered on the floor, she remembered the previous night's battle.

Since Barney never got home until well past nine, she no longer made dinner. Last night though she'd made a light snack. Working in the kitchen gave her something to do as she planned how to tell him she was leaving. When he arrived home she changed her mind about speaking to him. He was so drunk he could barely walk.

As he stumbled into the living room, he knocked over a lamp on the end table by the armchair. Instead of righting the lamp, Barney picked it up, yanked the cord from the adapter, and threw the lamp on the floor. "I hate that bloody thing. Why don't we have stuff I like, love?"

"Barney," Sarah cried, as she picked up the largest pieces of broken porcelain. "You chose that lamp. I thought you liked it."

"I don't. Make me a drink, love. And I want dinner on a tray in the living room."

"Dinner? Barney, it's past ten."

"What difference does that make? I'm hungry. Can't a man get a meal in his own home? What do you do all day, Sarah? Does looking pretty take up all your time? Don't tell me dinner's too much to expect at the end of long, hard day."

Sarah chose her words carefully. She couldn't let Barney see she was perturbed. If he detected any weakness, he'd attack. "Dinner was ready at seven. When you weren't home by nine, I asked the servants to dispose of it. Care for some appetizers?"

Barney grabbed her by the arm and pulled her towards the chair. "You'll make dinner. You owe me for the life of leisure I supply. I'm the one who spends his day in a place he hates."

So do I, Sarah thought. She tried to free herself from Barney's grasp. Bruises were starting to show on her arm. "What do you want?" she asked.

"I want a steak," he said as he flung his arm backwards, letting go of Sarah half-way through the motion.

Sarah was so intent on listening to Barney, she missed the rapidity of his actions until it was too late. She fell against the molding of the doorway, hitting her head on the corner. She sniffed back her tears. She wouldn't give him the satisfaction of knowing how much the fall hurt. From his sickening grin she thought it would please him. She stood, forced a smile, and walked slowly into the kitchen.

When she was alone, she rubbed her right hand against her head and felt for a lump. Instead, she found traces of blood. She opened a drawer for a plastic bag, took ice from the freezer, and made a compress. She sat down, put the ice pack on her head, and let her tears fall. The sounds of Barney making another drink echoed in her head. While she steadied herself, she thought.

Barney's enthusiasm for his job had abated, as she knew it would. Two months before, Sarah had first become aware of the subtle changes. It would have been easy to miss them had she not seen it all before. An angry comment that Geoff or Kevin was too tough a taskmaster was the first indication. Then Barney spent a week closeting himself in his study after work, claiming he was working on something that "would show those two they don't know it all." After that, the serious drinking began. Barney could no longer get out of bed without a shot of vodka in his orange juice.

The pattern was similar to the deterioration of his previous assignments. The time limit she and Tim had set made it harder to tolerate Barney's behavior. Since this was the last time she'd face Barney's drunken rages, she had expected to be inured to them.

He came home from work smelling like a brewery. He laughed off his condition as the byproduct of an evening spent entertaining shippers. Sarah knew that was his fantasy. It wasn't a business necessity that Barney get drunk. He was compelled to prove he could best Geoff at something.

With each passing day, Sarah dreaded her newly found social life. In the past, she'd avoided social contact when Barney's drinking worsened. Now though, her social life was part of her plan. The knowing glances, the whispers behind her back, even the pitying stares must be endured gracefully.

Each time she was invited to play bridge or go to lunch, she was physically ill at the prospect. In the beginning she kept her head high, smiled, and acted as if nothing were wrong. When she could take the parody no longer, when the comments were no longer said in hushed tones, she allowed her pain to show.

Yesterday, she'd gone to bridge with red-rimmed eyes. Janet Adams asked what was wrong, and Sarah burst into tears. After her sobs subsided, she said she and Barney had fought about his drinking. It was the truth. Arguments were their only form of communication. Barney overcame his feelings of worthlessness by abusing his wife.

The thought of staying with Barney was too horrible to bear. He killed off pieces of her each day. Given the facts, her decision to leave Barney was logical, sensible, and fully based in reality. *Why did she feel so guilty?*

She trembled as she looked at the living room. There was no sign of Barney. All that remained of the holocaust was a broken lamp, a used glass, and an empty gin bottle.

Sarah went into the kitchen. Instead of her husband, she saw the servants at the table.

"Where's Mr. Parker?"

"Mister go to work."

"I overslept. Please clean the mess in the living room."

One of the women left the room at Sarah's instruction. The other stared at Sarah. "Missy call Mrs. Taylor."

"Has she rung?"

"Missy not look feel good. Mrs. Taylor find doctor, lah."

Sarah's head hurt too much to follow the pigeon English. "Did Mrs. Taylor ring before I woke up?"

The woman shook her head and giggled. The behavior infuriated Sarah. It took patience to deal with the servants, patience she did not have. They spoke a language she didn't understand and laughed at the oddest times. More than that, nothing that went on in the house was a secret from them. Sarah hated the looks of pity they gave her.

She asked for a pot of tea. It was time she got dressed and faced the day. Her right hip throbbed. No doubt she'd bruised it when she fell. A warm bath would make her feel better. While she soaked in the tub, Sarah reviewed the facts. Try as she might, and she had no doubt that she'd tried; there was no way to make her marriage succeed. It was a sham. She was terrified to tell Barney she was leaving. His reaction would be physical. She wasn't certain she could withstand another attack.

Maybe she should ring Barney Senior and tell him what had happened. If he thought his son was out of control, he'd intervene. No, she thought, she'd ring Tim. Together they'd decide what was the best course of action.

Tim suggested that they meet at his flat after Barney rang each of them to tell them which movie they were seeing that evening. Sarah had forgotten it was Wednesday, movie night. Tim's idea was brilliant. When Barney rang, she told him she'd be out for the rest of the day and would meet him at the theatre. It was just past noon. She and Tim would have several hours together. That was more than enough time for them to come up with the solution to her dilemma.

All thoughts of her bruised and battered body were forgotten the second Tim took her in his arms. She expected they would make love. Instead, she fell asleep in Tim's arms. Tim dozed, too. They woke when his bedroom door flew open and Barney stormed in. Sarah pulled the sheet up to cover them.

Barney never said a word. He stared at them for a few seconds, then left. His behavior stunned both Sarah and Tim. Having been caught, they expected Barney to say something. His silent withdrawal, so different from his unbridled rages, made no sense.

"How could he say nothing?" Sarah asked.

"I don't know, luv. Perhaps he doesn't care."

Sarah considered Tim's words. She'd been caught in the ultimate betrayal. If Barney could take it so calmly, maybe Tim was right. "I know he suspected something months ago, but..."

Tim put his arms around Sarah. "But this is the first time we've been alone in four months."

Sarah closed her eyes and pictured Barney's grin the night before, when he let go of her arm, knowing she'd fall. Not only had his movement been planned, he reveled in the feeling of power. "It doesn't make sense. Barney thinks he's a failure. That's why he drinks. If he's drunk, he doesn't hurt each time he sees a new deficiency."

"Shh, Sarah. That's his problem, not ours."

Sarah turned to face Tim. She shook his arms off her shoulders and took his hands in hers. "Last night Barney threw me against a wall because I argued about making him dinner. Today, he walks in on the two of us and doesn't say a word. It doesn't make sense. How did he get in your flat?"

Tim paused for an answer. "I've no idea. There's no reason for Geoff to give him a key." Tim reached for the phone.

"Who are you calling?"

"Geoff. I want to know if he has his key with him."

“What difference does it make?"

"If Barney slipped the key off Geoff's key ring without him being aware, it means Barney suspected something. I think it's best we know what his mental state is before we decide how to handle things."

Sarah dressed while Tim dialed Geoff's work number. The call took less than two minutes. Tim looked puzzled when he hung up.

"I spoke to Kevin. The door shut behind Geoff just as the call went through. The movie night is canceled. Geoff's leaving town. He's coming home to pack, then he's off to see Tory."

"I'd best leave," Sarah said.

"Where will you go, luv? I don't think your house is the wisest place."

"That's the last place I'd go. It's what Barney expects. He thinks I'll come running home to him with a story how it wasn't what it looked like. I'll have a pot of tea at the Marco Polo and think."

"I'll go with you," Tim suggested as he got out of bed.

Sarah kissed Tim. "No. I need to sort through things. Alone. Meet me at the Coffee Shop at the Marco Polo once Geoff leaves. By then we'll both be thinking more clearly."

Sarah left the flat in a rush, fearful of bumping into Geoff. She walked along Grange Road in a daze, as the enormity of what had happened filled her head. If Geoff were on his way home, he couldn't have given Barney the key to the flat. How had he gotten in? More importantly, why had he gone to the flat in the first place? Had he called Tim to tell him that the movie night was canceled and found out that Tim was out of the office? That wouldn't mean that she and Tim were together. If Barney had come to the flat expecting to find them together, why had he left without a word? They had been so careful. He couldn't suspect that Sarah was leaving him. Anyway, he had no proof. All he would have was his word. How much credence would anyone put in the words of a lush?

By the time she reached the Marco Polo, Sarah was emotionally drained and physically exhausted. It was hot and muggy. She wasn't accustomed to walking any distance in the heat. She was so thirsty, her throat felt parched. The doorman gave her a quizzical look as she walked into the hotel. His face was the last conscious memory she had.

When she came to, she was lying on the plush lobby carpet. All she could see were faces above her, looking down. From her vantage point, the faces were distorted, elongated somehow. She shut her eyes and reopened them to see if it made a difference. This time, she saw eyes widened in horror. She opened her mouth, but no words came out. It was as if she'd been struck dumb as punishment for her sins.

She had no idea how long she'd been there. *What would the hotel do*, she wondered. If they looked through her purse, they'd find her driver's license with her name and address. She had to stop them before they rang the house on Cluny Road. She couldn't face Barney. The more distraught she became, the less sense she could make of her predicament.

She tried to stand. Her legs felt like rubber. They'd never hold her. She was crying so much that she could barely breathe through her tears. Sarah closed her eyes to block out her fear.

She was aware that she was being lifted and carried, but it was like she was watching it happen to someone else. It was a dream. It had to be. If she woke up, she'd be in bed with Tim.

The next time she opened her eyes, there was a wet cloth on her forehead, and she was lying on a small leather couch. The room was painted white. There was a nurse dressed in a white uniform with her. Her vision was no longer distorted. When she pushed her legs over the edge of the couch, she could feel the rug underneath her toes. The nurse helped her stand.

Sarah sighed in relief She asked where she was and what had happened. The nurse explained that she'd passed out; heat stroke they thought. She was still at the Marco Polo. Although they couldn't stop her from leaving, the nurse suggested she eat first. Sarah nodded. The throbbing in her temples might subside if she ate.

The nurse escorted her to a table and stayed with her until her meal arrived. Once she left, Sarah pushed the plate away. The smell made her queasy. She sipped several glasses of iced tea while she waited for Tim.

Chapter 51
TORY

Singapore
Wednesday, May 6. 1981

"You're certainly in your element," Tory teased as Chris gave her a guided tour of the offices of the Physicians Referral Service.

"I can't believe we're almost ready to open. Monday morning our advertisement runs in the *New Straits Times.* We'll be open for business in a week," Chris said with a self-satisfied grin.

Tory smiled at the gushed words. Chris had every right to be pleased. For the past two months, Chris had spent each day visiting doctors, explaining the service, showing them the information they had, and enrolling them.

"Don't forget about dinner Saturday night," Chris said as Tory headed towards the door.

"How could I forget? Geoff and I are thrilled to steal you and Kevin away for an evening. In a week, we'll have to wait in line for the privilege of even speaking to you. Will you remember your old friends when you're famous?"

Chris laughed and picked up the ringing phone. Tory thought it must be Kevin or one of the children. Realizing she didn't have the private phone number of the office, she waited for Chris to finish the call. To her surprise, Chris handed her the phone.

"Hello?" she said, expecting to hear Alison. With Chris so busy, Tory and Alison spoke daily. The boy in Alison's algebra class whom she had a crush on had finally realized she was alive.

Each afternoon Alison recounted the latest pearls of wisdom that came from his mouth.

"Can we meet for an early dinner? I'm in a bit of a rush."

The words caught her off guard. "Geoff?" she asked.

"Something's come up. I must leave in the morning. Can you make dinner tonight?"

"Sure. Pete's Place?"

"I've had my fill of the Hyatt. How about the Marco Polo? We haven't been to the Brasserie in ages. I've a few things to settle here. Shall I pick you up at Chris's office?"

"I'll meet you there. I may do some errands while I'm in town."

"Give me an hour. No. On second thought an hour and a half would be best. That way I can pack before we meet."

Tory looked at her watch. "Okay. See you about 6:15 p.m. at the Brasserie."

She handed the phone to Chris. "Thanks. Guess it's a good thing I stuck around."

Chris nodded. "Kev says dinner Saturday may be canceled. What's going on?"

Tory shrugged. "Geoff's going out of town. That's all I know. Why would dinner be canceled? We don't need Geoff to have dinner."

Chris shook her head. "We planned a dinner for two couples. It won't be the same if there's only three of us."

"Why not? The three of us have had dinner together plenty of times."

"Not at Maixims de Paris," Chris argued.

Tory nodded. "I agree that's a tad pricey for my pocketbook. I wouldn't mind a good Rijstaffel, though."

"But dinner was Geoff's idea."

Geoff's sudden departure mattered more to Tory than a missed dinner. "You're jumping to conclusions. We don't know for sure Geoff won't be back. If he isn't, the three of us can go to Alkaff Mansion. We'll hold Geoff to his promise of a celebratory dinner at Maxims."

"You're right. How are things with the two of you? Kev and I thought you were planning an announcement Saturday and that's what we were celebrating."

Tory threw up her hands in surrender. "You're an incurable romantic. Things are fine."

"You've been saying that for months. Tell me more."

There was no reason to keep their plans a secret. Tory had been looking for an opportunity to tell Chris. But between Chris's involvement in her new venture and the time she spent with Kevin and her children, Chris had little time left for her friends. Tory didn't feel slighted. She was pleased that Chris and Kevin were happy again. "Now that I'm in town to stay for a while, Geoff and I are getting a house together."

"And...?" Chris said, expectantly.

Tory shrugged. "Geoff's tired of sharing a flat with Tim. Since he's moving out, we thought we'd see what happened if we were together more. I'm keeping my place in Jurong to work in. That way, if we can't stand having someone underfoot all the time, I can move home."

Chris smiled. "I hear wedding bells."

"I don't think so. Geoff isn't in the market for anything that permanent. He's more dismissive of marriage than I."

"The two of you deserve each other."

"Probably. I've got to go. Give me the number here. We'll discuss dinner on Saturday."

Tory was walking up the circular driveway to the Marco Polo as Geoff pulled in. She waited at the entrance while he parked the car. They kissed and then walked hand in hand into the Brasserie.

Tory told Geoff about Chris's office. When he didn't answer, she looked at him. He was toying absently with his wine glass. His eyes scanned the room. It was what she called his thinking pose. "Where are you going?" she asked loudly enough to get his attention.

Geoff blinked. The question interrupted him. "I'm sorry. I was thinking."

"I could tell."

Geoff smiled. "How?"

"When you're deep in thought, your eyes dart around the room."

"Really? I'm not looking at anything in particular."

"Your mind's going a mile a minute though."

Geoff grinned and reached for her hand. "And what makes you say that?"

"You don't hear anything I say. I was telling you about how disappointed Chris was that you might not be here Saturday night."

Geoff frowned. "I leave for Greece in the morning. I doubt I'll be back by Saturday. Please reschedule dinner with the Taylors. Any other Saturday is fine with me. Are you annoyed?"

"Business is business. How long will you be away? I'll need to change our appointment with Madame Chang."

"Yes. Please do."

Although Geoff didn't say more, Tory was positive something else was on his mind. Before she could probe, dinner was served. They ate in silence.

While they sipped their cognac, Geoff smiled at Tory, "I've been alone for a long time. It's a way of life I'm comfortable with."

Tory nodded silently. She didn't trust herself to say anything. Geoff planned to say good-bye and this was the preamble.

"Singapore has been an eye-opening experience for me. Things are never what they seem on the surface. I don't think I fully understood that until recently."

Tory shrugged.

"How much have I told you about my childhood?"

"You moved to Auckland when you were ten."

"London had been devastated by the war. We lived with my mother's family in a small row house. There were twelve of us in the place. My parents and I shared a bedroom. They fought at night, in whispers, so no one would hear them. I always woke up. My mother wanted to emigrate and make a fresh start in another country. My father didn't want to leave. When the opportunity came, we moved."

Tory wanted to grab Geoff by the throat and drag the words out of his mouth. This story of his childhood had nothing to do with saying farewell.

"In London I thought they argued because of the cramped quarters. Nothing changed in New Zealand, except they stopped whispering. I'd lie in bed and listen to their bitter, angry words. One day, when I was thirteen, my father left for work in the morning and never came home."

"What happened to him?"

"I don't know."

Tory reached for Geoff's hand. Momentarily, she forgot her apprehension about where the tale was leading. How would it feel to not know where your father was?

Geoff sipped his cognac. Tory stared at him, trying to decipher what his revelation meant. He was waiting for her to say something. "I'm sorry. Have you ever tried to find him?"

Geoff shook his head. "Until recently, I never thought it mattered. He left without a word. Obviously, he had no interest in me. Lately though, he's been on my mind. I wonder if I'm any more capable of close attachments than he was."

"Geoff, if you want to change your mind about sharing a house, it's okay with me."

Geoff squeezed her hand. "At the moment, I'm not certain what I want. I thought I'd mull things over in Greece. May we discuss it when I return?"

Tory nodded. Her stomach was in knots. Geoff looked at her expectantly, like he was waiting for her to say something to make it easier. Why couldn't she find soothing words to tell him that whatever he decided would be fine with her? Because she had a vested interest in the verdict. "Not a problem. Will you stay at my place tonight?"

Geoff shook his head. "It took me longer to finish things in the office than I anticipated. I've yet to pack. Thought I'd run you to Jurong, review the contract that's in question, and make an early night of it. Do you mind?"

Tory looked at her watch. It wasn't quite eight o'clock. "Why don't I save you the trip to Jurong? I can get the bus from here."

Geoff eyed her suspiciously. "You're annoyed with me."

"No, Geoff. As you said, you're accustomed to living alone. So am I. This isn't an arrangement to be entered into lightly."

"Let me drive you home."

Tory shook her head. "There's no need. It's still light. There'll be a bus on the half-hour. We'll both get to bed early."

"Are you certain you don't mind?"

They kissed good-bye in the lobby. Instead of going out the main exit, Tory went downstairs. If she walked along the lower level shops, she could minimize her time outdoors. Even though it was evening, the heat would still be oppressive. As she walked past the Coffee Shop, Tory thought she saw Sarah. Once she got a newspaper and a magazine, she walked past the Coffee Shop again. There was no mistaking the woman now. It was Sarah.

Since the Marco Polo was outside the Central Business District's barricades, it was not part of the city center. The location made it a popular meeting spot. Tory decided to go in and see if she could schedule a photo shoot next week. As she neared the table, she saw a pile of shredded napkins. Whoever Sarah was waiting for was late. Tory walked to the chair on the opposite side of the table, and put her hands on it. "Mind if I join you a sec?"

Sarah appeared not to hear. Tory gave her an appraising look. Something was wrong. Sarah's dress was wrinkled and her eyes stared, unfocused. She was ripping another napkin with a bruised hand. Although her dress had long sleeves, Tory detected bruising beneath the thin silk. The marks were new, mostly dark brown. It was a familiar sight. How many times had Tory concealed discolored skin with long sleeves or pancake makeup?

Tory was enraged. Any man who beat a woman was a monster. She forgot Geoff. All Tory could focus on was keeping Sarah from going back to Barney. She thought of calling Chris, and then changed her mind. Sarah would be humiliated if her friends knew what was going on.

Tory pulled back the chair and snapped her fingers in front of Sarah's eyes. "I thought I saw you. Mind if I join you?"

Sarah jumped and looked around the restaurant furtively. "What are you doing here?"

"Geoff and I had dinner upstairs. I planned to hop the bus, so I went to the Sundry Shop to pick up some reading material." Tory held up the brown paper bag to prove her point. "Are you waiting for someone?"

Sarah started to nod, then stopped, and shook her head. "I was. I guess he's not coming."

Tory willed herself to speak calmly. "It's nearly 8:30 p.m. When were you supposed to meet Barney?"

Tears welled in Sarah's eyes. She went to brush her cheek and winced. Her fingers were wet. As they moved across her face, her makeup came off, revealing another abrasion. "I can't go home," Sarah wailed.

"That's for sure," Tory added. "Why don't you come with me? We can talk about another shoot I'd like you to set up."

Sarah sat motionless.

Tory took matters into her hands. It was obvious Sarah was too distraught to understand what was happening. Tory motioned for the check, grabbed some bills from her wallet, stood, pulled Sarah's chair out, and eased her up. Since Sarah's right side looked to have taken the worst of her attack, Tory put her arm around Sarah's left shoulder, and led her to the side exit. It would be easy to hail a taxi from the queue. They were less likely to bump into anyone they knew on the side street.

Except for her tears, Sarah was silent in the cab. Her head leaned against Tory's shoulder. Until she saw the lump on her head, Tory wondered about Sarah's disorientation. A concussion would explain it. She must get Sarah to safety and find out how badly she was hurt.

The taxi stopped. Tory paid the driver and led Sarah into the small buildings. "There's no elevator. Can you manage four flights of stairs?"

Sarah was silent. She held on to the banister and took the steps slowly. Tory walked behind Sarah in case she stumbled. Several times, Sarah looked over her shoulder, as if to make certain Tory was behind her.

By the time they reached the top floor, Sarah was out of breath. Tory held Sarah with one hand, fumbled for her key, unlocked the door, flipped a switch, walked in, and motioned for Sarah to follow. When Sarah didn't move, Tory sighed and pulled her inside as gently as she could. Sarah followed like a sleepwalker. In her bedroom, Tory sat Sarah on the bed. She opened a bureau drawer, took out a nightshirt, and tossed it at Sarah. Automatically, Sarah started to unbutton her dress and put on the threadbare cotton shirt.

While Sarah changed, Tory went into the kitchen. As she waited for the kettle to boil, she opened the cupboards looking for arnica and green grass oil. Sarah's head should be treated. She took a clean tea towel from a drawer, considered for a moment, and then ripped it in half. It was a shame to ruin a good towel, but it made less sense to use two.

When the kettle whistled, Tory fixed chamomile tea. Then she dropped one of the towel halves in the sink and poured boiling water on it. She picked the hot towel up by her fingertips and waited for the water to go down the drain. She twisted the rag to remove the excess water, folded it in half, put it back in the sink, opened the arnica bottle, and poured it liberally on the white cotton. Arnica relieved swelling and helped heal bruises and sore muscles. She poured a few drops in a mug before adding the tea.

She took out a tray, put two mugs and the teapot on it, added a small plate with the folded arnica cloth and the bottle of green grass oil. She held the second cloth in her hand as she picked up the tray.

Sarah sat huddled against the carved headboard, almost in a fetal position. Slowly, so as not to frighten her, Tory put the tray on the nightstand and offered Sarah a mug of tea. "It's hot. It may be a tad bitter. It will help you sleep."

When Sarah took the mug, Tory picked up the arnica cloth, held it so Sarah could see it. "You hurt your head. This will make it feel better." Gently, she placed the compress on the lump.

The way Sarah sat, the nightshirt was bunched up at her hips. There was no mistaking the marks on Sarah's leg. The yellow bruising indicated that this wasn't the first time Barney had hit Sarah. He was clever though, most of his wrath centered where it wouldn't show when she was dressed.

Tory looked away. The memories of what Sarah must feel were too close to home. She picked up a mug, sipped her tea, and thought. She told Sarah, "I'll be in the other room working. If you need anything, holler."

Chapter 52
SARAH

Singapore
Thursday, May 7, 1981

Sarah woke with a start at 5 a.m. She looked around the room and tried to remember where she was. The last thing that was clear was bursting into tears at bridge on Tuesday. She had other vague recollections, but they must have been dreams. She got out of bed slowly and walked towards the door. Timidly, she turned the handle. When the door opened, she was speechless.

The room was huge, and at first, it looked like a jungle. There were large bushes in the corners and along the windowed wall. The other walls were covered with huge photos. The wood floor was a jumble of area carpets in varying shades of blue and green. The room was empty. Before she could decide what to do, Tory came through a door Sarah hadn't seen. She carried a cellophane bag in her right hand.

"You're up. Good. You were still asleep when I left. How're you feeling this morning?"

"Where am I?" she asked.

"My place." Tory shrugged. "Last night, you weren't coherent. The only thing you said that I understood was you couldn't go home."

Sarah's head throbbed. Maybe that was why nothing made sense. *Did I work with Tory yesterday?* The other times Sarah had set up displays for Tory, they'd worked in Sarah's kitchen. *Why did we work here?* Slowly, it started coming to her. The memories were fragmented: Barney throwing her against the wall while he sneered, then his finding her and Tim in bed. She shivered. "Does anyone know I'm here?"

Tory shook her head.

Sarah sighed in relief. "Thank goodness. I guess I owe you an explanation."

Tory waved her hand and shook her head vigorously. "Let's get one thing straight right now. I don't ask questions and you don't have to volunteer. Those are the house rules. If you need a place to crash for a while, you know where the bedroom is."

Sarah was dumbfounded. She couldn't believe anyone would take her in after what she'd done.

"The bathroom is the first door on the left, the next is the kitchen. My darkroom's on the right. That room's off limits. Other than that, if you see something you want, take it. If you can't find what you want, ask."

"Why?"

"'Cause I know where things are," Tory laughed nervously. She shifted her parcel back and forth between her hands.

Sarah pouted. "That's not what I meant. Why would you let me stay here? Surely you want to know what happened."

"I know all I need to know. I could've picked up the phone last night and gotten the details if I'd wanted them. You look like you could use a hiding place. This is a good place for that. The only person who comes here is Geoff, and he's out of town."

Sarah was not sure what to believe. Tory must know more than she let on. Little escaped her watchful eye. If she knew about the episode with Tim, her offer of sanctuary was a ruse. Sarah put her hand to her aching head.

"If your head still hurts, I'll make you another compress," Tory offered. She put her parcel on the table and beckoned Sarah to take the outstretched chair. "Sit down. I'll make tea. Are you hungry? I've been to the fish market."

The thought of fish for breakfast was nauseating. Sarah was queasy enough. Gingerly, she shoved the fish wrapped in white paper as far away from her as possible. "What I'd like are headache tablets. My head is killing me."

Tory nodded. "I'm not surprised. You have quite a lump. I have some stuff that'll help." Tory picked up the parcel and went into the kitchen.

While Sarah waited, she felt her head. The bump must be from hitting her head on the molding of the doorway. She tried to put the pieces of the puzzle together. Barney and she had fought Tuesday night. Wednesday he found her in Tim's arms. She went to the Marco Polo. Tim never showed, but Tory had. *Why didn't Tim come to the Marco Polo? What will I do now? I can't stay here. But, where can I go? How long will it be before Barney starts looking for me?* Her aching head was made worse by all the unanswered questions.

Tory returned with a cup of tea. Sarah took a sip and spit it out. The brew had an acrid taste. "That stuff is disgusting."

"It's fennel seed tea. It's good for your stomach. After that you should take a warm bath in Epsom salts and baking soda."

"Do you sit up nights dreaming up these concoctions? I've never heard of any of them."

Tory poured herself a mug of tea. "This is chamomile tea. It will calm you. After you finish what's in your cup, try some. They're old-fashioned elixirs. I was raised on stuff like this."

Slowly Sarah drained her cup. Once she knew what to expect, the taste wasn't so bad. Tory had made a comment in Penang about herbal cures. Her stomach was feeling better. Maybe Tory's ideas weren't so farfetched. When she put her cup down, Tory handed her another cup. This tea was nicer.

Tory got up and returned a few minutes later. "I've turned on the water in the bath. The towels are clean. I've left a bottle of green grass oil on the ledge. If you rub it on your bruises, they won't hurt as much."

Sarah paled. "How'd you know?"

"That's not important. There'll be time to talk after you feel better. I doubt you're very clear about things right now. I left a kimono in there that might fit."

Sarah poured more tea in her cup before going to the bathroom. The water was wonderfully soothing. She started to nod off and stopped herself. This wasn't the time to sleep. She needed to make plans. But the water was so inviting. What did it matter if she closed her eyes for a minute or two? Sarah woke when the water was cold.

As she got out of the tub, she saw the bottle of green grass oil. There was no harm in using it. Tory's other remedies had helped. If only she could get rid of her headache, she could think clearly. When she put on the kimono, she laughed. It was meant to be knee length and it practically hit the floor. The short sleeves reached her wrists.

Tory had left a toothbrush, still in its wrapper, on the sink. After using it, Sarah picked up the comb that had been next to the toothbrush, ran it through her hair, and wrapped a towel around her head, turban style. She was surprised at how much better she felt.

Tory was typing furiously on an electric typewriter that looked out of place in the room's jungle motif. She didn't look up when Sarah walked in the room. The phone rang. Tory swore to herself and turned a switch on an answering machine. "Whoever you are, leave a message," she said angrily.

"Have you been getting a lot of calls?" Sarah asked with trepidation.

Tory looked up. "Are you ready for that compress now? You look better."

Sarah felt well enough to realize Tory was being evasive. "My head aches. May I have a cup of tea? If you've some time, I'd like to talk. I know you said I didn't have to explain anything. And that's not what I want to do."

Tory jumped up from her desk. "No problem. I could use a break. What type of tea would you like? I do have conventional brews."

"My life's falling apart and you're worrying about what type of tea to serve?" The conversation was ludicrous. Tory must be uncomfortable. She was harboring the adulterous wife of a man who worked for her lover.

When Tory came back with the tea tray, she placed it on the coffee table. She motioned Sarah to sit on the couch, handed her the compress, pointed to some dry toast, and poured the tea.

"I thought you might be hungry. If you're not, don't worry, I'll feed it to the birds."

Sarah leaned her head against the back of the sofa and closed her eyes a minute. The compress eased the throbbing a bit. "Who's rung about me?"

Tory lounged on a carpet. She shrugged and rubbed the deep pile one way, then the other, and appeared fascinated with the effects it had on the shades of colors.

Sarah was not about to be put off. "You turned on your answering machine. Since Chris complains she wasted her money buying it for you last Christmas, you must be avoiding calls. If I know what you already know, it would make it easier for me to fill in the blanks."

Tory nibbled on her lower lip. When she spoke, her voice was a monotone. "Chris called. Barney called her last night, frantic, because you didn't come home. He was pretty drunk, so she ignored him. This morning, when Barney didn't show up at work, Kev called your house. Mai Liu answered. She said Barney was asleep in his chair and you hadn't come in last night. Kev called Chris. She's worried. I told her not to call anyone until she heard from me. Then Tim called and asked if I'd seen you at the Marco Polo." She poured herself a cup of tea. "I denied knowing anything."

"I can't go home to Barney."

"I'm glad you see that. We would've had a battle if you even considered it."

"Why would Chris wait for you to call her back?"

Troy shrugged. "I know how to find things out. She knows that. Singapore's a rumor mill. Before she alerts anyone to your absence, she wants to be sure she knows enough to be able to do damage control if necessary. From what I've seen, I think you should have left long ago."

Sarah nibbled on a piece of toast while she considered what had and hadn't been said. "I know you must have told me last night, but I've forgotten. Why were you at the Marco Polo?"

"Geoff and I met there for dinner. He wanted to make an early night of it, so I said I'd take the bus home. When I saw you, I decided to check your availability for another layout."

"So he didn't go to his flat to pack first? That explains it. Did Tim say anything other than asking if you and I'd met last night?"

"He told me he knew you left the Marco Polo with a tall, blonde woman. He said you should call him, so he could explain the mixed signals. He said you'd know what he meant."

Sarah nodded. Tim hadn't forsaken her. He'd waited for Geoff, who met Tory before he went to the flat. She looked at the phone and hesitated. She didn't want Tory to hear their conversation.

Tory followed Sarah's eyes, stood up and stretched. "I'm going to take a shower and wash my hair." She lifted the ends of her waist-length hair, and smiled. "It takes a long time to wash this mangy mop. Can you amuse yourself for an hour?"

Sarah nodded. The second Tory closed the bathroom door; Sarah pulled the phone to the couch and dialed Tim's office. He answered on the first ring, as if he'd been waiting.

"Tim, it's Sarah."

"She gave you the message. I was afraid she mightn't. What on earth possessed you to go with her last night, luv? Geoff didn't get home until late. The second he came in, I was out in a flash. You've got to get out of Tory's. Immediately."

"Why'? Tim, she's been so nice to me."

"I've told you before. Tory sees too much."

"I can't go back to Barney. He'll kill me if I tell him I'm leaving."

"Come here. Geoff's out of town. He was closeted in his bedroom on the phone when I got back last night. This morning he said he'd not be back until next week some time."

"It's safer here. Barney has a key to your place."

"Geoff let himself in with his key last night."

"Tim, if Barney could get in once, he can do it again. As long as Tory will let me stay, I'm better off here. I need to work through some things."

"Will you return to Australia with me? I must let the company in Adelaide know about their job offer by tomorrow."

"Make whatever decision's in your best interest. I must return to Sydney. That's where Trey is."

"When can I see you?"

"I need to think, Tim. I'll ring when I've sorted through everything."

"Sarah, luv, please ring if you need anything."

"I promise. Bye, Tim."

Sarah sat pensively. She wanted to see Tim. At the same time, it was more important she address the rest of her life. Barney would call the police when he sobered up enough to realize she still wasn't home. Safe as Tory might think her flat was Sarah couldn't remain here forever.

When Tory walked into the living room, she pointed to the tea tray. "Shall I make a fresh pot?"

Sarah nodded. It would give her time to decide how to explain. When Tory returned, Sarah told her everything that had happened since she arrived in Singapore. To her amazement, Tory listened intently and never interrupted, even when told about Barney walking in on her and Tim. "My marriage is over. There's no way I can deny it any longer. What will happen to Trey? No doubt Barney will use my infidelity to keep him."

"I think there are more serious matters to be considered than who says what in a divorce court."

"Are you nervous having me stay with you? Barney can be violent."

Tory stared out the window. "My father was a bully, especially when he drank. I know how to take care of myself. Those are lessons you never forget. As to Barney showing up here, it won't happen. Except for Geoff, no one knows where I live. There are apartments on each corner where I meet people."

"What has to be decided?"

"First you have to decide who goes public first. The fact that you're not at Cluny Road will be on the jungle drum before nightfall. Then Barney's drinking should be addressed. Chris might have some ideas about that. After that you need to think about where you go from here."

Sarah panicked at the thought of leaving. "How long can I stay?" she asked through her tears.

"As long as you want. I didn't mean what I said the way it sounded. Let me see if I can rephrase it." Tory paused, then continued. "You need to think about what to do with the rest of your life. Your son deserves at least one parent who's not a member of the walking wounded."

"What about Tim?"

"That's your call."

"Would it be all right if I invited Chris over? I don't feel well."

Tory went to her desk and pulled out her appointment book. "She's at her office. Tell her I'll meet her where Suradmin usually drops me off."

Before Sarah could answer, Tory had picked up a camera and was out the door.

Chapter 53
TORY

Singapore
Thursday, May 7, 1981

Tory waited while the doorman announced her. The man was so accustomed to seeing her at the apartment building with Geoff that he would have let her go up the elevator, had she not insisted he buzz Tim.

"He said go right up, Miss Winslow."

Tory paced the tiled elevator floor while the car made its ascent to the penthouse.

Tim opened the door before she reached it. "Where's Sarah? I thought she'd be with you."

Tory stormed into the apartment, went to the kitchen, took a glass, went to the bar, and poured herself a tall scotch. After a large gulp, she put the glass down, turned to Tim, and hit him as she cried. "Sarah's in a hospital, where she belongs. You bastard. How could you not know what was going on? You were her lover. Damn it! Why didn't you stop him?"

Tim picked the glass up from the counter. "You've had one too many. I've no idea what you're rambling on about. What hospital is Sarah in?"

Tory grabbed back the glass and stormed to the sofa. "Tim, you and I go back a long time. I'm not the timid, shy girl you met. So I'm willing to believe you're not the superficial, shallow boy I remember."

"Where is Sarah? What's going on? It's past midnight."

Tory looked at her watch: 12:15. A new day. Maybe it would be better one. She sipped her drink and thought. This would have to be approached logically. "Did you know Barney hit Sarah?"

The stunned look on Tim's face was all the answer Tory needed.

"You were her lover. Didn't you ever look at her body?"

"Sarah and I hadn't been together in four months. Wednesday was the first time. She fell asleep when we got to bed. I noticed some bruises, but she told me he'd shoved her into the wall. Once Barney walked in, I forgot all about it." Tim stood. "He hit her? I'll kill the bugger."

"You'll have to stand in line for the honor. How serious are you about Sarah?"

"I love her."

"So did her husband. And tonight she's in a hospital."

"I want to marry her. We had it all planned."

"She told me. Are your intentions honorable?" Tory stopped and put her hand to her mouth. "I can't believe I just said that. Sarah's had a rough time. The last thing she needs is you turning up, if you're not prepared for what's in front of her."

Tim stood and glared at Tory. "Don't you ever get tired of being sanctimonious? You're the sorriest excuse for a woman I've ever met. How would you have the slightest idea what Sarah needs or wants?"

"Been there, done it. Sarah sees you as the knight in shining armor who's going to make the world beautiful for her. If you're not up to the role, bow out gracefully. Now. As I recall your white charger doesn't like going uphill."

"As you said earlier, your memory of me may not be up to speed. I love Sarah." Tim grabbed her glass and took a swig. "Will you tell me what happened? When I spoke to Sarah she was at your flat."

"I tried everything I could think of to make Sarah feel better." Tory sniffed back her tears. "Nurturing isn't my strong suit. She had a lump on her head. All I remember about head injuries is you have to careful the person doesn't go into a coma when they sleep. I sat on the floor and watched her sleep all night.

"In the morning, she was a little better. I was scared. I got Sarah to suggest calling Chris. I thought with her nursing background, Chris would know what to do." Tory took a sip from the glass.

"Chris examined her and said she had an enlarged kidney. She thought Barney must've kicked her. We got Sarah to a hospital." Tory shook and waited for her tears to slow. "Tim, she's got needles stuck in her arm. She looks so small and fragile in the bed."

Tim got up, poured another drink, and handed it to Tory. She smiled weakly. "Chris must've called Kevin, 'cause he met us. Once we knew Sarah was safe, Kev took Chris and me to the canteen for coffee. We had to decide what to do about Barney. Kev called Trans Oil and got the number for Barney's parents. They'll be here tomorrow."

"Where is he now?"

"At the house. He's out cold. Kev's there, in case he wakes up."

"Where's Chris?"

"She went home. Even though the doctor said Sarah wouldn't wake up until morning, I stayed, in case he was wrong. The more I sat there, the angrier I got. We all ignored what was going on. We closed our eyes to Barney's drinking. None of us saw what he was doing to his wife. How could we have been so blind? He could've killed her."

"Tory, how were we to know? It's not something you think about. You don't expect wife beating, not in our world. It happens to other people."

Tory shook her head. "I should've known. All the signs were there. I didn't pick up on them."

"Stop blaming yourself. There was no way you could know. Sarah's safe. That's all that matters."

"What happens to Sarah now? Barney will be gone once his parents get here. They're coming with a doctor from a rehab hospital."

"She wants to go to Sydney for her son. I put in my resignation this morning. She and I will go together once she's well enough."

Tory smiled. Maybe Tim had grown up. This wasn't the Tim she remembered. "Can I tell her that tomorrow?"

"Tell me where she is. I'll tell her myself"

Tory shook her head. "She doesn't know I'm here. I'll see her tomorrow and tell her we spoke. What she does about calling you is her decision."

Chapter 54
SARAH

Singapore
Friday, May 8, 1981

The first thing Sarah saw when she woke was Tory asleep in a chair. Before she could say anything, Chris walked in with flowers.

"How are you feeling this morning?"

"Where am I?" Sarah asked.

"Mount Elizabeth Hospital. You needed more than Tory's bromides."

Tory walked over to the bed. "Did I make anything worse?" she asked. There was fear in Tory's eyes.

Chris put her hand out to reach for Tory. "No. But, you should have called for the cavalry sooner."

"When I saw the bruise on Sarah's hand and arm, I went on automatic pilot. Everything I did for her, I'd done for others or myself hundreds of times. I'm sorry you felt excluded."

"Excluded? I'm a nurse. I would have gotten her here sooner."

"It never dawned on me to call anyone. That's not the way we dealt with this at home."

Sarah coughed. "Will you stop quarreling?"

Chris turned and smiled. "I'm sorry. We're both worn out. Barney's folks will be here late this afternoon. They plan to take him home with them."

Sarah paled at the mention of her husband's name. "What will they do?"

"About what?" Tory asked. "You're staying here. They can't make you leave."

Chris nodded. "Sarah, they know you're in a hospital because of what their son did. Violet wanted to be certain you were getting the best care money could buy. We assured her you were. She said she'd like to see you. Tory told her, in no uncertain terms, that it was your call. If you didn't agree, we'd never tell them where you are." Chris smiled broadly. "You know it's impossible to get information from Tory."

"Right." Sarah paused. Momentarily she might be safe. Where would she go when she got out?

Chris arranged her flowers in a vase. "I only stopped by for a minute. I have to go to work. I'll check in on you later. Tory, are you coming?"

Tory shook her head. "I think I'll stay with Sarah 'til the doctor gets here." She turned to Sarah. "That is, if you don't mind?"

When Chris left, Sarah sat puzzled, waiting for Tory to say something. There must be a reason she lagged behind. Tory looked horrible. She was in the clothes she'd worn the day before. There were dark circles under her eyes. "I should thank you," Sarah offered.

Tory shook her head. "I owe you an apology. I should've realized what Barney was capable of. I saw Tim last night. He's ready to go back to Sydney with you."

Sarah breathed a sigh of relief. "I'm glad. It will be easier for me if he's there."

"Sarah, I'm not trying to be difficult. Honest. But are you sure you want Tim?"

The question startled Sarah. She paused. "I love Tim, I know I do. Sometimes, though, I wonder if that's enough. I don't want to go to him because I hate where I am or because I don't have anyplace to go."

Tory shuddered. "Those are two of the worst reasons I can think of to do anything. Did you marry Barney because you loved him or to get out of the house?"

Sarah paled. "A little of both. Everyone told me I should love him. So I thought I did."

Tory grimaced. "Sarah, stop living your life for other people. You'll never find happiness in other people's dreams."

Sarah resented Tory's smug attitude. She understood nothing but the life she led. "I was raised to be a wife. It's all I know how to do." Her tone was petulant.

"Bull. You're a marvelous cook; you have a good eye for color, style, fashion, and decorating. There must be a million things you could do if you wanted. The only thing that holds you back is fear."

Sarah closed her eyes to think. "You make it sound easy."

Tory shook her head. "I'm sorry. It's not, and I know that only too well. It's damned hard. But it's the only way to find happiness."

"What do I tell Tim? It sounds so wishy-washy: I love you, but I'm not sure."

"I love you, but I need time to think." Tory's eyes lit up as she spoke. "It makes a great deal of sense when you think about it. Can I let Tim know where you are?"

Sarah shook her head. "I'll ring him. How are things with Geoff?"

"I told you once my independence is what appealed to Geoff. All he was interested in was the chase. Now that he has what he thought he wanted, he isn't sure he really wants it."

"You're wrong. Geoff's solid like you. He'll be there if you leave room for him in your life. Now if you wouldn't mind leaving, I must call Tim. I want to tell him what I plan to do."

Chapter 55
TORY

Singapore
Saturday, May 16, 1981

Tory stood with Geoff at the newly opened Changi Airport. They made an odd pair. He was smiling and cheerful. She was downcast and glum. This was the third time Tory had been to the airport in two days, and she was tired.

Sarah and Tim had left yesterday. To give herself more time to think, Sarah had insisted on flying home alone. She would go to Sydney, file for divorce, get her son, and put her life together. Tim would give her space, although he, too, was relocating to Sydney.

Tim and Sarah's had been a tearful parting. Tory felt like an intruder, although they each claimed that they wanted her there. Sarah had been upset after Tim left. She insisted on returning to town, rather than spend five hours at Changi waiting for her flight.

Barney and his parents had just left. Barney was on his way to an exclusive sanatorium to dry out. His mother and father flanked him as he sat at the airport. All he could talk about was the day Sarah would come to her senses and come back to him.

Geoff returned from Greece three days earlier. This was the first time that Tory had seen him. According to the jungle drum, he'd been to Immigration. Tory knew that he too would leave soon. He hadn't said as much, but you knew some things intuitively, without ever having them put in words.

As they walked towards the car park, Geoff slipped his arm across her back. "Are you cross?" he asked when she stiffened at his touch.

"No. Weary of good-byes," she offered weakly. Geoff had steadfastly refused to accompany her to the airport to see Sarah or Tim off. The previous night after Sarah had gone, Tory called Geoff and asked him to go with her to see Barney off. At first he insisted that he had paperwork to finish and would have to give it a miss. This morning he called, said he'd changed his mind, and offered to go with her.

As they drove along Loyang Avenue, Geoff looked over and grinned. His happiness grated on Tory's nerves. He'd been euphoric since his return. He would call her several times a day, claiming to be swamped at work. At the same time, it was obvious he was pleased about something. At first, she tried to convince herself that she misunderstood -- that he was simply happy to be back at work. When he picked her up at noon, she couldn't ignore her fears any longer. He looked calmer than she'd ever seen him. It was more than happiness; it was a look of freedom.

Tory was sick of people coming and going. It had been her life for years. Now there had been too many partings. Geoff's would be the hardest of all.

"Care to stop at Raffles? We've not been there in a long time."

She shrugged. It was the ideal place to end things. Leave it to Geoff to remember where it began.

They walked into the old white hotel. Tory stared at the large floor tiles. Geoff paused at the photo gallery. He reached towards Tory's shoulders, drew her to him, and pointed. "Remember these? You were right, after all. They do look odd. It was a different time."

Tory's eyes darted from the photos and back to Geoff. He was in white cotton slacks and a short-sleeved madras shirt. The shirt combined various hues of red, pink and purple; it was a striking combination against his tanned skin and black hair. *I'll miss him*, she thought silently.

She tried to memorize him so she'd never forget him. It was important. She had no idea how much time there'd be before he left. The Taylors were planning to go on leave in July and August. Most likely he'd stay until Kevin returned. That would give them three months. They would have so little time. Once he was gone, his memory would be all she'd have to get through the long, lonely nights.

Geoff's hand passed in front of her face and she blinked. Geoff was staring at her. "I get dreamy here," she said.

He laughed and kissed her cheek. "Where do you disappear to when you go off like that?"

"The photos . . . how much times change."

"So do people." He moved his arm around her waist and led her down the hall. "I promised you a drink. Shall we go? You choose -- the Long Bar or outside?"

Tory let Geoff decide. She dawdled a moment to glance over her shoulder at the photos one more time. The people looked content and happy with their lives. Maybe they weren't so odd after all.

Tory played with the paper umbrella from her drink. She was desperate to hear what Geoff had to say. At the same time, she was afraid she'd cry when he told her.

Geoff took the umbrella from her hand, laid it on the table, and grasped her hands in his. "I owe you an explanation for running off like I did."

Tory shook her head. "It was business."

"I needed to see my father. To find out why he'd left and never been in touch. It was important. You'd gone home to face your fears. When you returned, you were ready to give us a go. Suddenly I was the one with cold feet." He smiled and loosened his grip on her hands. "Please believe me, that I love you was never a question in my mind. I hoped, if I sussed out what happened with my father, I'd understand what bothered me."

"Did you?"

Geoff nodded. "I think it's best I finish telling you about my youth. The year after my father left, my mother sent me to a boarding school in England. She moved to Hamilton and remarried two years later. She obliterated her past when she moved 130 kilometers. My father was gone, and I was safely ensconced in England.

"By the time I was in university, she had a whole new life. She and my stepfather had two children. They were the perfect suburban family. There was nothing for me in New Zealand, so I didn't return. Oh, I was welcome in their house, but I didn't belong there. I was from a different world. After university, I joined Trans Oil in the UK and lived in London for ten years."

"I thought you lived in Auckland until you moved here."

"Tory, please allow me to finish. Do you remember the first time we met?"

"In Jurong on the way to Sentosa," she grinned at him. When he shook his head, she thought again. "At the Taylors' the night before? No, I'm positive we didn't meet then. I only had eyes for Tim that night."

"It was years before. I was living in Auckland. Trans Oil held a marketing conference in Singapore. The first evening, they organized a harbor cruise and you were the tour guide. You were the most beautiful woman I'd ever seen and you were so utterly self-contained. All evening I watched blokes put the hard word on you. You rebuffed them all with a laugh. You led tours in the evenings, and on the weekends for small groups of us who wanted to see more of the city than the inside of restaurants and bars. Does any of this sound familiar?"

Tory giggled. "January 1974. How could I ever forget? Chris and I had just come back from Bangkok. I was wiped out. She'd run me ragged. She had to see and buy everything. When we landed, the MD of Trans Oil was with Kevin at the airport. He was in a panic. The head of PR had come down with hepatitis, and this ten-day conference started the next night. Trans Oil had been one of my first clients and, reluctantly, I agreed to fill in."

Her eyes lit up. "I knew there was something familiar about you when we met. You went to the zoo with me on Saturday morning."

"Right. You had the most fascinating stories about all the animals. You talked to them, knew their habits, their names, what they liked and disliked. It was amazing. I thought you the best tour guide in the world. When I returned to Auckland, I forgot about you.

"When I came back to Singapore, I explored a great deal. I wanted to learn all there was about this island. I'd walk around the city while I worked out a detail or mulled over an idea. I saw you frequently, in very odd places. It didn't seem to matter where I went. Every time I looked up, you and your camera were there. It was quite unsettling really. I was certain you were the woman from the conference. Thanksgiving night I discovered you were Tim's friend. He'd spoken of you often.

"The day we met at the Hyatt, I began to see a different you than the one Tim described. There was a real person there, one I very much wanted to know. But you had this impregnable wall around you. Even your eyes said do not disturb. That second time we went out, after I dropped you at your flat, I was livid at the way you kept me at bay. At the same time, I was intrigued. As I drove home, I realized how similar we were. You were as hostile as I. Neither of us wanted to be hurt, so we each lashed out, before anyone got close."

Despite her fears about what was to follow, Tory smiled at his adroit description. "We're a pair all right."

Geoff returned her smile. "Like you, I found Singapore enchanting. Superficially, it's the perfect blend of tropical paradise and modern city. Underneath the veneer, it's not that way at all. The rush to modern times has left people without a clue about their new roles. Then there are the expats. They cluster together in enclaves and hide behind their masks of civility. What happened with Barney and Sarah attests to that."

Tory couldn't understand the circuitous route Geoff was taking. When would he summon the courage to get the words out? The time he was taking made the situation worse for her. If she weren't careful, she'd be in tears any second.

"I blamed Singapore for what I saw. You were angry and so was I. It must be Singapore. It couldn't have been a problem within either of us.

"Every time we seemed to make progress, one of us pulled back. The afternoon on Pulau Sakeng, when you showed me how you'd lived, I finally understood how frightened you were. You clammed up when I asked questions. In London you opened up a bit. I knew then you hadn't told me the entire truth, but it was a start. When we came back to Singapore, we got caught up in our careers. There was never enough time for us to give it a go. That day on the boat, when you told me the undiluted version of your past, I saw how hard it must be for you to trust anyone. I also realized how difficult it was for you to go home and confront your past. I felt the cowardly lion in comparison."

Tory eyed Geoff skeptically.

"I've not had much contact with my mother in years. That Monday I rang her, asked about my father and what had happened between them. It's the first time we've spoken about it."

"What did she say?"

"That they'd been mismatched from the start. As the years progressed, it became apparent their marriage was a mistake. When it became intolerable, they divorced. Neither of them could face telling me the truth. They agreed my father would pack his things and go while I was at school."

Tory sat bolt upright in her chair. Finally, Geoff had said something of importance. "And she knew where your father was?"

He nodded. "London. I vowed that the next time I went to Greece I'd stop in London and pay him a visit. For a year I'd practically commuted to Greece, and now I was firmly planted in Singapore. It was quite ironic, really. Ultimately there was a problem with a contract and I went to Greece, although the matter could just as easily have been resolved by phone. If it hadn't been for your example of facing up to your nightmares, I might have let my own continue to plague my nights. I've always blamed myself for my father's leaving."

"What happened when you saw him?"

"We had a long talk over one too many bottles of wine."

"Why hadn't he been in touch?"

"Since I never asked about him, he chose not to interfere. He returned to London and started a new life."

Tory was stunned. "Why didn't your mother let him know you were there?"

Geoff grinned. "There was no reason to. They'd each gone on to happier places. All I would ever be was a reminder of their failed marriage. Until I spoke to them, I never understood. I thought there was something wrong with me. I must have been the cause of their turning their backs on me. Now I see that it had to do with their inability to face reality. It wasn't me at all."

Tory frowned. Geoff's tale confused her.

Geoff reached for her hand. "Last night, I asked if you'd like to go away, once Kev and I get things sorted out at the office. We could go anywhere you want. I figure if you try, you should be able to find two weeks in your calendar."

Tory's dark eyes clouded and she shook her hand free from his grasp. "Could you translate that question for me, please? I left my Jack Armstrong decoder ring at home."

"What?"

"Two weeks. Is that the normal payment for what we've had? I don't know the formula you're using to score our love affair. Is two weeks good or bad? I'd like to know how I rated as a lover."

"What are you talking about?"

"Give me a break. You've never lied to me before. Please don't start now. You're leaving. The two weeks is to say good-bye. It beats a teary farewell at Changi. Believe me, I've had enough of those in the past two days to last a lifetime."

Geoff laughed. "You can be a fruit loop at times. What makes you think I'm leaving?"

"You've been to Immigration."

Geoff reached for Tory's hands and refused to speak until he captured them both. "My passport was stolen in Athens. I went to Immigration to transfer my work permit."

"Then why your sudden interest in a trip?"

"Have you listened to anything I've said?" he demanded.

Tory nodded, her face a puzzled frown.

"I want to marry you. Two weeks seems appropriate for a honeymoon. If you wish more time, you must let me know."